INSTRUCTOR'S MANUAL

to accompany

COMPLETE BUSINESS STATISTICS

Third Edition

Amir D. Aczel

Prepared by

Richard Duffy

Massachusetts Institute of Technology

IRWIN

Chicago • Bogotá • Boston • Buenos Aires • Caracas
London • Madrid • Mexico City • Sydney • Toronto

Printed in the United States of America.

ISBN 0-256-21844-7

1 2 3 4 5 6 7 8 9 0 WCB 3 2 1 0 9 8 7 6

PREFACE

This *Instructor's Manual* has been prepared to serve as a resource for course planning. There are two parts to the manual.

The first part contains sample syllabi for various course structures. There are, of course, a wide variety of options as to how you can select material from this text, so this cannot be complete. However, we have provided an outline for each of the most common course setups we have seen.

The second part of this manual contains solutions to all the problems in each chapter. Note that the answers to most odd-numbered problems appear in Appendix B of the text for student use.

The *Student Problem Solving Guide for use with Complete Business Statistics, 3/e* by Michael Sklar is another resource you may wish to review. The SPSG is available for sale to students either separately or at a discounted price packaged with the text. It contains detailed explanations of representative problems from each section. An index is provided in the front of the *Guide* which lists the topics of the worked out problems.

We hope that you and your students enjoy using the third edition of *Complete Business Statistics*, and we welcome your comments.

Contents

BUSINESS REPLY MAIL
FIRST CLASS MAIL   PERMIT NO. 17   HOMEWOOD, IL

POSTAGE WILL BE PAID BY ADDRESSEE

RICHARD D. IRWIN

1333 Burr Ridge Pky.
Burr Ridge, IL 60521-0084

ATTENTION: C. Tuscher

(fold)

(fold)

IRWIN

Please use this postage-paid form to report any errors that you find in the Instructor's Manual to accompany COMPLETE BUSINESS STATISTICS, Third Edition. Be as specific as possible and note which changes should be made. We will do our best to address them in subsequent printings and future editions. Thank you.

NOTE: Extra copies of this form appear at the end of this manual.

Attention: C. Tuscher

Name_____School_____

Office Phone_____

Please fold and seal so that our address is visible.

SUGGESTED SYLLABUS NUMBER 1

(EASY)

FOR A ONE-SEMESTER FIRST COURSE IN APPLIED STATISTICS FOR STUDENTS OF BUSINESS, ECONOMICS, AND RELATED AREAS [UNDERGRADUATE]

1. All topics from Chapter 1. Remark: I personally prefer to start the course with Chapter 2 on probability, and to teach these topics just before Chapter 5. However, as a colleague put it, Chapter 1 offers a "painless introduction" to descriptive statistics before getting to the harder material on probability.

2. Chapter 2: Sections 2-1 through 2-6. These important sections cover the introduction to probability, basic definitions, rules, conditional probability, and independence of events. The rest of the topics in this chapter are left to the discretion of the instructor. [One week or more] Remark: In a course at this level, I personally skip Section 2-7 on combinatorial concepts, but I do teach Section 2-8 on the law of total probability and Bayes Theorem.

3. Chapter 3: Sections 3-1, 3-2, and 3-3. These sections cover the basic definitions and properties of random variables, expected values, variance and standard deviation. The more advanced topics in Section 3-3 on expected value of a function of a random variable, Chebyshev's theorem, and the variance of a linear function of a random variable may be skipped at this level. Include Section 3-4 on the binomial distribution, at the desired level of coverage. Section 3-5 on other discrete probability distributions may be skipped. Section 3-6 on continuous random variables should be covered. [About one week.]

4. Chapter 4: Teach Sections 4-1 through 4-5 on the use of the normal probability distribution. In a basic course, I would leave out Sections 4-6 and 4-7, which cover more advanced material. [One week or less.]

5. Chapter 5: Sections 5-1 to 5-3, covering the important ideas of sampling and sampling distributions; the central limit theorem. In a basic course I would cover very briefly the concepts in Section 5-4 on properties of estimators. I would then cover Section 5-5 on degrees of freedom. [One week.]

6. Chapter 6: Sections 6-1 to 6-4 on confidence intervals, their meaning and their construction, and the t distribution. I prefer to leave out Section 6-5 on the finite population correction factor. Cover at least part of Section 6-6 on the chi-square distribution; you may leave out confidence intervals for the population variance. Give at least *some* discussion of the subject of

Section 6-7, sample size determination. In an elementary course, Section 6-8 on one-sided confidence intervals may be skipped; however, I prefer to include it because of the important connection of this topic with one-tailed tests persented later in Chapter 7. Students who understand one-sided confidence intervals tend to have a better understanding of one-tailed (and two-tailed) tests. [One week or more.]

7. Chapter 7: Thoroughly cover Sections 7-1 to 7-7 on two-tailed tests, one-tailed tests, and the p-value. If you skipped Section 6-5 in Chapter 6, you may safely skip Section 7-8 on the f.p.c.f.; and if you skipped the discussion of estimating the population variance in Section 6-6, you may leave out tests about the population variance, Section 7-9. I would always give at least *some* discussion of power and the probability of a Type II error, Section 7-10. The extent of coverage, however, depends on how much time you want to devote to this topic. Depending on the extent of your discussion of sample size determination in Section 6-7, give some explanation of this topic in the context of hypothesis tests, Section 7-11. Have students read Section 7-12 on how hypothesis testing works. This will enhance their understanding after having completed most of this chapter, and it will warn them about possible pitfalls. [Two weeks.]

8. Chapter 8: When I am rushed in a basic course, I skip most of this chapter because ANOVA in Chapter 9 and chi-square tests in Chapter 14 can provide tests for many of the situations here. At least the first part of Section 8-6 must be presented, however, because here we introduce the F distribution. I would recommend including as much material as you can out of Sections 8-1 to 8-5 on the various two-sample tests for means and proportions. [Less than one week.]

9. Chapter 9: You should probably cover most of the material in Sections 9-1 to 9-4 on ANOVA. I personally feel that the ANOVA procedure *must* be followed by further analysis, and I therefore always cover Section 9-5. Section 9-6 defines the different modes and experimental designs. You may skip it, but the section is short and should not take too much time to cover. I would give at least some discussion of Two-Way ANOVA in Section 9-7. In a basic course, you may safely skip the rest of the chapter, on blocking and experimental design. [One to two weeks.]

10. Chapter 10: Cover Sections 10-1 through 10-7 on simple linear regression and correlation analysis. If you did *not* cover Chapter 9, you cannot explain Section 10-8 on the use of an ANOVA table in regression analysis (in Chapter 11 on multiple regression you will need this concept), so make sure you cover ANOVA first. I would give at least some discussion of residual plots and their use, Section 10-9, but you may choose to cover this material after starting Chapter 11. Explain Section 10-10 on prediction, prediction intervals, and confidence intervals for the conditional mean of Y. [One to two weeks.]

11. Chapter 11: Cover Sections 11-1 through 11-5 on the multiple regression model and its use. Give at least some discussion of the problem of multicollinearity (more about it in Section 11-11). In a basic course, I would not cover much of the material in other sections of this chapter, but the more time you can afford for coverage of these topics, the better! (These topics

include qualitative variables, polynomial regression, transformations, residual autocorrelation, and more. Cover what you can, depending on your choice.) You should discuss at least the second half of Section 11-13 on variable selection methods since most of your students who will end up using multiple regression analysis will probably be using the STEPWISE routine and they should understand what it does. [One or two weeks.]

12. Chapter 14: I would recommend covering Section 14-10 on contingency tables and a chi-square test for independence, as well as Section 14-11 on a chi-square test for equality among proportions. These sections do not have to be covered at the end of the course, you may discuss them any time after you have presented the chi-square distribution and hypothesis tests. Other topics in Chapter 14, a goodness of fit test and a variety of nonparametric methods, may be selected depending on available time and your own preference. [Less than one week.]

SUGGESTED SYLLABUS NUMBER 2

(EASY, MORE COMPREHENSIVE)
FOR A TWO-QUARTER SEQUENCE OF COURSES IN APPLIED
STATISTICS FOR STUDENTS OF BUSINESS, ECONOMICS,
AND RELATED AREAS [UNDERGRADUATE]

First Quarter:

1. Cover most topics of Chapter 1. These should include Sections 1-1, 1-2, 1-3, and 1-4 as a minimum, and any other of the further topics in the chapter. [One week.]

2. Chapter 2: Cover most of the chapter. [Two weeks.]

3. Chapter 3: Sections 3-1, 3-2 and 3-3. The more advanced topics in Section 3-3 on expected value of a function of a random variable and the variance of a linear function of a random variable may be skipped at this level. Section 3-4 on the binomial distribution. Section 3-5 on other discrete probability distributions may be skipped. Cover Section 3-6 on continuous random variables. [About one week.]

4. Chapter 4: Cover entire chapter. [One week or more.]

5. Chapter 5: Cover entire chapter. [One week or more.]

6. Chapter 6: Sections 6-1 to 6-4 on confidence intervals, their meaning and their construction, and the t distribution. (You may leave out Section 6-5 on the finite population correction factor.) Section 6-6 on the chi-square distribution and confidence intervals for the population variance. Section 6-7 on sample size determination. Section 6-8 on one-sided confidence intervals may be skipped. I prefer to include it because of the important connection of this topic with one-tailed tests presented later in Chapter 7.[Two weeks.]

7. Chapter 7: Thoroughly cover Sections 7-1 to 7-7 on two-tailed tests, one-tailed tests, and the p-value. If you skipped Section 6-5 in Chapter 6, you may skip Section 7-8 on the f.p.c.f. Include a discussion of power and the probability of a Type II error, Section 7-10. Cover Section 7-11 on sample size determination. Explain Section 7-12 on how hypothesis testing works. [Two weeks.]

Second Quarter:

1. Chapter 8: Cover entire chapter. Possibly leave out the latter part of Section 8-3 on a small-sample test for difference between population means. [One week or more.]

2. Chapter 14: Cover Sections 14-9 through 14-11 on chi-square analysis. Also cover as many nonparametric methods as you desire. Choose from among Sections 14-1 to 14-8. [One to two weeks.]

3. Chapter 9: Cover Sections 9-1 to 9-7 on One-Way and Two-Way ANOVA. You may skip the rest of the chapter on blocking and experimental design. [Two weeks.]

4. Chapter 10: Cover entire chapter. [Two weeks.]

5. Chapter 11: Cover Sections 11-1 through 11-5 and a selection of the further topics in the chapter, depending on your choice. These should include at least a brief discussion of the topics in Sections 11-6 to 11-9, testing the validity of the model, using a regression model for prediction, qualitative independent variables, and a discussion of polynomial terms in a regression model. If time permits, include Section 11-12 on the Durbin-Watson test, and Section 11-13 on variable selection methods. [Two weeks or more.]

6. If time permits, include your choice of topics on forecasting from Chapter 12. [One week, if possible.]

SUGGESTED SYLLABUS NUMBER 3

(COMPREHENSIVE)
FOR A TWO-SEMESTER SEQUENCE OF COURSES IN APPLIED
STATISTICS FOR STUDENTS OF BUSINESS, ECONOMICS,
AND RELATED AREAS
[UNDERGRADUATE]

First Semester:

1. Chapter 1. Cover the entire chapter. [One week or more.]

2. Chapter 2: Cover the entire chapter. [Two weeks.]

3. Chapter 3: Cover the entire chapter. [One to two weeks.]

4. Chapter 4: Cover the entire chapter. [One week or more.]

5. Chapter 5: Cover entire chapter. [One week or more.]

   Note: you may want to include Chapter 13 on quality control and improvement here .

6. Chapter 6: Cover the entire chapter. [Two weeks.]

7. Chapter 7: Cover the entire chapter. [Two weeks or more.]

8. Chapter 8: Cover the entire chapter. [One week or more.]

9. Chapter 14: Cover Sections 14-9 through 14-11 on chi-square analysis and as many nonparametric methods as you desire. [One to two weeks.]

Second Semester:

1. Chapter 9: Cover the entire chapter. [Two weeks or more.]

2. Chapter 10: Cover the entire chapter. [Two weeks.]

3. Chapter 11: Cover most of the chapter—your choice of the advanced topics. See Syllabus 2. [Over two weeks.]

4. Cover your choice of topics from Chapter 12 on index numbers, and forecasting. [One week.]

5. Chapter 11. Choose from among the forecasting methods.

6. Cover Chapter 13 on Quality Control and Improvement. [One week].

7. Chapter 15: Cover the entire chapter. If pressed for time, you may choose to teach either Sections 15-1 through 15-4 on Bayesian statistics, or Sections 15-4 through 15-8 on decision analysis. [One to two weeks.]

8. Chapter 16: Select some topics on sampling methods. [Remaining time.]

SUGGESTED SYLLABUS NUMBER 4
(INTERMEDIATE-LEVEL, ACCELERATED)
FOR A ONE-SEMESTER FIRST COURSE IN APPLIED STATISTICS
FOR STUDENTS OF BUSINESS, ECONOMICS, AND RELATED AREAS
[MBA or other GRADUATE]

1. Selected topics from Chapter 1. These should include Sections 1-1, 1-2, 1-3, and 1-4 as a minimum. [One week or less.]

2. Chapter 2: Cover entire chapter [Two weeks.]

3. Chapter 3: Cover entire chapter. [One week.]

4. Chapter 4: Cover entire chapter. [One week.]

5. Chapter 5: Cover entire chapter. [One week.]

6. Chapter 6: Cover Sections 6-1 to 6-4 on confidence intervals, their meaning and their construction, and the t distribution. Possibly leave out Section 6-5 on the finite population correction factor. Cover Section 6-6 on the chi-square distribution and confidence intervals for the population variance. Teach Section 6-7 on sample size determination. I would recommend covering Section 6-8 on one-sided confidence intervals. [One week.]

7. Chapter 7: Thoroughly cover all the sections of this chapter. [Two weeks.]

8. Chapter 8: Cover most or all sections of this chapter. [Less than one week.]

9. Chapter 9: Cover Sections 9-1 to 9-7. Time permitting, you may cover the rest of the chapter, including blocking and experimental design. [One week.]

10. Chapter 10: Cover the entire chapter. [One week.]

11. Chapter 11: Cover Sections 11-1 through 11-5 on the multiple regression model and its use. Give at least some discussion of the problem of multicollinearity (Section 11-11). Include as many advanced topics as desired. [One week.]

12. Cover Chapter 13: All, [One week.]

13. Chapter 14: Sections 14-9 to 14-11. Include some of the sections on nonparametric methods. [One week.]

In this course, concentrate on the many involved problems with strong business-analysis emphasis found throughout the book. Also include the Cases.

SUGGESTED SYLLABUS NUMBER 6

(INTERMEDIATE-LEVEL)
FOR A TWO-SEMESTER SEQUENCE OF COURSES IN APPLIED
STATISTICS FOR STUDENTS OF BUSINESS, ECONOMICS, AND
RELATED AREAS (NO PRIOR BACKGROUND IN STATISTICS)
[MBA or other GRADUATE]

This is similar to syllabus number 3, except that more of the optional, advanced topics may be included, and the pace may be somewhat faster than that of the undergraduate course, allowing the more extensive coverage for the same allotted class time. Concentrate on the more involved and more challenging problems, and on the Cases.

SUGGESTED SYLLABUS NUMBER 7

(ADVANCED, COMPREHENSIVE)
FOR A THREE-SEMESTER SEQUENCE OF COURSES IN APPLIED
STATISTICS FOR STUDENTS OF BUSINESS, ECONOMICS, AND
RELATED AREAS (NO PRIOR BACKGROUND IN STATISTICS)
[MBA, other MASTER program, or DOCTORAL program for
non-statistics business majors.]

Cover the entire book, possibly leaving out Section 11-15 on the matrix approach to multiple regression analysis.

I would evenly divide the material in the book into three equal parts and devote each semester to one part. You may choose to teach Chapters 1 through 6 in the first semester, Chapters 7 through 11 in the second semester, and Chapters 13 through 17 in the third semester. You may switch the order of the advanced chapters, however, this book assumes that Chapter 9 on ANOVA is taught before the regression chapters.

SUGGESTED SYLLABUS NUMBER 7

(INTERMEDIATE-LEVEL)
FOR A ONE-SEMESTER COURSE
[UNDERGRADUATE or GRADUATE.]

1. Cover Chapter 1. [One week.]

2. Quickly review Chapters 2 through 8. [Two weeks.]

3. Thoroughly cover Chapter 10. [Two weeks or more.]

4. Cover entire Chapter 11. [Two weeks.]

5. Cover entire Chapter 12. [One to two weeks.]

6. Cover entire Chapter 13. [One week.]

7. Cover entire Chapter 9, concentrating on experimental design in the second half of the chapter. [Two weeks or more.]

8. Cover Chapter 16.

A one-quarter variation of this course is also possible by deleting some topics and/or accelerating the discussion of others.

CHAPTER 1

1-1.   1. quantitative/ratio
    2. qualitative/nominal
    3. quantitative/ratio
    4. qualitative/nominal
    5. quantitative/ratio
    6. quantitative/interval
    7. quantitative/ratio
    8. quantitative/ratio
    9. quantitative/ratio
    10. quantitative/ratio
    11. quantitative/ordinal

1-2.   Data are based on numeric measurements of some variable, either from a data set comprising an entire population of interest, or else obtained from only a sample (subset) of the full population. Instead of doing the measurements ourselves, we may sometimes obtain data from previous results in published form.

1-3.   The weakest is the Nominal Scale, in which categories of data are grouped by qualitative differences and assigned numbers simply as labels, not usable in numeric comparisons. Next in strength is the Ordinal Scale: data are ordered (ranked) according to relative size or quality, but the numbers themselves don't imply specific numeric relationships. Stronger than this is the Interval Scale: the ordered data points have meaningful distances between any two of them, measured in units. Finally is the Ratio Scale, which is like an Interval Scale but where the ratio of any two specific data values is also measured in units and has meaning in comparing values.

1-4.   a.
Investment Objective:	qualitative, nominal
Net Asset Value:	quantitative, ratio
Offer Price:	quantitative, ratio
NAV Change:	quantitative, ratio
Total Return Year to Date:	quantitative, ratio
Maximum Initial Charge:	quantitative, ratio
Total Expense Ratio:	quantitative, ratio
Ranking:	quantitative, ordinal

1-5.   Ordinal.

1-6. A qualitative variable describes different categories or qualities of the members of a data set, which have no numeric relationships to each other, even when the categories happen to be coded as numbers for convenience. A quantitative variable gives numerically meaningful information, in terms of ranking, differences, or ratios between individual values.

1-7. The people from one particular neighborhood constitute a non-random sample (drawn from the larger town population). The frame of 100 people would be a random sample.

1-8. A sample is a subset of the full population of interest, from which statistical inferences are drawn about the population, which is usually too large to permit the variable(s) to be measured for *all* the members.

1-9. A random sample is a sample drawn from a population in a way that is not *a priori* biased with respect to the kinds of variables being measured. It attempts to give a representative cross-section of the population.

1-10. Nationality: qualitative. Length of intended stay: quantitative.

1-11. Ordinal. The colors are ranked, but no units of difference between any two of them are defined.

1-12.

Income:	quantitative, ratio
Number of dependents:	quantitative, ratio
Filing singly/jointly:	qualitative, nominal
Itemized or not:	qualitative, nominal
Local taxes:	quantitative, ratio

1-13. Lower quartile = 25th percentile = data point in position $(n + 1)(25/100) =$ $34(25/100) =$ position 8.5. (Here $n = 33$.) Let us order our observations: 109, 110, 114, 116, 118, 119, 120, 121, 121, 123, 123, 125, 125, 127, 128, 128, 128, 128, 129, 129, 130, 131, 132, 132, 133, 134, 134, 134, 134, 136, 136, 136, 136.
Lower quartile $= 121$
Middle quartile is in position: $34(50/100) = 17$. Point is 128.
Upper quartile is in position: $34(75/100) = 25.5$. Point is 133.5.
10th percentile is in position: $34(10/100) = 3.4$. Point is 114.8.
15th percentile is in position: $34(15/100) = 5.1$. Point is 118.1.

65th percentile is in position: $34(65/100) = 22.1$. Point is 131.1.

IQR $= 133.5 - 121 = 12.5$.

1-14. First, order the data:

$-1.2, 3.9, 8.3, 9, 9.5, 10, 11, 11.6, 12.5, 13, 14.8, 15.5, 16.2, 16.7, 18$

The median, or 50th percentile, is the point in position $16(50/100) = 8$. The point is 11.6.

First quartile is in position $16(25/100) = 4$. Point is 9.

Third quartile is in position $16(75/100) = 12$. Point is 15.5.

55th percentile is in position $16(55/100) = 8.8$. Point is 12.32.

85th percentile is in position $16(85/100) = 13.6$. Point is 16.5.

1-15. Order the data:

$38, 41, 44, 45, 45, 52, 54, 56, 60, 64, 69, 71, 76, 77, 78, 79, 80, 81, 87, 88, 90, 98$

Median is in position $23(50/100) - 11.5$. Point is 70.

20th percentile is in position $23(20/100) = 4.6$. Point is 45.

30th percentile is in position $23(30/300) = 6.9$. Point is 53.8.

60th percentile is in position $23(60/100) = 13.8$. Point is 76.8.

90th percentile is in position $23(90/100) = 20.7$. Point is 89.4.

1-16. Order the data: 1, 1, 1, 2, 2, 2, 3, 3, 4, 4, 5, 5, 6, 6, 7.

Lower quartile is the 25th percentile, point in position $16(25/100) = 4$. Point is 2.

The median is in position $16(50/100) = 8$. The point is 3.

Upper quartile is in position $16(75/100) = 12$. Point is 5.

IQR $= 5 - 2 = 3$.

60th percentile is in position $16(60/100) = 9.6$. It is 4.

1-17. The data are already ordered; there are 16 data points. The median is the point in position $17(50/100) = 8.5$. It is 51.

Lower quartile is in position $17(25/100) = 4.25$. It is 30.5.

Upper quartile is in position $17(75/100) = 12.75$. It is 194.25.

IQR $= 194.25 - 30.5 = 163.75$.

45th percentile is in position $17(45/100) = 7.65$. Point is 42.2.

1-18. The mean is a central point that summarizes all the information in the data. It is sensitive to extreme observations. The median is a point "in the middle" of the data set and does not contain all the information in the set. It is resistant to extreme observations. The mode is a value that occurs most frequently.

1-19. Mean, median, mode(s) of the observations in Problem **1-13**:

$$\text{Mean} = \bar{x} = \frac{1}{n} \sum x_i = 126.63$$

Median $= 128$

Modes $= 128, \ 134, \ 136$ (all have 4 points)

1-20. For the data of Problem **1-14**:

Mean $= 11.2533$

Median $= 11.6$

Mode: none

1-21. For the data of Problem **1-15**:

Mean $= 66.954$

Median $= 70$

Mode $= 45$

1-22. For the data of Problem **1-16**:

Mean $= 3.466$

Median $= 3$

Modes $= 1$ and 2

1-23. For the data of Problem **1-17**:

Mean $= 199.875$

Median $= 51$

Mode: none

1-24. For the data of Example 1-1:

Mean $= 163,260$

Median $= 166,800$

Mode: none

1-25. For the Delaware Group 'Offer Price' data in Problem **1-4**:

Mean = 13.001

Median = 11.94

1-26. Measures of variability tell us about the spread of our observations.

1-27. The most important measures of variability are the variance and its square root— the standard deviation. Both reflect all the information in the data set.

1-28. For a sample, we divide the sum of squared deviations from the mean by $n - 1$, rather than by n.

1-29. For the data of Problem **1-13**, assumed a sample:

Range $= 136 - 109 = 27$

Variance $= 57.74$

Standard deviation $= 7.5986$

1-30. For the data of Problem **1-14**:

Range $= 18 - (-1.2) = 19.2$

Variance $= 25.90$

Standard deviation $= 5.0896$

1-31. For the data of Problem **1-15**:

Range $= 98 - 38 = 60$

Variance $= 321.38$

Standard deviation $= 17.927$

1-32. For the data of Problem **1-16**:

Range $= 7 - 1 = 6$

Variance $= 3.98$

Standard deviation $= 1.995$

1-33. For the data of Problem **1-17**:

Range $= 1,209 - 23 = 1,186$

Variance $= 110,287.75$

Standard deviation $= 332.096$

1-34. $n = 33$, $\bar{x} = 126.64$, $s = 7.60$, so $\bar{x} \pm 2s = [111.44, 141.84]$; this captures 31/33 of the data points, so Chebyshev's theorem holds. The data set is not mound-shaped, so the empirical rule does not apply.

1-35. $n = 15$, $\bar{x} = 11.253$, $s = 5.090$, so $\bar{x} \pm 2s = [1.074, 21.433]$; this captures 14/15 of the data points, so Chebyshev's theorem holds. The data set is not mound-shaped, so the empirical rule does not apply.

1-36. $n = 22$, $\bar{x} = 66.95$, $s = 17.93$, so $\bar{x} \pm 2s = [31.09, 102.81]$; this captures *all* the data points, so Chebyshev's theorem holds. The data set is not mound-shaped, so the empirical rule does not apply.

1-37. $n = 15$, $\bar{x} = 3.467$, $s = 1.995$, so $\bar{x} \pm 2s = [-0.524, 7.457]$; this captures *all* the data points, so Chebyshev's theorem holds. The data set is not mound-shaped, so the empirical rule does not apply.

1-38. $n = 16$, $\bar{x} = 199.9$, $s = 332.1$, so $\bar{x} \pm 2s = [-464.3, 864.1]$; this captures 15/16 of the data points, so Chebyshev's theorem holds. The data set is not mound-shaped, so the empirical rule does not apply.

1-39.

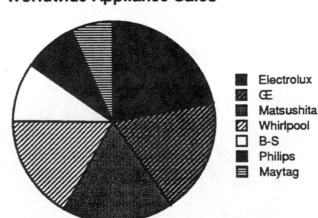

Worldwide Appliance Sales

- Electrolux
- GE
- Matsushita
- Whirlpool
- B-S
- Philips
- Maytag

1-40.

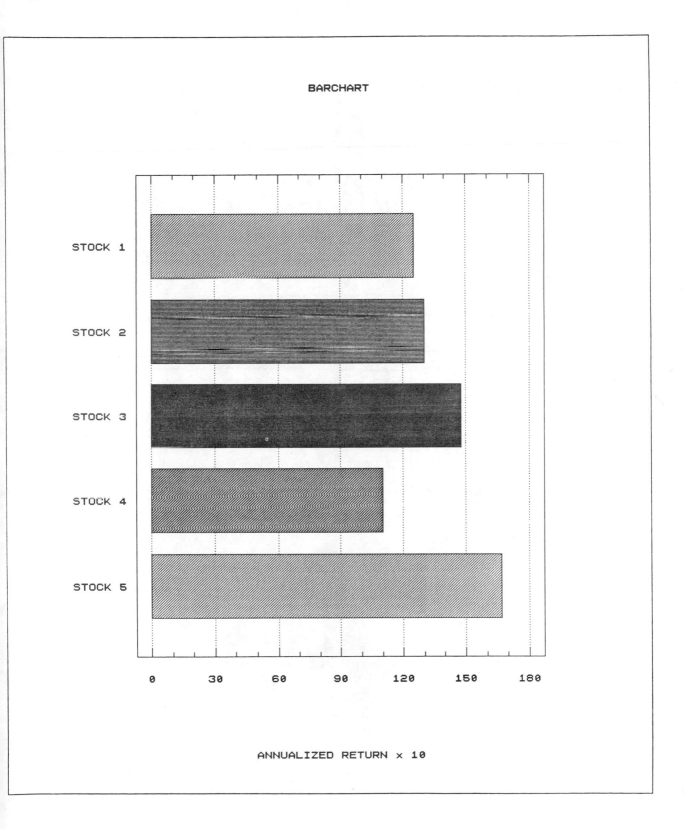

1-41.

Endowment in $Billions

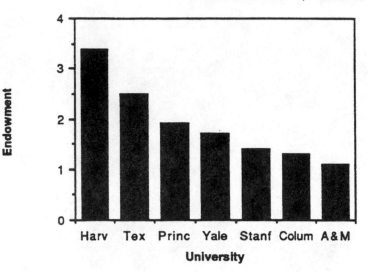

1-42.

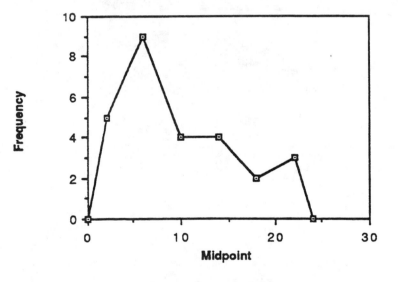

1-43. A pie chart giving relative amounts in each category of the nominal variable 'web-browsing application'. Netscape Navigator dominates, being the choice of just over 3/4 of the users in the survey.

1-44.

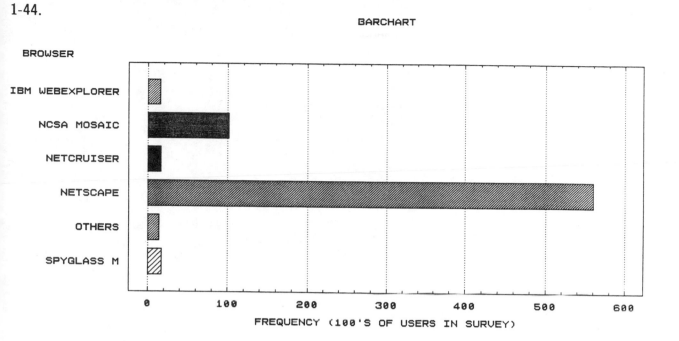

1-45. Time plot of the variable 'average hourly pay of factory workers', giving the specific range of values on the vertical axis.

1-46. Using SYSTAT:

```
5    5
5    6
5    88
6    01
6    23
6
6 H 6777
6    89
7    00
7 M 222333
7    455
7 H 667
7    889
8
8    22
8    4
```

1-47.

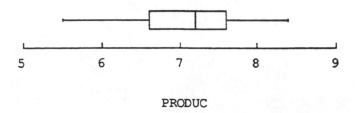

PRODUC

There are no outliers. The distribution is skewed to the left.

1-48. A stem-and-leaf display is a quickly drawn type of histogram useful in analyzing data. A box plot is a more advanced display useful in identifying outliers and the shape of the distribution of the data.

1-49. Using SYSTAT:

```
    0   5
***OUTSIDE VALUES***
    3    234
    3    578
    4 H 2234
    4 M 567788899
    5 H 01223
    5    5678
    6    3
***OUTSIDE VALUES***
    7    8
```

1-50.

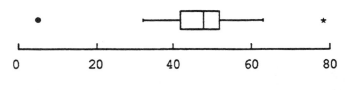

PERCENT

The data are narrowly and symmetrically concentrated near the median (IQR and the whisker lengths are small), not counting two extreme outliers.

1-51. Data set #1 has small values, clustered together and right-skewed. Data set #2 has larger values, wider-spread, and right-skewed. Set #3 is similar to #2 but more symmetric. Set #4 has largest values, wide-spread, and left-skewed.

1-52.

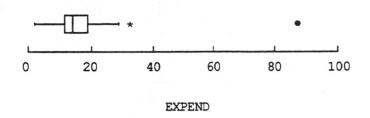

EXPEND

The outlier is Haiti. The conditions in Haiti may explain why this is an outlier. The suspected outlier is Guadeloupe.

1-53. Using SYSTAT:

```
1 H 0011111223444
1   55689
2 M 022333
2   567789
3 H 0122234
3   78
4   012
4   7
5   23
```

The distribution is right-skewed.

1-54. Outliers are detected by looking at the data set, constructing a box plot or stem-and-leaf display. An outlier should be analyzed for information content and not merely be rejected.

1-55. The median is the line inside the box. The hinges are the upper and lower quartiles. The inner fences are the two points at a distance of 1.5(IQR) from the upper and lower quartiles. Outer fences: same but at a distance of 3(IQR). The box itself represents 50% of the data.

1-56.

Mine A:		Mine B:	
3	24	2	34
3	57	2	89
4 H	123	3 H	24
4 M	55689	3	578
5 H	123	4 M	034
5		4 H	789
6	0	5	012
OUTSIDE VALUES		5	9
7	36		
8	5		

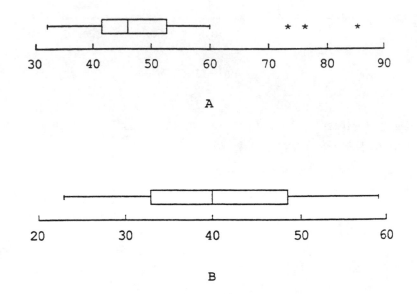

Values for Mine A are smaller than for Mine B, right-skewed, and there are three outliers. Values for B are larger and the distribution is almost symmetric. There is larger variance in B.

1-57. No. You need to use statistical inference.

1-59. $\bar{x} = 74.7$ $s = 13.944$ $s^2 = 194.43$

1-60. $\mu = 504.688$ $\sigma = 94.547$

1-61. Group data in Problem **1-60** into classes:

class	count
$300 \leq x < 400$	6
$400 \leq x < 500$	10
$500 \leq x < 600$	9
$600 \leq x < 700$	7

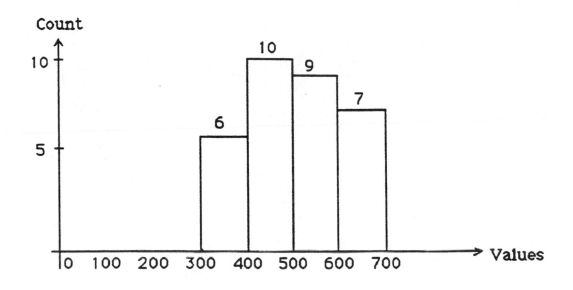

1-62.   Order the data: 344, 347, 359, 390, 396, 398, 400, 412, 441, 452, 455, 457, 474, 476, 477, 499, 504, 505, 530, 544, 560, 566, 580, 582, 587, 600, 606, 613, 632, 633, 641, 690

Range $= 690 - 344 = 346$

90th percentile lies in position: $33(90/100) = 29.7$. It is 632.7.

First quartile is in position $33(25/100) = 8.25$. It is $412 + (441 - 412).25 = 419.25$.

Middle quartile is in position $33(50/100) = 16.5$. It is 501.5.

Third quartile is in position $33(75/100) = 24.75$. It is $582 + 5(.75) = 585.75$.

1-63.

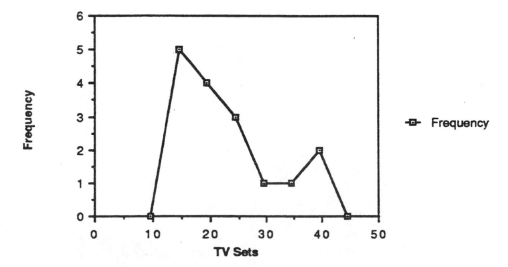

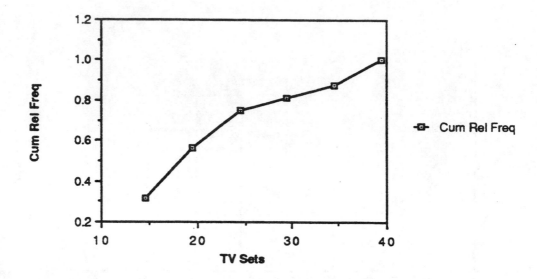

1-64. Stem-and-leaf display:

```
1     24
1  H  56789
2  M  023
2  H  55
3     24
3
4     01
```

1-65.

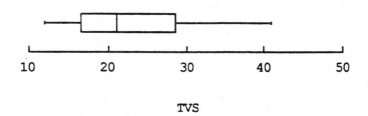

TVS

The data set is skewed to the right.

1-66.
```
        1    012
     ***OUTSIDE VALUES***
        1    9
        2    11
        2 H  22233
        2 M  455
        2    6677
        2 H  889
        3    0
        3    2
        3    45
        3    7
     ***OUTSIDE VALUES***
        6    2
```

1-67.

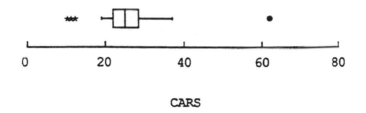

There are four outliers. These can also be seen from the stem-and-leaf display of the previous problem.

1-68.

BARCHART

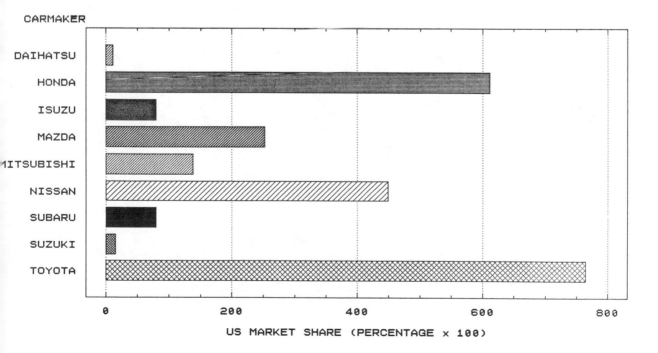

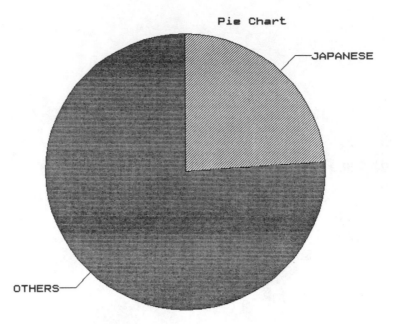

Pie Chart

JAPANESE

OTHERS

1-69.	industry group	mean	median	range	s^2	s
1-70.	Apparel & Shoes	21.59	20.30	47.7	132.19	11.50
	Home Furnishings	11.71	10.15	33.8	82.45	9.08
	Gas Distributors	10.52	10.85	12.6	12.33	3.51
	Software	21.23	20.25	34.2	129.89	11.40
	Personal Products	20.46	17.35	50.4	154.94	12.45
	International Oils	10.94	10.60	7.7	5.66	2.38

Some of the medians reported in the published table differ from those calculated here; this is due to a slightly different method used in the case of an even number of data points, and to the treatment of missing data. In all cases except Personal Products, the mean is very close to the median, due to the fairly uniform, symmetric distribution of the data within each industry group. The two measures are appoximately equal in meaning here, except in Personal Products where the top 2 or 3 products are outliers in the large group.

1-71.

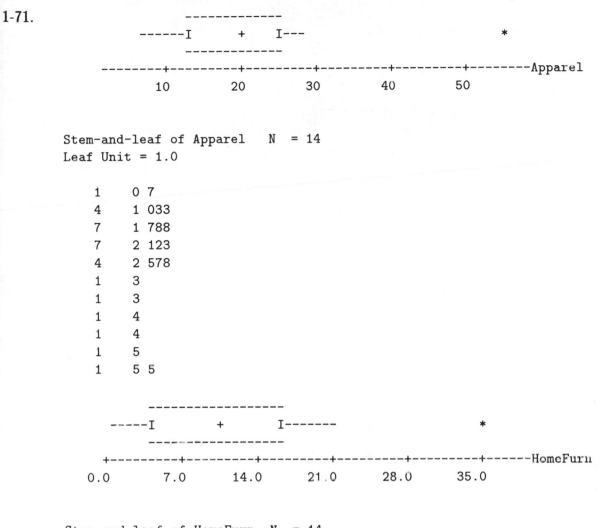

```
                   --------------
        ------I       +      I---                              *
      --------+---------+---------+---------+---------+-------Apparel
              10        20        30        40        50
```

```
Stem-and-leaf of Apparel   N  = 14
Leaf Unit = 1.0

       1     0 7
       4     1 033
       7     1 788
       7     2 123
       4     2 578
       1     3
       1     3
       1     4
       1     4
       1     5
       1     5 5
```

```
                 --------------------
        -----I         +         I-------                      *
           ---------------------
         +---------+---------+---------+---------+---------+------HomeFurn
        0.0       7.0      14.0      21.0      28.0      35.0
```

```
Stem-and-leaf of HomeFurn  N  = 14
Leaf Unit = 1.0

       4     0 1334
       7     0 688
       7     1 112
       4     1 6
       3     2 00
       1     2
       1     3 4
```

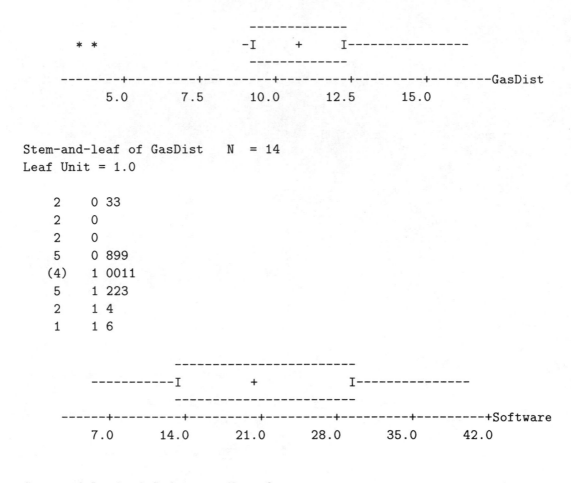

```
                          -------------
       * *                 -I    +     I-----------------
                          -------------
       --------+---------+---------+---------+---------+--------GasDist
             5.0       7.5       10.0      12.5      15.0


Stem-and-leaf of GasDist   N  = 14
Leaf Unit = 1.0

      2      0 33
      2      0
      2      0
      5      0 899
     (4)     1 0011
      5      1 223
      2      1 4
      1      1 6

                       -----------------------
           -----------I       +          I---------------
                       -----------------------
       ------+---------+---------+---------+---------+---------+Software
            7.0       14.0      21.0      28.0      35.0      42.0


Stem-and-leaf of Software  N  = 8
Leaf Unit = 1.0

      2      0 59
      2      1
      4      1 66
      4      2 4
      3      2 7
      2      3 0
      1      3 9
```

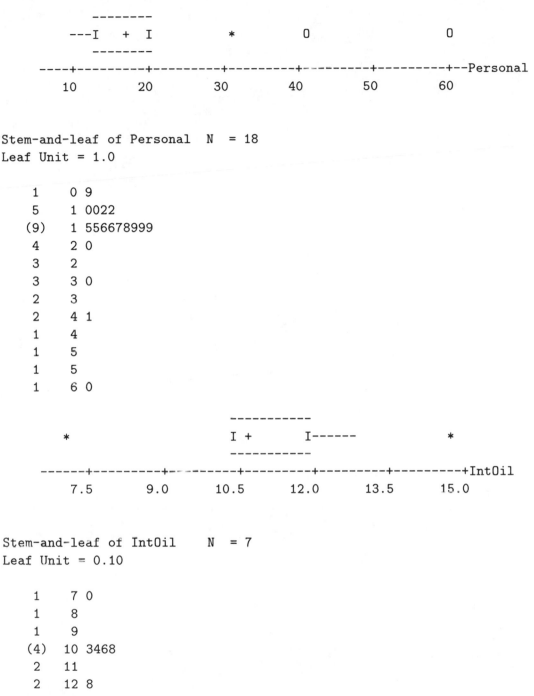

```
           --------
     ---I  +  I             *            0                   0
           --------
     ----+---------+---------+---------+---------+---------+--Personal
        10        20        30        40        50        60


Stem-and-leaf of Personal  N  = 18
Leaf Unit = 1.0

     1     0 9
     5     1 0022
    (9)    1 556678999
     4     2 0
     3     2
     3     3 0
     2     3
     2     4 1
     1     4
     1     5
     1     5
     1     6 0


                                     -----------
         *                          I +       I------             *
                                     -----------
     ------+---------+---------+---------+---------+---------+IntOil
        7.5       9.0       10.5      12.0      13.5      15.0


Stem-and-leaf of IntOil    N  = 7
Leaf Unit = 0.10

     1     7 0
     1     8
     1     9
    (4)   10 3468
     2    11
     2    12 8
     1    13
     1    14 7


                  ---------
         --------I +    I--------- *  **          0   0
                  ---------
     --+---------+---------+---------+---------+---------+----ALL
        0        12        24        36        48        60
```

For the data set as a whole, the outliers are only those values above 34.

1-72. Overall:

mean = 16.37

median = 13.00

mode = 10.6

range = 59.20

st. dev. = 10.65

first quartile = 10.3, third quartile = 19.9

10th percentile = 5.98, 90th percentile = 29.16

1-73. The mean = 9.153 is quite close to the median = 9.13, but rather less than the national average. This indicates that mortgage rates tend to be lower in large cities than elsewhere.

1-74. $s^2 = 0.0299$, $s = 0.1729$. Chebyshev's theorem applies in all cases. This data set has two modes, and $\bar{x} \pm 2s = [8.807, 9.498]$ captures 21/24 of the points, or only 87.5%. The empirical rule does not hold here.

1-75. Rates have two modes: 9.00 and 9.25

Points have the single mode 3.00

1-76.
```
                                -------------------
                ----------------I        +         I-----------------
                                -------------------
        ------+---------+---------+---------+---------+---------+---------+MthlyPay
           592.0      600.0     608.0     616.0     624.0     632.0
```

No outliers or unusual cities.

1-77.
```
Stem-and-leaf of MthlyPay   N  = 24
Leaf Unit = 1.0

      1    59 0
      1    59
      8    60 3333333
      8    60
     (6)   61 000000
     10    61 7777777
      3    62 3
      2    62
      2    63 00
```

```
Stem-and-leaf of Points     N  = 24
Leaf Unit = 0.10

      1       1 5
      1       1
      1       1
      5       2 0000
      5       2
      9       2 5555
     (4)      2 7777
     11       2 8
     10       3 00000
      5       3 223
      2       3 5
      1       3
      1       3
      1       4 0
```

```
Histogram of MthlyPay    N = 24

Midpoint    Count
    590        1   *
    595        0
    600        0
    605        7   *******
    610        6   ******
    615        7   *******
    620        0
    625        1   *
    630        2   **
```

```
Histogram of Points     N = 24

Midpoint    Count
    1.6        1   *
    2.0        4   ****
    2.4        4   ****
    2.8        5   *****
    3.2        8   ********
    3.6        1   *
    4.0        1   *
```

Monthly Payment is symmetrically distributed with two modes; Points is a somewhat left-skewed distribution.

1-78.   A right-skewed distribution with large standard deviation greatly influenced by the
        single point = 100.

1-79. Bar graphs showing change over time. The units on the vertical axis of the Sales graph, however, are ten times as large as those on the Profits graph (e.g., 4 billion in Sales is at the same height as 400 million in Profits), so be careful.

1-80. Time plot, show an increasing trend of the S&P Stock Index for the period shown. Fairly close to a straight linear increase.

1-81. Bar graph showing change over time. The numbers are percentage changes, not absolute dollar amounts, which makes comparison of different quarters a little less straightforward. Note the truncated representation of 1994 first quarter, which would normally be shown more than twice as tall as the previous quarter's number.

1-82. $\mu = 18.80$ $\qquad \sigma = 40.47$

1-83.

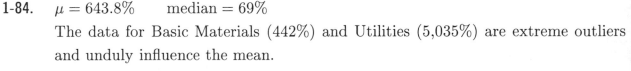

1-84. $\mu = 643.8\%$ $\qquad$ median $= 69\%$
The data for Basic Materials (442%) and Utilities (5,035%) are extreme outliers and unduly influence the mean.

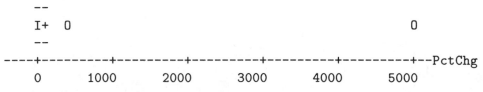

1-85. Paperbacks are much more variable: they have a sample variance of 5.24, compared to 0.93 for the hardcovers. A possible reason is the greater number of different paperbacks that are published compared to hardcovers, allowing more opportunities for outliers in the sales trends.

1-86. If the values were proportional to the heights, then the California icon would be almost 4 times as tall as each of the three icons on the right. Instead it's only about twice as tall: thus the values are proportional to area. This may be a subtle point when quickly inspecting the graphic for its numerical information content.

1-87. $\mu = 101,141.4$, which is a little smaller than the listed USA median of 107,900.

1-88. The median table entry is 89,300, considerably less than the USA median. This is due to the different population groupings. The median table entry is the middle value out of just 133 values, each being the median price within a city; but each of those cities has a different number of houses. If we knew all the individual house prices for each of the cities, pooling and ordering all those data could very well result in a middle value which is not contained in the "median city" or which is in that city but is not the middle value of that particular city's values in the pool.

1-89. Medians are used to minimize the influence of outliers.

1-90.

```
              -------
     ----I +   I------- * **    *     0                      0
              -------
     ----+---------+---------+---------+---------+---------+ -Price
     60000      120000    180000    240000    300000    360000
```

Honolulu and San Francisco are the two extreme outliers; Anaheim is the most extreme of the nearer outliers. No doubt the higher prices in cities such as these are due to the very great demand for residences in such desirable locations.

Case 1. Coupon, Amount Issued, Recent Price, Yield to Put, Yield to Maturity, and Yield Sacrifice are all quantitative/ratio variables. Maturity Date and Date of First Put are quantitative/interval variables. Issuer is a qualitative/nominal variable. Moody's Rating is a quantitative/ordinal variable.

The important variables here are Yield to Put, Yield to Maturity, and Yield Sacrifice, for making comparisons among the differing results from buying these bonds, keeping them to maturity, exercising the put option before maturity, or buying similar bonds with no put option.

Using MINITAB:

	N	MEAN	MEDIAN	TRMEAN	STDEV	SEMEAN
Put	10	7.256	7.370	7.301	0.698	0.221
Maturity	10	7.7580	7.6700	7.7625	0.3158	0.0999
Sacrific	10	0.652	0.555	0.625	0.331	0.105

	MIN	MAX	Q1	Q3
Put	6.100	8.050	6.718	7.823
Maturity	7.2300	8.2500	7.5350	8.0775
Sacrific	0.330	1.190	0.392	0.980

```
                                 ---------------------------
          -----------------------I            +          I-------
                                 ---------------------------
          ------+---------+---------+---------+---------+---------+Put
            6.30      6.65      7.00      7.35      7.70      8.05
```

```
                              ---------------------------
           ----------------I     +              I----------
                              ---------------------------
          --+---------+---------+---------+---------+---------+----Maturity
          7.20      7.40      7.60      7.80      8.00      8.20
```

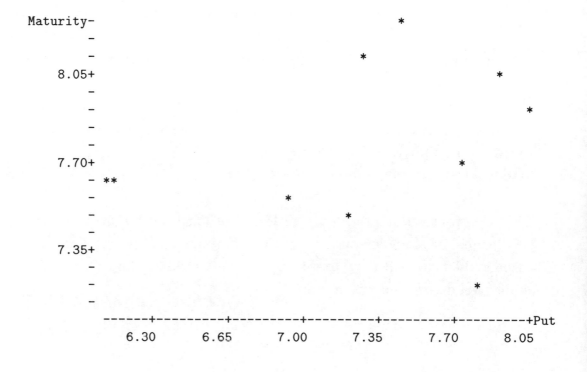

```
  Maturity-                                      *
         -
         -                                  *
    8.05+                                                *
         -
         -                                                    *
         -
         -
    7.70+                                           *
         - **
         -                              *
         -                                  *
         -
    7.35+
         -
         -                                            *
         -
         -
          ------+---------+---------+---------+---------+---------+Put
              6.30      6.65      7.00      7.35      7.70      8.05
```

CHAPTER 2

2-1. Objective and subjective.

2-2. An event is a set of basic outcomes of an experiment. The union of two events is the set containing all basic outcomes that are either in one event or in the other, or in both. The intersection of two events is the set of basic outcomes that are members of both events.

2-3. The sample space is the universal set pertinent to a given experiment. It is the set of all possible outcomes of an experiment.

2-4. The probability of an event is a measure of the likelihood of the occurrence of the event. When sample points are equally likely, the probability of the event is the relative size of the set comprising the event within the sample space.

2-5. The union $G \cup F$ is the event that the baby is either a girl, or is over 5 pounds (of either sex). The intersection $G \cap F$ is the event that the baby is a girl over 5 pounds.

2-6. The union is the event that the player scores in the game with A, or in the game with B, or in both. The intersection is the event that the player scores in both games.

2-7. The union $A \cup B$ is the event of getting the grad school acceptance or the job offer or both. The intersection $A \cap B$ is the event of receiving both.

2-8. $R \cup T$ is the event that a randomly chosen person is exposed to the ad on the radio or the ad on television, or both. $R \cap T$ is the event that a randomly chosen person is exposed to the ad on the radio and the ad on television.

2-9. $S \cup B$: purchase stock or bonds, or both.
$S \cap B$: purchase stock and bonds.

2-10. P(being killed by terrorists) $= 39/28{,}000{,}000 = 0.00000139$ (about 1 in 718,000).
P(dying in an automobile accident) $= 1/5{,}300 = 0.0001887$.

2-11. One suitcase lost every 2 days; 2 flights per day; 200 passengers per flight; on average 2 pieces of luggage per passenger: $2 \times 200 \times 2 \times 2 = 1{,}600$.

P(losing a suitcase) $= 1/1{,}600 = 0.000625$

2-12. Since there are only 37 possible outcomes, the probability of winning is $1/37 = 0.027$, better odds (for the player) than the American version. Because of this, the house admission fee makes sense.

2-13. Roughly: Highest $= 0.80$, Moderate $= 0.50$, Low $= 0.10$.

2-14. At each level of radon, the risk of contracting lung cancer as implied by the chart is the number of people reported in the second column divided by the sample size 1,000:

Radon Level	Risk of Contracting Lung Cancer
20 pCi/L:	8/1,000 (0.008)
10 pCi/L:	4/1,000 (0.004)
8 pCi/L:	3/1,000 (0.003)
4 pCi/L:	2/1,000 (0.002)
2 pCi/L:	1/1,000 (0.001)
1.3 pCi/L:	$< 1/1{,}000$ (< 0.001)
0.4 pCi/L:	$< 1/1{,}000$ (< 0.001)

2-15. Yes. The measured radon level can only be at one of any of the levels shown, at most.

2-16. The table in Problem **2-14** compares the highest risk of lung cancer, 8/1,000, to "the risk of being killed in a violent crime" which we will assume is the same thing as "being murdered." But 0.008 is much greater than $9/100{,}000 = 0.000009$. The explanation is that the lung cancer risk pertains to the whole span of time of living in a house with the given radon level, which may be many years; the CNN Business News statistic pertains to just one year.

2-17. 0.85, for example, is a typical "very likely" probability.

2-18. More like to occur than not to occur.

2-19. The team is very likely to to win.

2-20. P(first shopper detected) + P(second detected) − P(both detected)
$$= 0.98 + 0.94 - 0.93 = 0.99$$

2-21. **a.** The two events are mutually exclusive.

b. Let O, D be the events: machine is out-of-control, down (respectively). Then we need $P(O \cup D) = P(O) + P(D) - P(O \cap D) = 0.02 + 0.015 - 0 = 0.035$

c. $P(\overline{D}) = 1 - P(D) = 1 - 0.015 = 0.985$
This event and D are mutually exclusive.

2-22. $P(F) + P(> 50) - P(F \ \& \ > 50) = \dfrac{12 + 2 - 2}{20} = 0.6$

$P(< 30) = 2/20 = 0.1$

2-23. $P(T \cup R) = P(T) + P(R) - P(T \cap R) = 0.25 + 0.34 - 0.10 = 0.49$

2-24. $P(S \cup B) = P(S) + P(B) - P(S \cap B) = 0.85 + 0.33 - 0.28 = 0.90$

2-25. $P(\text{VT} \cup \text{CE}) = \dfrac{380 + 412 - 357}{550} = 0.7909$

2-26. **a.** In the one-year performance column, 4 of the 7 indexes were losses, so the probability is 4/7.

b. All but two of percentage figures in the 10-year column are > 200, so the probability is 5/7.

c. P(yield $\geq 5\%$) + P(3-year gain $\geq 35\%$) − P(both) = $(3 + 4 - 1)/7 = 6/7$.

d. Yes; none of the seven indexes both lost money during the last year and had a yield of at least 4%.

2-27. $P(M \cup H) = P(M) + P(H) - P(M \cap H) = \dfrac{11 + 8 - 5}{28} = \dfrac{1}{2} = 0.500$

2-28. $P(M \mid R) = .80$ $P(R) = 0.4$ $P(M \cap R) = (0.8)(0.4) = 0.32$

2-29. $P(L \cap D) = 0.12$ $P(L) = 0.20$ $P(D \mid L) = P(L \cap D) / P(L) = .12/.20 = 0.60$

2-30. $P(N \mid D) = 0.25$
$P(D) = 0.10$
$P(N \cap D) = P(N \mid D) P(D) = (.25)(.10) = 0.025$
2.5% of the packages do not arrive on time.

2-31.

	East	South	Mid-west	West	row total
Hospital	75	128	29	52	284
Phys. visit	233	514	104	251	1102
Outpatient	100	326	65	99	590
col. total	408	968	198	402	1976

a. $P(M) = 198/1976 = 0.1002$

b. $P(E) = 408/1976 = 0.2065$

c. Mutually exclusive events: $P(M \cup S) = P(M) + P(S) = (198 + 968)/1976 = 0.59$

d. $P(H) = 284/1976 = 0.144$

e. $P(S \mid H) = P(S \cap H) / P(H) = \dfrac{128/1976}{284/1976} = 0.451$

f. $P(P \mid E) = P(P \cap E) / P(E) = \dfrac{233/1976}{408/1976} = 0.571$

g. $P(W \mid O) = P(W \cap O) / P(O) = \dfrac{99/1976}{590/1976} = 0.168$

h. $P(E \cup O) = P(E) + P(O) - P(E \cap O) = (408 + 590 - 100)/1976 = 0.454$

i. $P(H \cup S) = P(H) + P(S) - P(H \cap S) = (284 + 968 - 128)/1976 = 0.569$

2-32. $P(A \mid H) = 0.94$ $P(H) = 0.65$
$P(A \cap H) = P(A \mid H) P(H) = (.94)(.65) = 0.611$

2-33. **a.** $P(I) = 119/246 = 0.484$

b. $P(D) = 112/246 = 0.455$

c. $P(I \cap D) = 34/246 = 0.138$

d. $P(\overline{I} \cap \overline{D}) = 49/246 = 0.199$

e. $P(D \mid I) = P(D \cap I)/P(I) = 0.138/0.484 = 0.285$

f. $P(I \mid \overline{D}) = P(I \cap \overline{D})/P(\overline{D}) = \dfrac{85/246}{134/246} = 0.634$

g. $P(D \cup I) = P(D) + P(I) - P(D \cap I) = 0.455 + 0.484 - 0.138 = 0.801$

2-34. Let E, S denote the events: top Executive made over \$1M, Shareholders made money, respectively. Then:

a. $P(E) = 3/10$

b. $P(\overline{S}) = 3/10$

c. $P(E \mid \overline{S}) = P(E \cap \overline{S})/P(\overline{S}) = \dfrac{2/10}{3/10} = 2/3 = 0.667$

d. $P(S \mid E) = P(S \cap E)/P(E) = \dfrac{1/10}{3/10} = 1/3 = 0.333$

2-35. Let S, D, P denote the events: patient slept in the following hour, patient was given the drug, and patient was given a placebo (respectively). Then:

	Drug	Placebo	row total
Sleep	18	12	30
No sleep	32	38	70
col. total	50	50	100

a. $P(S) = 30/100 = 3/10$

b. $P(S \mid P) = P(S \cap P)/P(P) = \dfrac{12/100}{50/100} = 12/50 = 6/25 = 0.24$

c. $P(D \mid S) = P(D \cap S)/P(S) = \dfrac{18/100}{30/100} = 18/30 = 3/5 = 0.60$

2-36. For any single executive, P(believes) = P(does not believe) = 1/2. By independence, the probability that all 5 executives polled do not believe is $(1/2)^5$, the product of the individual probabilities for each of the 5 executives.

P($\geq$ 1 executive believes) = 1 – P(none believe) = $1 - (1/2)^5 = 31/32 = 0.969$

P(all 5 believe) = $(1/2)^5 = 1/32 = 0.0313$

2-37. P(at least one broken)

$= 1 - P(\text{both not broken}) = 1 - (99/100)^2$ (by independence)

$= 0.0199$.

Another way to solve the problem:

P(at least one broken) = $P(B_1 \cup B_2)$

$= P(B_1) + P(B_2) - P(B_1 \cap B_2)$

$= P(B_1) + P(B_2) - P(B_1) P(B_2)$ (by independence)

$= (.01) + (.01) - (0.01)^2 = 0.0199$

2-38. P(at least one job) = 1 – P(no jobs)

$= 1 - \dfrac{2}{3}\dfrac{2}{3}\dfrac{2}{3}\dfrac{5}{6}\dfrac{5}{6}\dfrac{19}{20}\dfrac{19}{20}$ (by independence)

$= 0.8143$

2-39. Assume independence:

P(at least one arrives on time) = 1 – P(all three fail to arrive)

$= 1 - (1 - 0.90)(1 - 0.88)(1 - 0.91) = 0.99892$

2-40. For a flight in a modern aircraft, we have P(not crashing) = 1 – P(crashing) = $1 - \dfrac{1}{500,000} = \dfrac{499,000}{500,000}$. Since the flights are independent events, the probability of no crashes in any of N flights is $\left(\dfrac{499,000}{500,000}\right)^N$. Thus:

P($\geq$ 1 crash in the next 20) = 1 – P(no crashes in the next 20)

$= 1 - \left(\dfrac{499,000}{500,000}\right)^{20} = 1 - (0.999998)^{20} = 0.00004$

P($\geq$ 1 crash in the next 50) = 1 – P(no crashes in the next 50)

$= 1 - \left(\dfrac{499,000}{500,000}\right)^{50} = 1 - (0.999998)^{50} = 0.00010$

P($\geq$ 1 crash in the next 100) = 1 – P(no crashes in the next 100)

$= 1 - \left(\dfrac{499,000}{500,000}\right)^{100} = 1 - (0.999998)^{100} = 0.00020$

2-41. Using the notation of Problem **2-35**:

$$P(D)\,P(S) = \frac{50}{100}\frac{30}{100} = 0.15$$

$$P(D \cap S) = \frac{18}{100} = 0.18 \neq 0.15$$

Thus the two events are not independent.

2-42. Referring to Problem **2-31**:

$$P(H)\,P(M) = \frac{284}{1976}\frac{198}{1976} = 0.01440$$

$$P(H \cap M) = \frac{29}{1976} = 0.01467 \neq 0.01440$$

Thus the two events are not independent (though they're very close).

2-43. Referring to Problem **2-33**:

$$P(D)\,P(I) = \frac{112}{246}\frac{119}{246} = 0.2202$$

$$P(D \cap I) = \frac{34}{246} = 0.1382 \neq 0.2202$$

Thus the two events are not independent.

2-44. Referring to Problem **2-34**:

$$P(E)\,P(\overline{S}) = \frac{3}{10}\frac{3}{10} = 0.09$$

$$P(E \cap \overline{S}) = \frac{2}{10} = 0.20 \neq 0.09$$

Thus the two events are not independent. There may be some sort of relationship between them as a general rule, if seen in all firms.

2-45. P(getting at least one disease) $= 1 - $ P(getting none of the three)

$= 1 - $ P(not getting mal.) P(not getting schist.) P(not getting s.s.)

$= 1 - \big(1 - $ P(getting mal.)$\big)\big(1 - $ P(getting schist.)$\big)\big(1 - $ P(getting s.s.)$\big)$

$= 1 - \left(1 - \dfrac{110,000,000}{2,100,000,000}\right)\left(1 - \dfrac{200,000,000}{600,000,000}\right)\left(1 - \dfrac{25,000}{50,000,000}\right)$

$= 1 - (0.9476)(0.6667)(0.9995) = 0.3686$

2-46. There are four components, with 0.85 reliability each:

P(device works) = P(all four components work) $= (0.85)^4 = 0.522$

2-47. The device works if at least one out of three works.

P(device works) = 1 − P(all components fail)

= 1 − (1 − 0.96)(1 − 0.91)(1 − 0.80) = 0.99928

2-48. Assume independence:

$1 - (0.25)^3 = 0.9844$

2-49. Since 1/4 of the items are in any particular quartile, and assuming independent random samples with replacement so that all four choices have the same probability of being in the top quartile,

P(all four in top quartile) = $(1/4)^4 = 1/256 = 0.0039$

P(at least one from bottom quartile) = 1 − P(all four from top three quartiles) =
$1 - (3/4)^4 = 175/256 = 0.684$

2-50. $(55)(30)(21)(13) = 450{,}450$ sets of representatives.

2-51. $9! = (9)(8)(7)(6)(5)(4)(3)(2)(1) = 362{,}880$ different orders.

2-52. $n\mathbf{P}r = \dfrac{n!}{(n-r)!} = \dfrac{15!}{(15-8)!} = (15)(14)(13)(12)(11)(10)(9)(8) = 259{,}459{,}200$

2-53. $6\mathbf{P}3 = \dfrac{6!}{(6-3)!} = \dfrac{6!}{3!} = (6)(5)(4) = 120$ ordered choices.

2-54. $\dbinom{7}{2} = \dfrac{7!}{(7-2)!\,2!} = 21$ pairs.

2-55. Only one possible combination of 3 elements chosen from the 14 parts consists of the 3 faulty ones. So since any 3-element combination is equally likely to be picked,

the probability = $1 \,/\, \dbinom{14}{3} = 1 \,/\, \dfrac{14!}{3!\,11!} = 1/364 = 0.00275$

2-56. Only one of the $\dbinom{36}{6}$ combinations wins, so the probability of guessing it is

$1 \,/\, \dbinom{36}{6} = 1 \,/\, \dfrac{36!}{6!\,30!} = 1/1{,}947{,}792 = 0.000000513$

2-57. How many ways of guessing a set of 6 of the numbers from 1 to 36 will have 5 correct and 1 wrong? If $W = \{w_1, w_2, \ldots, w_6\}$ is the winning combination, then there are 6 choices of which w_i is *not* in the guessed combination, and 30 possible wrong guesses in place of w_i (since the one wrong guess can be any of the numbers from 1 to 36 that are not in W). So $(6)(30) = 180$ possible combinations match exactly 5 of the winning numbers. Thus the probability of making such a guess is

$$180 \Big/ \binom{36}{6} = 180/1{,}947{,}792 = 0.0000924$$

2-58. For the next Mazda of this model to be identical to yours, it needs to be an old model with your same engine (old models had 2 choices), same hood (4 choices), same steering wheel (9 choices), same wheels (6 choices), same color (7 choices), same seats (79 choices), and same body type (2 choices). If we assume that every possible combination of these choices exists and that within each category each choice is equally likely, then the probability of a randomly chosen combination being the same as yours is $1/(2 \cdot 4 \cdot 9 \cdot 6 \cdot 7 \cdot 79 \cdot 2) = 1/477{,}792 = 0.00000209$

2-59. Let T, R be the events: successful takeover, resignation of a board member.

$P(T \mid R) = 0.65 \qquad P(T \mid \overline{R}) = 0.30 \qquad P(R) = 0.70$

$P(T) = P(T \mid R)\,P(R) + P(T \mid \overline{R})\,P(\overline{R}) = (.65)(.70) + (.30)(.30) = 0.545$

2-60. Let A, S be the events: the drug is approved, the drug has side effects.

$P(A \mid \overline{S}) = 0.95 \qquad P(A \mid S) = 0.5 \qquad P(S) = 0.2 \qquad P(\overline{S}) = 0.8$

$P(A) = P(A \mid S)\,P(S) + P(A \mid \overline{S})\,P(\overline{S}) = (.5)(.2) + (.95)(.8) = 0.86$

2-61. Let D, B be the events: deal is concluded, competitor makes a bid.

$P(D \mid \overline{B}) = 0.45 \qquad P(D \mid B) = 0.25 \qquad P(B) = 0.40 \qquad P(\overline{B}) = 0.60$

$P(D) = P(D \mid \overline{B})\,P(\overline{B}) + P(D \mid B)\,P(B) = (.45)(.60) + (.25)(.40) = 0.37$

2-62. Let S, E be the events: property is sold, economy improves.

$P(S \mid E) = 0.9 \qquad P(S \mid \overline{E}) = 0.5 \qquad P(E) = 0.7$

$P(S) = P(S \mid E)\,P(E) + P(S \mid \overline{E})\,P(\overline{E}) = (.9)(.7) + (.5)(.3) = 0.78$

2-63. Let F, A be the events: ships sail full this summer, dollar appreciates against European currencies.

$$P(F \mid \overline{A}) = 0.92 \qquad P(F \mid A) = 0.75 \qquad P(A) = 0.23$$
$$P(F) = P(F \mid A)\,P(A) + P(F \mid \overline{A})\,P(\overline{A}) = (.75)(.23) + (.92)(.77) = .8809$$

2-64. Let O, G be the events: door should open, green light appears.

$$P(O) = 0.9 \qquad P(G \mid O) = 0.98 \qquad P(G \mid \overline{O}) = 0.05$$

$$P(O \mid G) = \frac{P(G \mid O)\,P(O)}{P(G \mid O)\,P(O) + P(G \mid \overline{O})\,P(\overline{O})} = \frac{(.98)(.9)}{(.98)(.9) + (.05)(.1)} = 0.9944$$

2-65. Let S, E be the events: the alarm sounds, there is an emergency situation.

$$P(S \mid E) = 0.95 \qquad P(S \mid \overline{E}) = 0.02 \qquad P(E) = 0.004$$

$$P(E \mid S) = \frac{P(S \mid E)\,P(E)}{P(S \mid E)\,P(E) + P(S \mid \overline{E})\,P(\overline{E})} = \frac{(.95)(.004)}{(.95)(.004) + (.02)(.996)} = 0.1602$$

2-66. Let I, H, M, L be the events: indicator rises; economic situation is high, medium, low.

$$P(I \mid H) = 0.6 \qquad P(I \mid M) = 0.3 \qquad P(I \mid L) = 0.1$$
$$P(H) = 0.15 \qquad P(M) = 0.70 \qquad P(L) = 0.15$$

$$P(H \mid I) = \frac{P(I \mid H)\,P(H)}{P(I \mid H)\,P(H) + P(I \mid M)\,P(M) + P(I \mid L)\,P(L)}$$

$$= \frac{(.6)(.15)}{(.6)(.15) + (.3)(.7) + (.1)(.15)} = \frac{0.09}{0.09 + 0.21 + 0.015} = 0.2857$$

2-67. Let I, O be the events: test indicates oil, oil really is present.

$$P(I \mid O) = 0.85 \qquad P(I \mid \overline{O}) = 0.10 \qquad P(O) = 0.4$$

$$P(O \mid I) = \frac{P(I \mid O)\,P(O)}{P(I \mid O)\,P(O) + P(I \mid \overline{O})\,P(\overline{O})} = \frac{(.85)(.4)}{(.85)(.4) + (.10)(.6)} = .85$$

2-68. Let I, S be the events: test indicates success, product really is successful.

$$P(I \mid S) = 0.75 \qquad P(I \mid \overline{S}) = 0.15 \qquad P(S) = 0.6 \qquad P(\overline{S}) = 0.4$$

$$P(S \mid I) = \frac{P(I \mid S) P(S)}{P(I \mid S) P(S) + P(I \mid \overline{S}) P(\overline{S})} = \frac{(.75)(.6)}{(.75)(.6) + (.15)(.4)} = .8824$$

2-69. Let MM, FF, MF denote the events of reaching the two men, the two women, the married couple (respectively). Let W be the event that a woman answers the door. Then:

$P(MF) = 1/3$	$P(W \mid MF) = 1/2$	$P(MF \cap W) = 1/6$
$P(MM) = 1/3$	$P(W \mid MM) = 0$	$P(MM \cap W) = 0$
$P(FF) = 1/3$	$P(W \mid FF) = 1$	$\underline{P(FF \cap W) = 1/3}$
		$P(W) = 1/2$

$$P(MF \mid W) = \frac{P(MF \cap W)}{P(W)} = \frac{1/6}{1/2} = 1/3$$

2-70.   **a.** P(at least one right) $= 1 - $ P(all three wrong) $= 1 - (1 - 0.03)^3 = 0.0873$

b. $0.03^3 = 0.000027$

2-71. P(≥ 1 out of 5 misdirected) $= 1 - $ P(none misdirected)
$= 1 - [\text{P(a single call not misdirected)}]^5 = 1 - (199/200)^5 = 0.0248$

2-72. $(0.02)(1/200) = 1/10,000 = 0.0001$

2-73. $P(A \cup B) = 0.4 + 0.3 - 0.1 = 0.6$

2-74. $P(C \cup S) = 0.15 + 0.10 - 0.05 = 0.20$

2-75. Let C, J be the events: pass CPA exam, get job offer.
$P(C) = 0.6 \qquad P(C \cap J) = 0.4$
$P(J \mid C) = P(C \cap J) / P(C) = 0.4/0.6 = 0.667$

2-76. $P(A) = 0.20 \qquad P(A \cap B) = 0.12$
$P(B \mid A) = P(A \cap B) / P(A) = 0.12/0.20 = 0.60$

2-77. Let P, I be the events: production increases, interest rates decline more than half a point.
$$P(P \mid I) = 0.72 \qquad P(I) = 0.25$$
$$P(P \cap I) = P(P \mid I)\,P(I) = (.72)(.25) = 0.18$$

2-78. Let EQ, SD be the events: engineering quality, sporty design rated among most important features.
$$P(EQ) = 0.35 \qquad P(SD) = 0.50 \qquad P(EQ \cap SD) = 0.25$$
$(.35)(.50) = .175 \neq .25$, therefore the two events are not independent.

2-79. The assumption of independence is justified by random sampling.
$$P(\text{all 3 people consider } EQ) = (.35)^3 = 0.0429$$
$P(\text{at least one person considers } EQ) = 1 - P(\text{none of the three consider } EQ) = 1 - (.65)^3 = 0.7254$

2-80. P(exposed to at least one mode of advertising)
$$= 1 - P(\text{not exposed to any of the 3})$$
$$= 1 - (.90)(.85)(.80) = 0.388$$

2-81. Let S, R be the events: see the ad in the *Wall Street Journal*, remember it.
$$P(S) = 0.6 \qquad P(R \mid S) = 0.85$$
$$P(S \cap R) = P(R \mid S)\,P(S) = (.85)(.6) = 0.51$$
51% of the people see and remember the advertisement.

2-82. $P(\text{defective}) = 0.1 \qquad$ 5 chips are chosen at random.
$$P(\text{none of the 5 are defective}) = (0.90)^5 = 0.59049$$
$$P(\text{at least one is defective}) = 1 - P(\text{none are defective}) = 0.40951$$

2-83. $P(\text{at least one color}) = 1 - P(\text{none of the colors}) \qquad$ By independence:
$$= 1 - (1 - 0.3)(1 - 0.2)(1 - 0.15) = 0.524$$

2-84. $(2/3)^5 = 0.132$
The choice is probably not random.

2-85. Let S, F, N, U be the events: subsidiary will be successful, political situation is favorable, neutral, unfavorable.

$P(S \mid F) = 0.55 \qquad P(S \mid N) = 0.3 \qquad P(S \mid U) = 0.1$

$P(F) = 0.6 \qquad P(N) = 0.2 \qquad P(U) = 0.2$

$P(S) = P(S \mid F) P(F) + P(S \mid N) P(N) + P(S \mid U) P(U)$

$= (.55)(.6) + (.3)(.2) + (.1)(.2) = 0.41$

2-86. Let L, A be the events: legislation is passed, authorization is granted.

$P(L \cap A) = 0.5 \qquad P(L) = 0.75$

$P(A \mid L) = P(L \cap A) / P(L) = 0.5/0.75 = 0.6667$

2-87. Let D, H be the events: customer defaults, economy is high.

$P(D \mid H) = 0.04 \qquad P(D \mid \overline{H}) = 0.13 \qquad P(H) = 0.65$

$P(D) = P(D \mid H) P(H) + P(D \mid \overline{H}) P(\overline{H})$

$= (.04)(.65) + (.13)(.35) = 0.0715$

2-88. 6/8, or 0.75. Simple inference from proportions observed in the past.

2-89. $P(\text{at least one booking}) = 1 - P(\text{none})$

$= 1 - (0.92)^{20} = 0.8113$

2-90. $P(\text{none are in error}) = (0.95)^{10} = 0.5987$

2-91. Let A, F, So, J, Se be the events: student got an A, student is a freshman, sophomore, junior, senior.

$P(Se \mid A)$

$= \dfrac{P(A \mid Se) P(Se)}{P(A \mid Se) P(Se) + P(A \mid F) P(F) + P(A \mid So) P(So) + P(A \mid J) P(J)}$

$= \dfrac{(.40)(.15)}{(.40)(.15) + (.20)(.30) + (.30)(.35) + (.35)(.20)} = 0.2034$

2-92. Let S, C be the events: product is successful, competitor produces similar product.

$P(S \mid \overline{C}) = 0.67 \qquad P(S \mid C) = 0.42 \qquad P(C) = 0.35$

$P(S) = (.67)(.65) + (.42)(.35) = 0.5825$

2-93. $P(\text{at least one error}) = 1 - P(\text{all 1,000 entries correct}) = 1 - (0.9992)^{1,000} = 0.5508$

2-94. Conceptually, in the hole-card game there is a card missing from the space of cards available for play by the players—the hole card itself, which is removed from play at the beginning. So, for example, if a player wants to make a draw and needs anything lower than a 4 in order not to go over 21, she can't be sure of the probability that the next card is in fact smaller than a 4 (given the cards already drawn and known to everyone), since the hole card may or may not be one of the remaining cards smaller than 4. In other words, the probability space represented by the deck (in a randomized order) used for the main play isn't exactly specified in the hole-card game (from any player's point of view), while this space is always based on the full 52-card deck in the regular game. *Practically* speaking, however, the probabilities involved vary only slightly, and their role in the outcome of the game should be more or less unnoticeable when averaged over a span of games.

2-95. Yes: $(0.9)(0.9)(0.95) = 0.7695$, which is greater than 70%.

2-96. Assume a large population so that the sampling can be considered as being done with replacement (i.e., removing one item does not appreciably alter the remaining number of data points on either side of the median). Then the first item drawn is on a particular side of the median, after which the second item has a $1/2$ probability of coming from the other side, since half of the points in the population are on one side and half are on the other by the definition of median. Thus the probability that the median will lie between the two points drawn is $1/2$.

2-97. Making the same assumptions as in Problem **2-96**, first count the number of ways that all n elements drawn could lie on the same side of the median: since the choices are independent (this being a random sample) and each of the $n-1$ choices after the first has probability $1/2$ of being on the same side of the median as the first choice, the number of such ways is $(1/2)^{n-1}$. The median will lie somewhere between the smallest and largest values drawn exactly when the above situation does *not* occur, so the desired probability is $1 - (1/2)^{n-1}$.

2-98. P(at least one paper accepted) $= 1 - $ P(no papers accepted)

$= 1 - $ P(first paper rejected) P(second paper rejected) $\cdots$

$= 1 - [1 - .14][1 - (.14)(.9)][1 - (.14)(.9)^2][1 - (.14)(.9)^3] \cdots$

$= 1 - (.86)(.874)(.8866)(.89794)(.908146) \cdots$

Using 800 iterations on a computer: $= 0.766660928$

2-99. We need a method that is fair *even if* the caller knows which way the coin is biased (since otherwise a single random call would still have probability 1/2 of matching the actual outcome). Here it is: the caller pre-selects one of *H-T* or *T-H* as the guessed sequence of outcomes of two consecutive flips. The coin is then flipped twice: if it results in two different outcomes, the caller attends the meeting iff his or her choice of the order of outcomes was correct. But if the two flips have the same outcome, then the coin is flipped twice again, repeated as needed until a pair of different outcomes is obtained. Note that even if the coin is much more likely to come up heads (and even if the caller knows this), the sequence *H-T* is equally likely as *T-H*: they both have probability $P(H)P(T)$, since the two tosses are independent.

2-100. All the possibilities for the sexes (in order) of 4 children:

```
FFFF  (all same)      MFFF  (3 and 1)
FFFM  (3 and 1)       MFFM  (2 and 2)
FFMF  (3 and 1)       MFMF  (2 and 2)
FFMM  (2 and 2)       MFMM  (3 and 1)
FMFF  (3 and 1)       MMFF  (2 and 2)
FMFM  (2 and 2)       MMFM  (3 and 1)
FMMF  (2 and 2)       MMMF  (3 and 1)
FMMM  (3 and 1)       MMMM  (all same)
```

Thus, by counting the above categories (since each of the 16 sequences of birth sexes is equally likely), the chance of all boys or all girls is $2/16 = 1/8$; chance of two of each is $6/16 = 3/8$; and the chance of three of one sex and one of the other is $8/16 = 4/8$. Marilyn is right in this case.

Case 2. Let R, C, A denote the events: system's radar detects an incoming missile, the Patriot missile explodes close to the incoming missile, incoming missle explodes in the air because of impact from Patriot fragments, repsectively. The data given are:

$$P(R) = 0.99 \qquad P(C \mid R) = 0.985 \qquad P(A \mid C) = 0.65$$

Since A can only happen if C does and C can happen only if R does, we have:

P(incoming missile totally destroyed in air)

$$
\begin{aligned}
= P(A) &= P(A \cap C) \\
&= P(C) P(A \mid C) \\
&= P(C \cap R) P(A \mid C) \\
&= \big[P(R) P(C \mid R) \big] P(A \mid C) \\
&= \big[(0.99)(0.985) \big] (0.65) \\
&= [0.9752](0.65) \\
&= 0.634
\end{aligned}
$$

Since $0.9752 = 40.96/42 \doteq 41/42$, it is probably this number that the President was referring to, i.e., $P(C \cap R)$—merely the probability that the Patriot detonates in close proximity to the incoming missile, *not* taking into account whether the latter then explodes or not.

CHAPTER 3

3-1.   **a.** $\sum P(x) = 1.0$

     b.

x	F(x)
0	0.3
1	0.5
2	0.7
3	0.8
4	0.9
5	1.0

     c. $P(X > 2) = 1 - F(2) = 0.3$

3-2.   **a.** $\sum P(x) = 1.0$

     b.

x	F(x)
0	0.01
1	0.10
2	0.40
3	0.60
4	0.80
5	0.90
6	1.00

     c. $P(X \leq 4) = F(4) = 0.80$

     d. $P(X \geq 2) = 1 - F(1) = 0.90$

3-3.   **a.** $\sum P(x) = 1.0$

     b.

x	F(x)
0	0.10
10	0.30
20	0.65
30	0.85
40	0.95
50	1.00

     c. $P(X > 20) = 1 - F(20) = 0.35$

3-4.   **a.** $P(2 \le X \le 4) = 0.2 + 0.2 + 0.3 = 0.7$

b.

x	$F(x)$
0	0.1
1	0.2
2	0.4
3	0.6
4	0.9
5	1.0

c. $\sum P(x) = 1.0$

3-5.

first die outcome:

	1	2	3	4	5	6
1	●	●	●	●	●	●
2	●	●	●	●	●	●
3	●	●	●	●	●	●
4	●	●	●	●	●	●
5	●	●	●	●	●	●
6	●	●	●	●	●	●

second die out-come:

X = sum of the two dice. Note from the sample space that one outcome leads to a sum of 2, two equally-likely outcomes lead to a sum of 3, three lead to a sum of 4, four to a sum of 5, five to a sum of 6, and six (the highest number of outcomes) lead to a sum of 7. Thus, the most likely sum is $x = 7$. Afterwards, the probabilities decline: five outcomes lead to a sum of 8, four to a sum of 9, three to a sum of 10, two to a sum of 11, and one outcome (two "sixes") leads to a sum of 12. We thus have the following probability distribution and cumulative distribution function:

x	$P(x)$	$F(x)$
2	1/36	1/36
3	2/36	3/36
4	3/36	6/36
5	4/36	10/36
6	5/36	15/36
7	6/36	21/36
8	5/36	26/36
9	4/36	30/36
10	3/36	33/36
11	2/36	35/36
12	1/36	1.0

3-6.   **a.** $\sum P(x) = 1.0$

      b.

x	$F(x)$
0	0.1
1	0.3
2	0.7
3	0.8
4	0.9
5	1.00

      c. $P(1 \le X \le 4) = F(4) - F(0) = 0.9 - 0.1 = 0.8$

      d. $P(\text{extra costs}) = P(X > 3) = 1 - F(3) = 0.2$

      e. $P(\text{no orders for 5 days}) = (0.1)^5 = 0.00001$

      f. $P(\text{extra costs for 2 days}) = (0.2)^2 = 0.04$

3-7.   **a.** $P(4 \le X \le 7) = P(4) + P(5) + P(6) + P(7) = 0.55$

      b.

x	$F(x)$
2	0.20
3	0.40
4	0.70
5	0.80
6	0.90
7	0.95
8	1.00

      c. $P(X \le 6) = F(6) = 0.9$

      d. $P(3 < X \le 6) = F(6) - F(3) = 0.9 - 0.4 = 0.5$

3-8.   **a.** $\sum P(x) = 1.0$

      b. $P(1 < X \le 3) = P(2) + P(3) = 0.6$

      c. $P(1 \le X \le 4) = \sum_{x=1}^{4} P(x) = 0.9$

      d.

x	$F(x)$
0	0.1
1	0.3
2	0.6
3	0.9
4	1.00

3-9. **a.** $\sum P(x) = 1.0$

b. $\sum\limits_{x=12}^{15} P(x) = 0.20 + 0.15 + 0.10 + 0.05 = 0.50$

c.

x	$F(x)$
9	0.05
10	0.20
11	0.50
12	0.70
13	0.85
14	0.95
15	1.00

3-10. For the random variable in Problem **3-1**:

$E(X) = 1.8$ $E(X^2) = 6$ $V(X) = 2.76$ $SD(X) = 1.661$

3-11. For Problem **3-2**:

$E(X) = 3.19$ $E(X^2) = 12.39$ $V(X) = 2.2139$ $SD(X) = 1.4879$

3-12. For Problem **3-3**:

$E(X) = 21.5$ $E(X^2) = 625$ $V(X) = 162.75$

3-13. For Problem **3-4**:

$E(X) = 2.8$ $E(X^2) = 10$ $V(X) = 2.16$ $SD(X) = 1.47$

3-14. E(sum of two dice) $= 7$. Derived as follows:

x	$P(x)$	$x\,P(x)$
2	1/36	2/36
3	2/36	6/36
4	3/36	12/36
5	4/36	20/36
6	5/36	30/36
7	6/36	42/36
8	5/36	40/36
9	4/36	36/36
10	3/36	30/36
11	2/36	22/36
12	1/36	12/36
		$252/36 = 7$

3-15. For Problem **3-6**:

$E(X) = 2.2$

$P(X > E(X)) = P(X > 2.2) = P(3) + P(4) + P(5) = 0.3$

3-16. For Problem **3-7**:

$E(X) = 4.05 \qquad E(X^2) = 19.15 \qquad V(X) = 2.7475 \qquad SD(X) = 1.6576$

3-17. By Chebyshev's theorem:

$P(|X - \mu| < k\sigma) \geq 1 - 1/k^2$

For $k = 4$, Probability $\geq 1 - 1/4^2 = 1 - 1/16 = 0.9375$

3-18. Three standard deviations. Because:

$8/9 = 1 - 1/3^2$, so $k = 3$ in Chebyshev's theorem.

3-19. $E(X) = 8.3 \qquad V(X) = 2.3$

$E(Y) = 8.4 \qquad V(Y) = 6.4$

Y is a riskier stock because $V(Y) > V(X)$ while $E(X)$ is close to $E(Y)$.

3-20. $P(X = 0)$ is 0.2.

a. The most likely outcome is $2,000 (prob. = 0.3)

b. Is the venture likely to be successful? Yes: $P(X > 0) = 0.6$

c. The long-term average is $E(X)$: $\qquad E(X) = +800$

d. A good measure of the risk is the standard deviation.

$E(X^2) = 2,800,000 \qquad V(X) = 2,160,000 \qquad SD(X) = 1,469.69$

3-21. The expected value of a random variable is the long-term average. Hence the airline must raise its fare by the expected value of a claim per passenger. The mean claim is: $E(X) = 0 \times P(\text{no claim}) + 600 \times P(\text{claim}) = 0 + 600(0.005) = \$3$

3-22. We use Equation (3-6) for a linear function of a random variable:

$E(aX + b) = aE(X) + b$

Hence: E(monthly cost of the operation)

$= 25,000 + 5,000\,E(X) = 25,000 + 5,000(4.05) = \$45,250$

3-23. Refer to Problem **3-4**. Operation cost: $C(X) = 300\sqrt{X}$

x	$P(x)$	$C(x)$	$C(x)\,P(x)$
0	0.1	0	0
1	0.1	300	30
2	0.2	424.26	84.85
3	0.2	519.62	103.92
4	0.3	600	180
5	0.1	670.82	67.08

$$465.85 = E(\text{cost})$$

3-24. In Problem **3-2**, penalty $= X^2$.

Find E(penalty). From Problem **3-11**: $E(X^2) = \$12.39$

3-25. The expected value of a random variable is the long-term average value of the random variable. It is the mean of the distribution of the random variable, its center of mass. Uses: a typical value of the random variable, a central value.

3-26. The variance is a measure of the spread or uncertainty of the random variable. The variance is the expected squared deviation of the value of the random variable from its mean. One use of the variance is as a measure of the risk of an investment.

3-27. The variance is a squared quantity, and thus in applications it has less meaning than its square root, the standard deviation. The standard deviation is in the original units of the problem.

3-28. Refer to Problem **3-22**.

Cost $= 25{,}000 + 5{,}000X$

By Equation (3-10): $V(aX + b) = a^2\,V(X)$

From Problem **3-16**, we know that $V(X) = 2.7475$, so:

$V(\text{Cost}) = (5{,}000)^2(2.7475) = 68{,}687{,}500$

$SD(\text{Cost}) = 8{,}287.79$

3-29. **a.** The assumption of a random sampling of 5 industries assures us $A = 0.75$ is constant, and independence of trials.

b. Using the Binomial Distribution table, with $p = 0.60$ and $n = 5$, we have
P(0 or 1 industry added workers) = $F(1) = 0.087$, so
P(2 or more industries added workers) = $1 - F(1) = 0.913$

c.

s	$F(s)$	$P(s)$
0	0.010	0.010
1	0.087	0.077
2	0.317	0.230
3	0.663	0.346
4	0.922	0.259
5	1.000	0.078

d. P(at least 1 added workers) $= 1 - $ P(none added any) $= 1 - $ P(0) $= 1 - 0.010$ (using the table from part **c.**) $= 0.99$. For more accuracy, compute P(0) $= \binom{5}{0}(0.6)^0(1 - 0.6)^5 = 0.01024$, giving the answer $1 - $ P(0) $= 0.98976$

e. $P(X = 3) = 0.346$

f. $E(X) = np = 5(0.6) = 3.0$

g. $V(X) = npq = 5(.60)(.40) = 1.2$

3-30. F is not binomial: N/n is not greater than 10 (the trials are not independent and p is not constant).

3-31. X is binomial if sales calls are independent of each other.

3-32. $E(X) = np = 100(.10) = 10$
$SD(X) = \sqrt{npq} = \sqrt{100(.10)(.90)} = 3.00$
By Chebyshev's theorem: $P(|X - \mu| < k\sigma) \geq 1 - 1/k^2$
$1 - 1/k^2 = 0.75$, so $k = 2$
$\mu - 2\sigma < X < \mu + 2\sigma$
$10 - 2(3) < X < 10 + 2(3)$
$4 < X < 16$ are the desired bounds.

3-33. X is not binomial because members of the same family are related and not independent of each other.

3-34. Bernoulli trials are a sequence of identical, independent trials each resulting in a success or a failure with constant success probability, p. A binomial random variable counts the number of successes in a sequence of n Bernoulli trials.

3-35. P(at least 5 were exposed) $= P(X \geq 5) = 1 - F(4)$, where $p = 0.20$ and $n = 10$,
$= 1 - .9672 = 0.0328$
P(at most 2 were exposed) $= P(X \leq 2) = F(2) = 0.6778$

3-36. P(at least 10 will submit a claim) $= P(S \geq 10) = 1 - F(9)$ where $n = 15$, $p = 0.30$
$= 1 - .9963 = 0.0037$
$E(X) = np = 15(.3) = 4.5$
$SD(X) = \sqrt{npq} = \sqrt{15(.3)(.7)} = 1.77$

3-37. Testing each item is a Bernoulli trial; define success as "nonconforming". So $p = 0.20$, $n = 20$. The lot is accepted if $X \leq 2$. The table gives $P(X \leq 2) = 0.206$, so $P(\text{rejection}) = 0.794$.

3-38. Bernoulli trials with $n = 5$, $p = \dfrac{3,000}{3,000 + 27,000} = 0.1$. The table gives $P(X \leq 1) = 0.9185$, so $P(X \geq 2) = 0.0815$. Out of ten customers, the expected number who get the American beer is $np = (10)(0.1) = 1$.

3-39. $n = 6$, $p = 0.05$, "success" being "negative comments". The table gives $P(X \leq 1) = 0.967$, so $P(X \geq 2) = 0.033$.

3-40. $n = 15$, $p = 0.7$. The table gives $P(X \leq 10) = 0.4845$.

3-41. $n = 100$, $p = 0.001$, so $\mu = np = 0.1$. Using $P(x) = \dfrac{\mu^x e^{-\mu}}{x!}$ gives
$P(0) = 0.905$, $P(1) = 0.0905$, $P(2) = 0.00452$, $P(3) = 0.000151$.

3-42. Since this is "sampling without replacement," we need the hypergeometric distribution with $N = 20$, $S = 7$, $n = 8$ for $x = 0, \ldots, 3$:

$$\sum_{x=0}^{3} \binom{S}{x}\binom{N-S}{n-x} / \binom{N}{n}$$

$$= \left[\binom{7}{0}\binom{13}{8} + \binom{7}{1}\binom{13}{7} + \binom{7}{2}\binom{13}{6} + \binom{7}{3}\binom{13}{5} \right] / \binom{20}{8}$$

$$= [(1)(1,287) + (7)(1,716) + (21)(1,716) + (35)(1,287)]/125,970 = 0.7492$$

3-43. Use the geometric distribution: $P(x = 3) = pq^{x-1} = (0.35)(0.65)^2 = 0.148$

3-44. Using the Poisson distribution with $\mu = 1$, we need

$$P(X \geq 2) = 1 - P(X \leq 1) = 1 - \left(\frac{\mu^0 e^{-\mu}}{0!} + \frac{\mu^1 e^{-\mu}}{1!} \right) = 0.2642$$

3-45. Use the hypergeometric distribution with $N = 15$, $S = 6$, $n = 10$. Note that $P(0)$, the probability that none of the ten randomly selected banks is foreign-owned, must be 0 since there are only 9 domestic banks in the entire space of 15 banks. Thus:

$$P(X \geq 3) = 1 - P(X \leq 2) = 1 - \sum_{x=1}^{2} \binom{S}{x} \binom{N-S}{n-x} / \binom{N}{n}$$

$$= 1 - \left[\binom{6}{1} \binom{9}{9} + \binom{6}{2} \binom{9}{8} \right] / \binom{15}{10}$$

$$= 1 - \left[(6)(1) + (15)(9) \right] / 3{,}003 = 0.953$$

3-46. Use the multinomial distribution with three categories: regular audit, with probability $p_1 = \frac{2{,}000{,}000}{100{,}000{,}000} = 0.02$; mail audit, with probability $p_2 = \frac{1{,}000{,}000}{100{,}000{,}000} = 0.01$; and no audit, with probability $p_3 = 1 - p_1 - p_2 = 0.97$. With $n = 50$ we need:

$$P(1, 1, 48) = \frac{50!}{1! \, 1! \, 48!} (.02)^1 (.01)^1 (.97)^{48} - 0.114$$

3-47. Using $\mu = np = \frac{1{,}800}{5{,}000} = 0.36$, calculate

$$P(X \leq 2) = \sum_{x=0}^{2} \frac{\mu^x e^{-\mu}}{x!} = e^{-0.36} \sum_{x=0}^{2} \frac{(0.36)^x}{x!} = 0.9940$$

3-48. Hypergeometric distribution with $N = 11$, $S = 4$, $n = 5$. Note that $P(5) = 0$ since there are only 4 tenured faculty members. A majority of a committee of 5 is 3 or more, so

$$P(X \geq 3) = P(3) + P(4) = \left[\binom{4}{3} \binom{7}{2} + \binom{4}{4} \binom{7}{1} \right] / \binom{11}{5} = 0.197$$

3-49. Geometric distribution with $p = 0.1$: $\mu = 1/p = 10$

3-50. A continuous random variable can take on any value in an interval of real numbers; a discrete random variable's possible values must comprise a finite or countably infinite set.

3-51. Probabilities are obtained as areas under the density function $f(x)$ graphed over the intervals in question.

3-52. $P(X = a)$ = area under $f(x)$ between a and a = area of a line segment = 0, regardless of its height (the value $f(a)$ in this case).

3-53. $F(x)$ = area under $f(y)$ from $-\infty$ (smallest y) to x.

3-54. **a.**

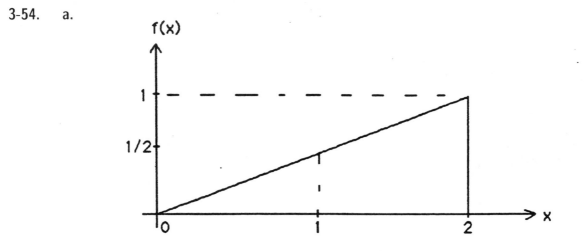

b. Area under $f(x)$ = area of a triangle = (base)(height)/2 = (2)(1)/2 = 1.00

c. $P(0 \le X \le 1)$ = area under $f(x)$ from 0 to 1

$$= \text{area of triangle from 0 to 1} = \frac{(1)(1/2)}{2} = 1/4 = 0.25$$

3-55. $f(x) = \begin{cases} 1/7 & \text{if } 0 \le x \le 7 \\ 0 & \text{otherwise} \end{cases}$

3-56. For the random variable in Problem **3-55**, $P(0 \le X \le 2)$ = area under $f(x)$ between 0 and 2 = 2(1/7) = 0.286

3-57. Intuitively, the "center of mass" under $f(x)$ is 3.5:

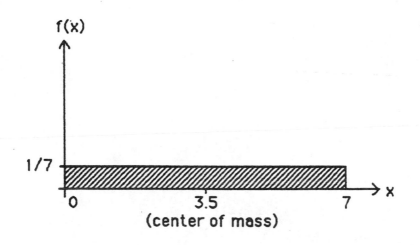

3-58. For the random variable in Problem **3-54**:

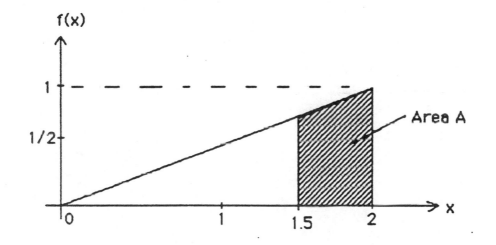

$$P(X > 1.5) = \text{area A} = 1 - \frac{(1.5)\,f(1.5)}{2} = 1 - \frac{(1.5)(\frac{1.5}{2})}{2} = 1 - 0.5625 = 0.4375$$

3-59. Since μ = mean time between arrivals = 3, we use $\lambda = 1/\mu = 1/3$:
$$P(X \geq 2) = 1 - F(2) = 1 - (1 - e^{-\lambda 2}) = e^{-2/3} = 0.5134$$

3-60. $\mu = 100$, so $\lambda = 1/\mu = 0.01$:
$$P(X \geq 65) = 1 - F(65) = 1 - (1 - e^{-\lambda 65}) = e^{(-0.01)65} = 0.522$$

3-61. $V = \mu$ for any exponential distribution, so $SD = \sqrt{V} = \sqrt{100} = 10$

3-62.   **a.** $\sum P(x) = 1.00$

b.

x	$F(x)$
0	.05
1	.10
2	.20
3	.35
4	.55
5	.70
6	.85
7	.95
8	1.00

c. $P(3 \le X < 7) = F(6) - F(2) = .85 - .20 = 0.65$

d. P(at most 5 tables will be sold) $= F(5) = 0.70$

e. $E(X) = 4.25$

f. $E(X^2) = 22.25 \qquad V(X) = 4.1875 \qquad SD(X) = 2.0463$

g. Using Chebyshev's theorem, 0.75 probability bounds on the number of tables sold daily: $1 - 1/k^2 = 0.75$, thus $k = 2$ and the bounds are $\mu \pm 2\sigma = 4.25 \pm 2(2.0463) = [0.1574, 8.3426]$. By comparison, from the actual distribution: $P(1 \le X \le 8) = 0.95$

3-63.   Use the Binomial Distribution table, $n = 20$, $p = 0.05$: $F(3) = 0.984$

3-64.   **a.** $\sum P(x) = 1.00$

b.

x	$F(x)$
0	.10
1	.30
2	.60
3	.75
4	.90
5	.95
6	1.00

c. $P(2 < X \le 5) = F(5) - F(2) = .95 - .6 = 0.35$

$P(3 \le X \le 6) = F(6) - F(2) = 1 - 0.6 = 0.40$

$P(X > 4) = 1 - F(4) = 1 - 0.9 = 0.1$

d. P(4 or 5 orders) $= P(4) + P(5) = 0.2$

e. By independence: $P(3) \times P(3) = (.15)^2 = 0.0225$

f. $E(X) = 2.4 \qquad E(X^2) = 8.2 \qquad V(X) = 2.44 \qquad SD(X) = 1.562$

3-65. **a.** Y is binomial: the number of "successes"—no orders—in $n = 52$ trials, where $p = 0.10$ and trials are independent.

b. $E(Y) = np = 52(.10) = 5.2$

3-66. **a.** $E(X) = 17.56875 \qquad$ Since bought at 17.25, profit per share $= 0.31875$; on 100 shares the profit is \$31.875 $\;\;(= 31\frac{7}{8})$

b. $E(X^2) = 308.76016 \qquad V(X) = 0.09918 \qquad SD(X) = 0.3149$
It is a measure of risk.

c. The limitation is in the assumption of the stationarity and independence of the stock prices.

3-67. $E(\text{Profit}) = E(1{,}200\,X - 1{,}750) = 1{,}200\,E(X) - 1{,}750 = 1{,}200(2.4) - 1{,}750 = \$1{,}130$
$V(\text{Profit}) = (1{,}200)^2 V(X) = (1{,}200)^2(2.44) = 3{,}513{,}600$
$SD(\text{Profit}) = 1{,}874.46$

3-68. **a.** Each of the 10 choices is made independently of the others, including the possibility that some titles may be chosen more than once among the 10 (i.e., the customer may end up with some duplicate copies), so that the probability of choosing a Multimedia title remains 60/400 for each title chosen.

b. $n = 10 \qquad p = 60/400 = 0.15 \qquad q = 0.85$
$P(0) = \binom{n}{0} p^0 q^{10} = (0.85)^{10} = 0.1969$
$P(1) = \binom{n}{1} p^1 q^9 = 10(0.15)(.85)^9 = 0.3474$
Therefore, $P(\text{at least 2 are Multimedia}) = 1 - P(0) - P(1) = 0.456$

3-69. **a.** $P(2 \text{ successes} \mid p = 0.4, n = 20) = F(2) - F(1) = 0.0031$

b. $F(2) = 0.0036$

c. Do not believe the advertisement. If the ad is true, then we have just observed a rare event. The probability of obtaining a result as extreme as what we have obtained, or more extreme, is 0.0036

d. $E(X) = np = 20(.4) = 8$

3-70. **a.** The distribution is binomial if the cars are independent of each other.

b.

x	$P(x)$
0	.5987
1	.3152
2	.0746
3	.0105
4	.0009
5	.0001

6 through 10 have probabilities smaller than .0001

c. $P(X \geq 2) = 1 - F(1) = 1 - .9139 = .0861$

d. $E(X) = np = 10(.05) = 1/2$ a car.

3-71. X is geometric.

3-72. X is not approximated well by a binomial random variable because N/n is less than 10. X is hypergeometric.

3-73. **a.** $f(x) = \begin{cases} 1/4 & \text{for } 5 \leq x \leq 9 \\ 0 & \text{otherwise} \end{cases}$

b. $P(X < 8) = 3/4 = 0.75$

c. $E(X) = 7$

3-74. **a.**

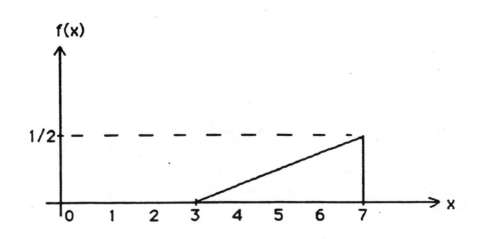

b. The area under $f(x)$ is the area of the triangle $=$ (base)(height)/2
$= (7 - 3)(1/2)(1/2) = 1$

c. $P(X > 5) = $ area of trapezoid from 5 to 7 $= 1 - $ area of triangle from 3 to 5
$$= 1 - 2 f(5)/2 = 1 - 2(1/4)(1/2) = 1 - 1/4 = 3/4 = 0.75$$

3-75. $p = 1,600/14,000 = 0.1143 \qquad n - 6 \qquad$ We need: $P(X \leq 3)$

$F(3)$ using approximate $p = 0.1$ is 0.9987

Now let's compute it exactly:

$$P(0) = \binom{6}{0}(.1143)^0(1 - .1143)^6 = .4828$$

$$P(1) = \binom{6}{1}(.1143)^1(.8857)^5 = .3738$$

$$P(2) = \binom{6}{2}(.1143)^2(.8857)^4 = .1206$$

$$P(3) = \binom{6}{3}(.1143)^3(.8857)^3 = \underline{.0207}$$

.9979, which is quite close to
the approximate answer.

3-76. $n = 15 \qquad p = 0.05 \qquad P(X \leq 3) = 0.9945$

3-77. The candidate needs the votes of at least 5 of the remaining 10 members.
P(get job) = P(get interview) P(get job | get interview)
$= 0.95 \, P(X \geq 5 \mid n = 10, p = .5) = (.95)[1 - F(4)]$
$= (.95)(1 - 0.377) = 0.59185$

3-78. **a.** $(0.44)(13.8) + (0.33)(10.4) + (0.23)(7.5) = 11.229$

b. $E(X^2) = 132.42 \qquad V(X) = 6.33 \qquad SD(X) = 2.52$
20/20: $(13.8 - 11.23)/2.52 = +1.02$
G.B.: $(10.4 - 11.23)/2.52 = -0.33$
M.C.: $(7.5 - 11.23)/2.52 = -1.48$

3-79. **a.** Based on the given data, P(closing date is May 26, 27, or 28)
$= (1 + 2 + 1)/18 = 0.222$

b. The weighted sum is $23\frac{8}{9} = 23.889$

3-80. Using the binomial distribution for $n = 20$, $p = 0.10$:
$P(X > 3) = 1 - F(3) = 1 - 0.867 = 0.133$

Expected value of the geometric distribution with $p = 0.1$ is $\mu = 1/p = 10$.

3-81.   **a.** $P(12) + P(13) + P(14) = 0.31$

  b. $E(X) =$ weighted sum is 10.980

  c. $E(X^2) = 122.080 \qquad V(X) = 1.520 \qquad SD(X) = 1.233$

3-82. $\lambda = 1/\mu = 1 \qquad F(X < 1/2) = 1 - e^{-\lambda/2} = 1 - e^{-0.5} = 0.3935$

3-83.   A binomial distribution with $n = 20, p = 0.70$; we want
  P(at least 5 five accept giving out birthdate) $= 1 - P(\leq 4 \text{ accept})$

$$= 1 - \sum_{x=0}^{4} P(\text{exactly } x \text{ accept}) = 1 - \sum_{x=0}^{4} \binom{20}{x}(0.70)^x(0.30)^{20-x}$$

$$= 1 - (3.487 \times 10^{-11} + 1.627 \times 10^{-9} + 3.607 \times 10^{-8} + 5.050 \times 10^{-7} + 5.008 \times 10^{-6})$$

$$= 1 - 5.55 \times 10^{-6} = 0.9999945$$

  (extremely close to 1.0)

3-84.   Using a multinomial distribution with probabilities $p_1 = 0.25$ (foreign drugs), $p_2 = 0.20$ (foreign drugs sold by Japanese companies), and $p_3 = 1 - p_1 - p_2 = 0.55$ (Japanese-made). With $n = 12$ we want

$$P(4, 4, 4) = \frac{12!}{4!\,4!\,4!}(0.25)^4(0.20)^4(0.55)^4 = 0.0198$$

Case 3. 1. According to the article, one third of the bank's employees became shareowners. We're looking at a binomial distribution with $n = 10$, $p = 1/3$, $q = 2/3$ (assume that $N/n \geq 10$ here, since we have no way of knowing the total number of bank employees). So:

$$P(\text{at most 2 of the 10 are shareowners}) = \sum_{k=0}^{2} \binom{10}{k}(1/3)^k(2/3)^{10-k}$$

$$= (1)(.667)^{10} + (10)(.333)(.667)^9 + (45)(.333)^2(.667)^8 = 0.2991$$

So P(at least 3 of the 10 are shareowners) $= 1 - 0.2991 = 0.7009$

2. Assuming that the four millionaires mentioned in the first paragraph are the only ones among the 700 total shareowners, we have $n = 100$, $p = 4/700 < 0.05$, so the Poisson approximation is usable, where $\mu = np = 4/7$. Then the probability of finding at most three millionaires in the sample of 100 is

$$P(X \leq 3) = \sum_{x=0}^{3} \frac{\mu^x e^{-\mu}}{x!} = e^{-4/7}\left(\frac{1}{1} + \frac{(4/7)}{1} + \frac{(4/7)^2}{2} + \frac{(4/7)^3}{6}\right)$$

$$= (0.5647)(1 + 0.5714 + 0.1633 + 0.0311) = 0.9972$$

3. Since there were 150 original shareholders, $p = 150/700 = 0.2143$, and we need the binomial probability P(5) for this p and $n = 15$:

$$\binom{15}{5}(0.2143)^5(1 - 0.2143)^{10} = (3{,}003)(0.0004518)(0.0897) = 0.1217$$

CHAPTER 4

NOTE: *A linear interpolation was used in the solution of most problems using the normal table. Thus small discrepancies may be found when comparing the answers with solutions obtained without an interpolation.*

4-1. $P(-1 < Z < 1) = 2(.3413) = 0.6826$
$P(-1.96 < Z < 1.96) = 0.95$
$P(-2.33 < Z < 2.33) = 0.9802$
$P(Z < 2.58) = 0.9951$
$P(-3 < Z < 3) = 0.9974$

4-2. $P(-2 < Z < 1) = .4772 + .3413 = 0.8185$

4-3. $P(-2.66 < Z < -0.89) = .4961 - .3133 = 0.1828$

4-4. $P(Z > 3.02) = .5 - .4987 = 0.0013$

4-5. $P(2 < Z < 3) = .4987 - .4772 = 0.0215$

4-6. $P(Z < -2.5) = .5 - .4938 = 0.0062$

4-7. $P(Z > -2.33) = .5 + .4901 = 0.9901$

4-8. $P(-2 < Z < 15) = $ a number very close to $.5 + .4772 = 0.9772$

4-9. $P(Z < -45) = $ a very small number, close to zero.

4-10. $P(-.01 < Z < .05) = .0199 + .0040 = 0.0239$

4-11. $P(-2 < Z < 2) = 2(.4772) = 0.9544$

4-12. $z = \pm 1.645$

4-13. Not likely. $P(Z < -4) = .5 - .49997 = 0.00003$

4-14. $P(Z > z) = 0.85$
$z = -1.036$ (approximately).

4-15. $P(Z < z) = 0.575$

$z = 0.19$

4-16. $P(Z > z) = 0.5$

$z = 0$

Do not need a normal table to find this: the Z variable has mean $= 0$ by definition.

4-17. $P(Z > z) = 0.28 \iff P(0 < Z < z) = 0.5 - 0.28 = 0.22$

$z = 0.583$ (approximately).

4-18. Look for $z > 0$ such that $P(0 < Z < z) = 0.40/2 = 0.20$: $\qquad z = \pm 0.524$

4-19. Look for $z > 0$ such that $P(0 < Z < z) = 0.95/2 = 0.475$: $\qquad z = \pm 1.96$

4-20. Look for $z > 0$ such that $0.5 - P(0 < Z < z) = 0.01/2 = 0.005$, which means $P(0 < Z < z) = 0.495$: $\qquad z = \pm 2.576$

(± 2.575 is the value obtained by a linear interpolation, ± 2.576 is more accurate.)

4-21. $P(|Z| > 2.4) = P(Z > 2.4 \text{ or } Z < -2.4) = 2\,P(Z > 2.4) = 2(.5 - .4918) = 0.0164$

4-22. $X \sim N(674, 55^2)$

$P(X < 600) = P\left(Z < \dfrac{600 - 674}{55}\right) = P(Z < -1.345) = .5 - .4107 = 0.0893$

4-23. $X \sim N(410, 2^2)$

$P(407 < X < 415) = P\left(\dfrac{407 - 410}{2} < Z < \dfrac{415 - 410}{2}\right) = P(-1.5 < Z < 2.5) = $
$.4332 + .4938 = 0.927$

4-24. $X \sim N(500, 20^2)$

$P(X > 555) = P\left(Z > \dfrac{555 - 500}{20}\right) = P(Z > 2.75) = .5 - .4970 = 0.003$

4-25. $X \sim N(-44, 16^2)$

$P(X > 0) = P\left(Z > \dfrac{0 - (-44)}{16}\right) = P(Z > 2.75) = 0.003$

4-26. $X \sim N(0, 4^2)$

$P(X > 2.5) = P\left(Z > \dfrac{2.5 - 0}{4}\right) = P(Z > .625) = .5 - .234 = 0.266$

4-27. $X \sim N(16, 3^2)$

$P(11 < X < 20) = P(-1.667 < Z < 1.333) = .4521 + .4088 = .8609$

$P(17 < X < 19) = P(.33 < Z < 1) = .3413 - .1306 = 0.2107$

$P(X > 15) = P(Z > -.33) = .5 + .1306 = 0.6306$

4-28. $X \sim N(45, 10^2)$

a. $P(X < 60) = P(Z < 1.5) = .5 + .4332 = 0.9332$

b. $P(X < 40) = P(Z < -.5) = .5 - .1915 = 0.3085$

c. $P(X > 70) = P(Z > 2.5) = .5 - .4938 = 0.0062$

4-29. $X \sim N(8,000, \; 1,000^2)$

$P(X \geq 9,322) = P(Z \geq 1.322) = .5 - .4069 = 0.0931$

4-30. $X \sim N(2.06, 0.08^2)$

a. $P(X > 2.10) = P(Z > .5) = .5 - .1915 = 0.3085$

b. $P(X < 1.90) = P(Z < -2.0) = .5 - .4772 = 0.0228$

c. $P(2.00 < X < 2.20) = P(-.75 < Z < 1.75) = .4599 + .2734 = 0.7333$

4-31. $X_{n.east} \sim N(6.90, 1.0^2)$ $X_{mtn} \sim N(4.31, 1.0^2)$

a. $P(X_{n.east} > 8.00) = P\left(Z > \dfrac{8.00 - 6.90}{1.0}\right) = P(Z > 1.10) = .5 - .3643 = 0.1357$

b. $P(X_{mtn} < 3.00) = P\left(Z < \dfrac{3.00 - 4.31}{1.0}\right) = P(Z < -1.31) = .5 - .4049 = 0.0951$

4-32. $X_{n.eng} \sim N(8.22, 1.0^2)$ $X_{ak} \sim N(7.10, 1.0^2)$ $X_{g.lks} \sim N(4.55, 1.0^2)$

$X_{s.east} \sim N(4.71, 1.0^2)$ $X_{plns} \sim N(4.40, 1.0^2)$ $X_{s.west} \sim N(4.21, 1.0^2)$

a. $P(X_{n.eng} > 7.00) = P\left(Z > \dfrac{7.00 - 8.22}{1.0}\right) = P(Z > -1.22)$

$= .5 + P(0 < Z < 1.22) = .5 + .3888 = 0.8888$

$$P(X_{ak} > 7.00) = P\left(Z > \frac{7.00 - 7.10}{1.0}\right) = P(Z > -0.10)$$

$$= .5 + P(0 < Z < 0.10) = .5 + .0398 = 0.5398$$

By independence, the probability of both is the product: 0.4798

b. $P(X_{g.lks} < 4.00) = P\left(Z < \dfrac{4.00 - 4.55}{1.0}\right) = P(Z < -0.55)$

$$= .5 - P(0 < Z < 0.55) = .5 - .2088 = 0.2912$$

$$P(X_{s.east} < 4.00) = P\left(Z < \frac{4.00 - 4.71}{1.0}\right) = P(Z < -0.71)$$

$$= .5 - P(0 < Z < 0.71) = .5 - .2611 = 0.2389$$

$$P(X_{plns} < 4.00) = P\left(Z < \frac{4.00 - 4.40}{1.0}\right) = P(Z < -0.40)$$

$$= .5 - P(0 < Z < 0.40) = .5 - .1554 = 0.3446$$

$$P(X_{s.west} < 4.00) = P\left(Z < \frac{4.00 - 4.21}{1.0}\right) = P(Z < -0.21)$$

$$= .5 - P(0 < Z < 0.21) = .5 - .0832 = 0.4168$$

By independence, the probability of all four is the product: 0.00999

4-33. $X \sim N(120, 44^2)$ $\qquad$ $P(X < x) = 0.56$
$P(Z < z) = 0.56$, thus:
$z = 0.15$
$x = \mu + z\sigma = 120 + (.15)(44) = 126.6$

4-34. $X \sim N(16.5, 0.8^2)$ $\qquad$ $P(X > x) = 0.85$
$P(Z > z) = 0.85$, thus:
$z = -1.04$
$x = \mu + z\sigma = 16.5 - 1.04(.8) = 15.67$

4-35. $X \sim N(19{,}500, 400^2)$ $\qquad$ $P(X > x) = 0.02$
$P(Z > z) = 0.02$, thus:
$TA = 0.48$ and $z = 2.054$
$x = \mu + z\sigma = 19{,}500 + 2.054(400) = 20{,}321.6$

4-36. $X \sim N(88, 5^2)$

$P(x_1 < X < x_2) = 0.98$

$P(-z < Z < z) = 0.98$ TA $= .98/2 = .49$

$x_1 = 88 - 2.33(5) = 76.35$

$x_2 = 88 + 2.33(5) = 99.65$

4-37. $X \sim N(32, 7^2)$ Find x_1, x_2 so that

$P(x_1 < X < x_2) = .99$ TA $= .99/2 = .495$

$z = \pm 2.576$

$x_{1,2} = 32 \pm 2.576(7)$

$= 13.97$ and 50.03

4-38. $X \sim N(-61, 22^2)$

$P(X > x) = 0.25$ TA $= .25$

$z = 0.675$ $x = -61 + 0.675(22) = -46.15$

4-39. $X \sim N(97, 10^2)$ $P(102 < X < x) = 0.05$

$P\left(\dfrac{102 - 97}{10} < Z < \dfrac{x - 97}{10}\right) = 0.05$

$P(0.5 < Z < z) = 0.05$

TA$(0.5) = 0.1915$. We need z such that TA$(z) = 0.1915 + 0.05 = 0.2415$

z is approximately 0.65

$x = 97 + (.65)(10) = 103.5$

Check: $P(102 < X < 103.5) = P(.5 < Z < .65)$

$= $ TA$(.65) - $ TA$(.5) = .2422 - .1915 = 0.0507$

4-40. $X \sim N(600, 10{,}000)$ $\sigma = \sqrt{10{,}000} = 100$

$P(X > x_1) = 0.01$ $z_1 = 2.326$

$x_1 = 600 + 2.326(100) = 832.6$

$P(X < x_2) = 0.05$ $z_2 = -1.645$

$x_2 = 600 - 1.645(100) = 435.5$

4-41. $X \sim N(25{,}000, 5{,}000^2)$

$P(X > x) = 0.15$

TA $= .35$ $z = 1.037$

$x = \mu + z\sigma = 25{,}000 + (1.037)5{,}000 = \$30{,}185$

4-42. $z = \pm 1.96$ $X \sim \mathrm{N}(27{,}009,\, 4{,}530^2)$

Interval: $27{,}009 \pm 1.96(4{,}530) = [18{,}130.2,\, 35{,}887.8]$

4-43. $X \sim \mathrm{N}(11.2,\, 0.6^2)$

0.99 probability implies $\mathrm{TA} = .99/2 = .495$

$z = \pm 2.576$

$x_{1,2} = 11.2 \pm 2.576(0.6) = 9.654,\, 12.746$

4-44. $X \sim \mathrm{N}(113,\, 4^2)$

0.95 probability of falling $< z$ means we want $\mathrm{TA} = .9500 - .5 = .4500$

$z = 1.645$

Therefore the cutoff $x = \mu + z\sigma = 113 + 1.645(4) = 119.58$

4-45. $X \sim \mathrm{N}(50,\, 5^2)$

0.90 probability of falling $> z$ (a negative value) means that the corresponding positive value $-z$ cuts off $TA = .9000 - .5 = .4000$, so

$z = -1.282$

Therefore the cutoff $x = \mu + z\sigma = 43.59$

4-46. $X \sim \mathrm{N}(129,\, \sigma^2)$ $\mathrm{P}(X > 142) = 0.3$

$\mathrm{P}\left(Z > \dfrac{142 - 129}{\sigma}\right) = 0.3$

$z = 0.524 = (142 - 129)/\sigma$

$\sigma = 24.81$ $\sigma^2 = 615.49$

4-47. $X \sim \mathrm{N}(\mu,\, 0.2^2)$

$\mathrm{P}(X < 0.5) = 0.65$ $z = 0.385$

$(0.5 - \mu)/0.2 = 0.385$

$\mu = .5 - (.2)(.385) = 0.423$

4-48. $X \sim \mathrm{N}(3{,}250,\, \sigma^2)$

$\mathrm{P}(X > 4{,}000) = 0.10$ $\mathrm{TA} = 0.4$ $z = 1.28$

$(4{,}000 - 3{,}250)/\sigma = 1.28$

$\sigma = (4{,}000 - 3{,}250)/1.28 = 585.94$

4-49. $X \sim \mathrm{N}(\mu, 560^2)$

$\mathrm{P}(X > 12{,}439) = 0.90 \qquad z = -1.28$

$(12{,}439 - \mu)/560 = -1.28$

$\mu = 12{,}439 + 1.28(560) = 13{,}155.8$

4-50. $X \sim \mathrm{N}(\mu, \sigma^2)$

$\mathrm{P}(X < 12) = 0.75 \qquad \mathrm{P}(X < 10) = 0.45$

Find z_1 such that $\mathrm{P}(Z < z_1) = .75$

Find z_2 such that $\mathrm{P}(Z < z_2) = .45$

$\mathrm{TA}_1 = .25 \qquad \mathrm{TA}_2 = .05 \quad z_2$ is negative

$z_1 = 0.674 \qquad z_2 = -0.126$

$$
\begin{aligned}
12 - \mu &= (.674)\sigma \\
\underline{10 - \mu} &= \underline{(-.126)\sigma} \\
2 &= 0.80\sigma \qquad \sigma = 2.5
\end{aligned}
$$

$12 - \mu = (.674)\sigma = 1.685$

$\mu = 10.315$

4-51. $\mathrm{P}(X > 4.9) = 0.65 \qquad \mathrm{P}(X < 4.2) = 0.25$

$z_1 = -.385 \qquad z_2 = -.675$

$\dfrac{4.9 - \mu}{\sigma} = -.385 \qquad \dfrac{4.2 - \mu}{\sigma} = -.675$

$$
\begin{aligned}
4.9 - \mu &= (-.385)\sigma \\
\underline{4.2 - \mu} &= \underline{(-.675)\sigma} \\
0.7 &= 0.29\sigma \qquad \sigma = 2.414
\end{aligned}
$$

$\mu = 4.9 + (0.385)\sigma = 5.829$

4-52. $\sigma = 1.75 \qquad \mathrm{P}(X > 7.4) = 0.55$

$X \sim \mathrm{N}(\mu, 1.75^2)$

$z = -0.126$

$\dfrac{7.4 - \mu}{1.75} = -0.126$

$7.4 - \mu = -0.2205$

$\mu = 7.6205$

4-53. $X \sim N(36{,}405, \sigma^2)$

$P(X > 45{,}000) = 0.05 \qquad z = 1.645$

$(45{,}000 - 36{,}405)/\sigma = 1.645$

$\sigma = 5{,}224.92$

4-54. $X \sim N(\mu, 46.2^2)$

$P(X < 4{,}048) = 0.9 \qquad z = 1.28$

$(4{,}048 - \mu)/46.2 = 1.28$

$\mu = 4{,}048 - 1.28(46.2) = \$3{,}988.86$ million

4-55. $X \sim N(5.2, \sigma^2) \qquad P(X < 7.0) = 0.80$

$P\left(Z < \dfrac{7.0 - 5.2}{\sigma}\right) = 0.80 \qquad z = 0.842$

$z = 1.8/\sigma = 0.842$

$\sigma = 2.138$

4-56. $X \sim N(\mu, \sigma^2)$

$P\left(Z > \dfrac{1.5 - \mu}{\sigma}\right) = 0.6 \qquad z_1 = -0.253$

$P\left(Z < \dfrac{2.1 - \mu}{\sigma}\right) = 0.9 \qquad z_2 = 1.282$

$1.5 - \mu = -0.253\sigma$

$\underline{2.1 - \mu = 1.282\sigma}$

$0.6 = 1.535\sigma \qquad \sigma = 0.391$ million

$\mu = 1.5 + 0.253\sigma = 1.599$ million

4-57. Assume independence of parties arriving for dinner.

$P(\text{success}) = 0.7$

$P(X > 15) = 1 - F(15) = F(4) \text{ [using } p = 0.3] = 0.2375$

Using a normal approximation:

$\mu = np = 20(.7) = 14 \qquad \sigma = \sqrt{npq} = 2.049$

$P(X > 15) = P(X > 15.5) \text{ [using a continuity correction]}$

$= P\left(Z > \dfrac{15.5 - 14}{2.049}\right) = P(Z > .732) = 0.2321$

4-58. Random sampling from large population implies a binomial distribution.

$n = 100 \qquad p = 0.4 \qquad \mu = np = 40 \qquad \sigma = \sqrt{npq} = 4.899$

$P(X \geq 20) = P(X > 19.5)$ [continuity correction]

$= P\left(Z > \dfrac{19.5 - 40}{4.899}\right) = P(Z > -4.18) > 0.99997$

4-59. $n = 45 \qquad p = 0.8 \qquad$ Assume independence of chips.

$\mu = 45(.8) = 36 \qquad \sigma = \sqrt{npq} = 2.683$

$P(X \geq 30) = P(X > 29.5)$ [cont. corr.] $= P(Z > -2.42) = 0.9922$

4-60. Assume independence of managers, and that managers from this company are the same as all others (i.e., $p = 0.6$ for them too).

$p = 0.6 \qquad n = 28 \qquad \mu = np = 16.8 \qquad \sigma = \sqrt{npq} = 2.592$

P(at least 1/2 will pass) is:

$P(X \geq 14) = P(X > 13.5)$ [cont. corr.]

$= P\left(Z > \dfrac{13.5 - 16.8}{2.592}\right) = P(Z > -1.273) = 0.8985$

4-61. Assume independence of students.

$p = 0.25 \qquad n = 1{,}889 \qquad \mu = np = 472.25 \qquad \sigma = \sqrt{npq} = 18.82$

$P(X \geq 500) = P(X > 499.5)$ [cont. corr.] $= P\left(Z > \dfrac{499.5 - 472.25}{18.82}\right)$

$= P(Z > 1.448) = .5 - .4262 = 0.0738$

4-62. Assume independence of executives.

$p = 0.75 \qquad n = 30 \qquad \mu = np = 22.5 \qquad \sigma = \sqrt{npq} = 2.372$

$P(X \geq 20) = P(X > 19.5)$ [cont. corr.] $= P\left(Z > \dfrac{19.5 - 22.5}{2.372}\right)$

$= P(Z > -1.265) = .5 + .3971 = 0.897$

4-63. Assume independence of earners chosen.

$p = 0.64 \qquad n = 50 \qquad \mu = np = 32 \qquad \sigma = \sqrt{npq} = 3.394$

$P(X \leq 30) = P\left(Z < \dfrac{30 - 32}{3.394}\right) = P(Z < -.589) = .5 - .2222 = 0.278$

4-64. $X \sim N(549, 68^2)$

$P(X > 500) = P\left(Z > \dfrac{500 - 549}{68}\right) = P(Z > -.72) = .5 + .2642 = 0.7642$

4-65. $X \sim N(785, 60^2)$

$$P(X > 800) = P\left(Z > \frac{800 - 785}{60}\right) = P(Z > .25) = .5 - .0987 = 0.4013$$

$$P(750 < X < 850) = P\left(\frac{750 - 785}{60} < Z < \frac{850 - 785}{60}\right)$$

$$= P(-.58333 < Z < 1.0833) = .2201 + .3606 = 0.5808$$

i.e., about 58% of all working days.

$$P(X < 665) = P(Z < -2) = .5 - .4772 = 0.0228$$

4-66. $X \sim N(650, 50^2)$

$$P(X > 700) = P\left(Z > \frac{700 - 650}{50}\right) = P(Z > 1) = .5 - .3413 = 0.1587$$

$$P(X < 750) = P\left(Z < \frac{750 - 650}{50}\right) = P(Z < 2) = .5 + .4772 = 0.9772$$

4-67. (Note that price is discrete: $48, 48\frac{1}{2}, 48\frac{1}{4}$, etc.)

$X \sim N(48, 6^2)$

$$P(X > 60) = P\left(Z > \frac{60 - 48}{6}\right) = P(Z > 2) = 0.0228$$

$$P(X < 60) = P(Z < 2) = 0.9772$$

$$P(X > 40) = P\left(Z > \frac{40 - 48}{6}\right) = P(Z > -1.33) = .5 + .4088 = 0.9088$$

$$P(40 < X < 50) = P(-1.33 < Z < .33) = .4088 + .1306 = 0.5394$$

Limitation: stock prices are very discrete.

4-68. $X \sim N(800{,}000, 10{,}000^2)$

$P(X > x) = 0.80$

$P(Z > z) = 0.80 \qquad \text{TA} = .30 \qquad z \text{ negative} \qquad z = -0.842$

$x = \mu + z\sigma = 800{,}000 - (.842)10{,}000 = 791{,}580$ barrels per day.

4-69. $X \sim N(8.95, 2^2)$

$P(X > x) = 0.90$

$z = -1.28$

$x = 8.95 - 1.28(2) = \$6.39$

4-70. $X \sim N(8, 0.5^2)$

find x_1, x_2 such that $P(x_1 < X < x_2) = 0.95$

$z_{1,2} = \pm 1.96$

$x_{1,2} = \mu + z_{1,2}\sigma = 8 \pm 1.96(.5) = [7.02, 8.98]$ percent.

4-71. $X \sim N(50{,}000, 3{,}000^2)$

Give 0.99 probability bounds:

$z = \pm 2.576$

Bounds are $50{,}000 \pm 2.576(3{,}000) = [42{,}272, 57{,}728]$

4-72. $X \sim N(2{,}348, 762^2)$

$P(X \geq x) = 0.85 \qquad z = -1.04$

$x = 2{,}348 - 1.04(762) = 1{,}555.52$

0.80 probability bounds: $z = \pm 1.28$

$x_{1,2} = 2{,}348 \pm 1.28(762) = [1{,}372.64, 3{,}323.36]$, i.e., they are 80% sure that anywhere from 1,373 to 3,323 people will sign up for the trip.

4-73. $X \sim N(12.1, 2.5^2)$

$P(X > x) = 0.75 \qquad z = -0.675$

$x = 12.1 - .675(2.5) = 10.4125\%$

$P(X < x') = 0.75 \qquad z' = 0.675$

$x' = 12.1 + (.675)(2.5) = 13.7875\%$

4-74. $X \sim N(15.6, 4.1^2)$

$P(X > x) = 0.95 \qquad z = -1.645$

$x = 15.6 - 1.645(4.1) = 8.8555$ KW.

4-75. $X \sim N(5.9, 0.8^2)$

$P(Z < z) = 0.95 \qquad z = 1.645$

$\mu + z\sigma = 7.22$

4-76. $.5 - \text{TA}(z = 3.000) = .5 - .4987 = .0013$, so the total area outside of $z = \pm 3.000$ is $2(.0013) = .0026$, or 0.26%. Thus, define "too many" items as "more than 0.26%". If noticeably more than 0.26% of the items are out of bounds, assuming the normal distribution for when the process is *in* control, then a very low-probability event is being observed and the distribution is probably not in fact a normal one, i.e., the process is probably *not* in control.

-77. $X \sim N(\mu, \sigma^2)$

$P(X > 671{,}000) = 0.45 \qquad P(X > 712{,}000) = 0.10$

$z_1 = 0.126 \qquad z_2 = 1.28$

$$0.126 = \frac{671{,}000 - \mu}{\sigma} \qquad 1.28 = \frac{712{,}000 - \mu}{\sigma}$$

$$671{,}000 - \mu = 0.126\sigma$$

$$\underline{712{,}000 - \mu = 1.28\sigma}$$

$$41{,}000 = 1.154\sigma \qquad \sigma = 35{,}528.596$$

$$\mu = 671{,}000 - 0.126\sigma = 666{,}523.4$$

-78. $X \sim N(\mu, \sigma^2)$

$P(X > 65) = 0.45 \qquad P(X > 70) = 0.15$

$z_1 = 0.126 \qquad z_2 = 1.0365$

$$\frac{65 - \mu}{\sigma} = 0.126 \qquad \frac{70 - \mu}{\sigma} = 1.0365$$

$$70 - \mu = 1.0365\sigma$$

$$\underline{65 - \mu = 0.126\sigma}$$

$$5 = .9105\sigma \qquad \sigma = 5.49$$

$$\mu = 70 - 1.0365\sigma = 64.31$$

-79. $X \sim N(\mu, \sigma^2)$

$P(X > 1{,}000) = 0.1 \qquad z = 1.28$

$P(X \geq 650) = 0.5 \qquad z = 0$

$$\frac{1{,}000 - \mu}{\sigma} = 1.28 \qquad \frac{650 - \mu}{\sigma} = 0$$

$$1{,}000 - 650 = 1.28\sigma$$

$$\mu = 650 \qquad \sigma = 273.44$$

-80. $X \sim N(4{,}500,\, 1{,}800^2)$

$P(X < x) = 0.80 \qquad z = 0.842$

$x = 4{,}500 + (.842)1{,}800 = 6{,}015.6$

-81. $X \sim N(34{,}750,\, 3{,}560^2)$

$P(X < x) = 0.75 \qquad z = 0.675$

$x = 34{,}750 + (.675)3{,}560 = 37{,}153$ papers.

4-82. $X \sim \mathrm{N}(42, 2.4^2)$

$P(X < x) = 0.98 \qquad z = 2.054$

$x = 42 + 2.054(2.4) = 46.9296$

that is, 46 minutes and 56 seconds after the hour.

4-83. $p = .30 \qquad n = 238 \qquad \mu = np = 71.4 \qquad \sigma = \sqrt{npq} = 7.07$

$P(X \geq 50) = P\left(Z > \dfrac{50 - 71.4}{7.07}\right) = P(Z > -3.027) = .5 + .4988 = 0.999$

4-84. $X \sim \mathrm{N}(\mu, 5.1^2)$

$P(X > 124.6) = 0.20 \qquad z = 0.842$

$\dfrac{124.6 - \mu}{5.1} = 0.842$

$\mu = 120.3$

$P(X < \mu) = 0.50$ (no matter what the distribution actually might be).

4-85. $X \sim \mathrm{N}(38, 11^2)$

$P(X > x) = 0.90 \qquad z = -1.28$

$x = 38 - 1.28(11) = 23.92$ months, so set warranty for 24 months (2 years).

4-86. (Redo Problem **3-69** using a normal approximation):

$p = 0.4 \qquad n = 20 \qquad \mu = np = 8 \qquad \sigma = \sqrt{npq} = 2.19$

We solve part (b):

$P(X \leq 2) = P(X < 2.5) \qquad$ [cont. correction]

$= P\left(Z < \dfrac{2.5 - 8}{2.19}\right) = P(Z < -2.51) = .5 - .494 = 0.006$

Exact probability (binomial) in the earlier problem is found to be 0.0036. (Here the approximation is not good because $npq < 9$.)

4-87. $X \sim \mathrm{N}(40{,}000, 10{,}000^2)$

$P(25{,}000 < X < 35{,}000) =$

$P\left(\dfrac{25{,}000 - 40{,}000}{10{,}000} < Z < \dfrac{35{,}000 - 40{,}000}{10{,}000}\right) = P(-1.50 < Z < -0.50)$

$= \mathrm{TA}(1.50) - \mathrm{TA}(0.50) = 0.242$

4-88. For any distribution (normal or not) with mean μ, $P(X \geq \mu) = 0.5$

-89. $X \sim N(1.5, \sigma^2)$ (using units of \$1 million)

$P(X > 1) = P\left(Z > \dfrac{1 - 1.5}{\sigma}\right) = 0.75$ $z = -0.675$

$\sigma = (1 - 1.5)/(-0.675) = 0.741$, i.e., \$741,000.

-90. For the normal approximation:

$n = 10{,}000$ $\mu = np = (10{,}000)(0.1) = 1{,}000$ $\sigma = \sqrt{npq} = 30$

$P(X \geq 800) = P\left(Z \geq \dfrac{800 - 1{,}000}{30}\right) = P(Z \geq -6.67)$

= a number very close to 1.

-91. $n = 30$ $p = 0.80$ $\mu = np = 24$ $\sigma = \sqrt{npq} = 2.191$

$P(X \geq 10) = P(X > 9.5)$ [cont. corr.] $= P\left(Z > \dfrac{9.5 - 24}{2.191}\right) = P(Z > -6.618) =$

1.00 (extremely close).

Case 4. a.

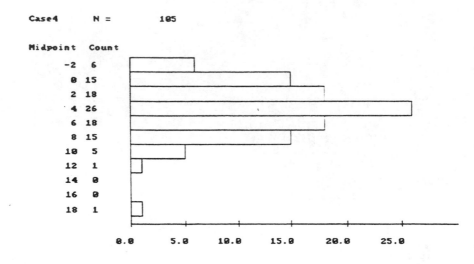

```
Case4      N =        105

Midpoint  Count
    -2   6
     0  15
     2  18
     4  26
     6  18
     8  15
    10   5
    12   1
    14   0
    16   0
    18   1

        0.0    5.0   10.0   15.0   20.0   25.0
```

For the sample: $\bar{x} = 4.170$ $s = 3.501$

Both values are slightly higher than those from the full set of stocks. Since $P(Z < -0.6745) = 0.25$ and $P(Z < 0.6745) = 0.75$, we see that for a normally distributed variable $X \sim N(4.170, 3.501^2)$ the corresponding values $x_{1,2}$ with $P(X < x_1) = 0.25$, $P(X < x_2) = 0.75$ are $x_{1,2} = 4.170 \mp (0.6745)3.501 = 1.809, 6.531$. Compare with the actual values from the sample data set:

   $Q_1 = 1.620$ $Q_3 = 6.289$ The agreement is good, and the data set seems to be quite close to a normal distribution.

b. If the pre-commission net return is X percent, then *after* the commission is deducted the new net return percentage is $(0.95)X$ when X is positive (since presumably the brokerage doesn't charge anything if you lose on the investment). Leaving aside the negative values, this change in the data set, with each point X being replaced by $(0.95)X$, would affect the overall symmetry somewhat since the amount of "shift," $X - (0.95)X$, is proportional to X. However the overall distribution should remain approximately normal.

CHAPTER 5

5-1. Parameters are numerical measures of populations. Sample statistics are numerical measures of samples. An estimator is a sample statistic used for estimating a population parameter.

5-2. $\bar{x} = 97.9225$ (estimate of μ)
$s = 51.8303$ (estimate of σ)
$s^2 = 2,686.38$ (estimate of σ^2—the population variance)

5-3. $\hat{p} = x/n = 5/12 = 0.41667$
(5 out of 12 accounts are over \$100.)

5-4. $\bar{x} = 15.333$ $\quad s = 2.5546$

5-5. $\hat{p} = x/n = 3/10 = 0.30$
Average of points $> 500 = 586.667$, i.e., \$586,667.

5-6. $\hat{p} = x/n = 11/18 = 0.6111$, where $x =$ the number of users of the product.

5-7. We need 25 elements from a population of 950 elements. Use the rows of Table 5-1, the rightmost 3 digits of each group starting in row 1 (left to right). So we skip any such 3-digit number that is either > 950 or that has been generated earlier in this list, giving us a list of 25 different numbers in the desired range. The chosen numbers are:

480, 11, 536, 647, 646, 179, 194, 368, 573, 595, 393, 198, 402, 130, 360, 527, 265, 809, 830, 167, 93, 243, 680, 856, 376.

5-8. We will use again Table 5-1, using columns this time. We will use right-hand columns, first 4 digits from the right (going down the column):

4,194   3,402   4,830   3,537   1305.

5-9. We will use Table 5-1, sets of 2 columns using all 5 digits from column 1 and the first 3 digits from column 2, continuing by reading down in these columns. Then we will continue to the set: column 3 and first 3 digits column 4. We skip any numbers that are $> 40,000,000$. The resulting voter numbers are:

10,480,150   22,368,465   24,130,483   37,570,399   1,536,020.

5-10. There are $7 \times 24 \times 60$ minutes in one week: $(7)(24)(60) = 10,080$ minutes. We will use Table 5-1. Start in the first row and go across the row, then to the next row (left to right using all 5 digits in each set), discarding any of the resulting 5-digit numbers that are $> 10,080$. The resulting minute numbers are:

1,536   2,011   6,243   7,856   6,121   6,907.

5-11. A sampling distribution is the probability distribution of a sample statistic. The sampling distribution is useful in determining the accuracy of estimation results.

5-12. Only if the population is itself normal.

5-13. $E(\bar{X}) = \mu = 125$ $SE(\bar{X}) = \sigma/\sqrt{n} = 20/\sqrt{5} = 8.944$

5-14. The fact that, in the limit, the population distribution does not matter. Thus the theorem is very general.

5-15. When the population distribution is unknown.

5-16. The Central Limit Theorem does not apply.

5-17. $\hat{P}$ is binomial. Since $np = 1.2$, the Central Limit Theorem does not apply and we cannot use the normal distribution.

5-18. $\mu = 1,247$ $\sigma^2 = 10,000$ $n = 100$

$$P(\bar{X} < 1,230) = P\left(Z < \frac{1,230 - 1,247}{100/10}\right) = P(Z < -1.7) = .5 - .4554 = 0.0446$$

5-19. $P(|\bar{X} - \mu| \geq 8) = 1 - P(|\bar{X} - \mu| < 8) = 1 - P(-8 < \bar{X} - \mu < 8)$

$$= 1 - P\left(\frac{-8}{55/\sqrt{150}} < Z < \frac{8}{55/\sqrt{150}}\right) = 1 - P(-1.78 < Z < 1.78)$$

$$= 1 - 2(.4625) = 0.075$$

5-20. $P(X \geq 3.6) = P\left(Z \geq \frac{3.6 - 3.4}{1.5/\sqrt{100}}\right) = P(Z \geq 1.333) = 0.0912$

5-21. $p = 0.70$ $\sqrt{p(1-p)/n} = 0.0324$

$$P(X \geq 0.80) = P\left(Z \geq \frac{0.80 - 0.70}{0.0324}\right) = P(Z \geq 3.086) = 0.001$$

5-22. $s = 4{,}500 \qquad n = 225$

$$P(|\bar{X} - \mu| < 800) = P\left(|Z| < \frac{800}{4{,}500/\sqrt{225}}\right) = P\left(\frac{-800}{4{,}500/15} < Z < \frac{800}{4{,}500/15}\right)$$

$$= P(-2.667 < Z < 2.667) = 2(.4961) = 0.9923$$

5-23. $p = 0.18 \qquad n = 200$

$$P(\hat{P} \geq .20) = P\left(Z \geq \frac{.20 - .18}{\sqrt{(.18)(.82)/200}}\right) = P\left(Z \geq \frac{.02}{.02717}\right) = P(Z \geq .736)$$

$$= .5 - .2692 = 0.2308$$

5-24. The claim is that $p = 0.58$. We have $n = 250$ and $x/n = 123/250 = 0.492$.

$$P(\hat{P} \leq .492) = P\left(Z \leq \frac{.492 - .58}{\sqrt{(.58)(.42)/250}}\right) = P(Z < -2.819) = 0.0024$$

5-25. Note that the given percentages are individual statistics, *not* population or sample proportions. $\mu = 67.5 \qquad n = 100 \qquad \sigma = 10$

Using the normal approximation:

$$P(\bar{X} \geq 70) = P\left(Z > \frac{70 - 67.5}{10/\sqrt{100}}\right) = P(Z \geq 2.50) = .5 - .4938 = 0.0062$$

5-26. $n = 16 \qquad \mu = 1.5 \qquad \sigma = 2$

$$P(\bar{X} > 0) = P\left(Z > \frac{0 - 1.5}{2/\sqrt{16}}\right) = P(Z > -3) = .5 + .4987 = 0.9987$$

5-27. $p = 1/7$

$$P(\hat{P} < .10) = P\left(Z < \frac{.10 - .143}{\sqrt{(1/7)(6/7)/180}}\right) = P(Z < -1.643) = .5 - .4498 =$$

0.0502, a low probability. The sample size, along with np and $n(1 - p)$, are large enough here that the sample distribution (over all the different samples of 180 people in the population) of the proportion of people who get hospitalized during the year is going to be pretty close to normal. Therefore, any one such sample proportion will be close to the predicted mean 1/7 with reasonable probability, and 1/10 is far enough away from that mean given our estimated sample standard deviation that the probability of falling even farther away than that from the mean is small.

5-28. $\mu = 700 \qquad \sigma = 100 \qquad n = 60$

$$P(680 \leq X \leq 720) = P\left(\frac{680 - 700}{100/\sqrt{60}} \leq Z \leq \frac{720 - 700}{100/\sqrt{60}}\right)$$

$$= 2\,\text{TA}(1.549) = 0.8786$$

5-29. $p = \mu = 0.35 \qquad \sigma = \sqrt{(0.35)(0.65)/500} = 0.0213$

$$P(|\hat{P} - p| > 0.05) = P(\hat{P} < 0.30) + P(\hat{P} > 0.40)$$

$$= P\left(Z < \frac{0.30 - 0.35}{0.0213}\right) + P\left(Z > \frac{0.40 - 0.35}{0.0213}\right)$$

$$= 1 - 2\,\text{TA}(2.344) = 0.0190$$

5-30. Estimator B is better. It has a small bias, but its variance is small. This estimator is more likely to produce an estimate that is close to the parameter of interest.

5-31. I would use this estimator because consistency means as $n \to \infty$ the probability of getting close to the parameter increases. With a generous budget I can get a large sample size, which will make this probability high.

5-32. $\hat{s}^2 = 1{,}287 \qquad s^2 = \left(\frac{n}{n-1}\right)\hat{s}^2 = \left(\frac{100}{99}\right)1{,}287 = 1{,}300$

5-33. Advantage: uses all information in the data.
Disadvantage: may be too sensitive to the influence of outliers.

5-34. Depends also on efficiency and other factors. With respect to the bias:
A has bias $= 1/n$
B has bias $= 0.01$
A is better than B when $1/n < 0.01$, that is, when $n > 1/0.01 = 100$

5-35. Consistency is important because it means that as you get more data, your probability of getting closer to your "target" increases.

5-36. $n_1 = 30$, $n_2 = 48$, $n_3 = 32$. The three sample means are known. The df for deviations from the three sample means are:
df $= n_1 + n_2 + n_3 - 3 = 30 + 48 + 32 - 3 = 107$

5-37. df $= n - 2$, because there are 2 restrictions: an intercept and a slope.

-38. No, because there are $n - 1 = 19 - 1 = 18$ degrees of freedom for these checks once you know their mean. Since 17 is one less, there is a remaining degree of freedom and you cannot solve for the missing checks.

-39. Yes. $(x_1 + \cdots + x_{18} + x_{19})/19 = \bar{x}$. Since 18 of the x_i are known and so is $\bar{x}$, we can solve the equation for the unknown x_{19}.

-40. $$S^2 = \frac{\sum (x_i - \bar{x})^2}{n - 1}$$

We divide the sum of the squared deviations from the mean by the df, which is equal to $n - 1$ to get a meaningful "average" squared deviation from the sample mean.

-41. $E(\bar{X}) = \mu = 1{,}065 \qquad V(\bar{X}) = \sigma^2/n = 500^2/100 = 2{,}500$

-42. $\sigma^2 = 1{,}000{,}000$
Want $SD(\bar{X}) \le 25$
$SD(\bar{X}) = \sigma/\sqrt{n} = 1{,}000/\sqrt{n}$
$1{,}000/\sqrt{n} \le 25$
$\sqrt{n} \ge 1{,}000/25 = 40$
$n \ge 1{,}600$. The sample size must be at least 1,600.

-43. $\mu = 53 \qquad \sigma = 10 \qquad n = 400$
$E(\bar{X}) = \mu = 53 \qquad SE(\bar{X}) = \sigma/\sqrt{n} = 10/\sqrt{400} = 0.5$

-44. $p = 0.5 \qquad n = 120$

$$SE(\hat{P}) = \sqrt{\frac{p(1 - p)}{n}} = \sqrt{\frac{(.5)(.5)}{120}} = 0.0456$$

-45. $E(\hat{P}) = p = 0.2$

$$SE(\hat{P}) = \sqrt{\frac{p(1 - p)}{n}} = \sqrt{\frac{(.2)(.8)}{90}} = 0.04216$$

5-46. $p = 0.5$ maximizes the variance of $\hat{P}$. **Proof:**

$$V(\hat{P}) = \frac{p(1-p)}{n}$$

$$\frac{dV(\hat{P})}{dp} = \frac{1}{n}\frac{d}{dp}(p - p^2) = \frac{1}{n}(1 - 2p)$$

Set the derivative to zero:

$$\frac{1}{n}(1 - 2p) = 0 \qquad\qquad 1 = 2p \qquad\qquad p = 1/2$$

The assertion may also be demonstrated by trying different values of p.

5-47. $n = 200 \qquad \mu = 50,000 \qquad \sigma = 8,000$

$$P(\bar{X} > 51,000) = P\left(Z > \frac{\bar{X} - \mu}{\sigma/\sqrt{n}} = \frac{51,000 - 50,000}{8,000/\sqrt{200}}\right)$$

$$= P(Z > 1.77) = .5 - .4616 = 0.0384$$

5-48. $P(\bar{X} \geq 1,000) = P\left(Z \geq \frac{1,000 - 1,065}{500/10}\right) = P\left(Z \geq \frac{-650}{500}\right)$

$$= P(Z \geq -1.3) = .5 + .4032 = 0.9032$$

We need to use the Central Limit Theorem for a normal distribution.

5-49. $\mu = 53 \qquad \sigma = 10 \qquad n = 400$

$$P(52 < \bar{X} < 54) = P\left(\frac{52 - 53}{10/20} < Z < \frac{54 - 53}{10/20}\right) = P(-2 < Z < 2) = 0.9544$$

5-50. $p = 0.5 \qquad n = 120$

$$P(\hat{P} \geq .45) = P\left(Z \geq \frac{.45 - .5}{\sqrt{(.5)(.5)/120}}\right) = P(Z \geq -1.095) = 0.8632$$

5-51. $n = 50 \qquad \mu = 2.2 \qquad \sigma = 0.5$

$$P(\bar{X} < 2.0) = P\left(Z < \frac{2.0 - 2.2}{0.5/\sqrt{50}}\right) = P(Z < -2.83)$$

$$= .5 - .4977 = 0.0023$$

5-52. $0.06 \le p \le 0.10$

$SE(\hat{P}) = \sqrt{p(1-p)/n} \le 0.03$

Assume $p = 0.06$:

$SE(\hat{P}) = \sqrt{(.06)(.94)/n} \le .03$

$(.06)(.94)/n \le .03^2$

$62.66 \le n$

Now assume the other extreme, $p = 0.10$:

$SE(\hat{P}) = \sqrt{(.1)(.9)/n} \le .03$

$(.1)(.9)/n \le .03^2$

$100 \le n$

Now, we also know that the function $SE(\hat{P})$ does not have a maximum point between $p = 0.06$ and $p = 0.10$ because the only maximum point of the function occurs at $p = 0.5$ (as we know from Problem **5-46**). Hence $SE(\hat{P})$ is monotonic between $p = 0.06$ and 0.10, and thus $n = 100$ is the minimum required sample size.

5-53.   Random samples from the entire population of interest reduce the chance of a bias and increase chance of being representative of the entire population. Also, we have a known probability of being within certain distances of the parameter of interest. We use a frame and a random number generator or a table of random numbers. A simple random sample is such that every possible set of n elements has an equal chance of being selected.

5-54.   A bias is a systematic deviation away from the target of estimation. A bias takes us away from the target parameter in repeated sampling. If the bias is small and variance of the estimator is also small, the bias may be tolerated, especially if the bias decreases as n increases.

5-55.   The sample median is unbiased. The sample mean is more efficient; it is also sufficient. This is why we prefer the sample mean. We must assume normality for using the sample median to estimate μ. The median is more resistant to outliers.

5-56. S^2 has $n-1$ in the denominator because there are $n-1$ degrees of freedom for deviations from the sample mean. Using $n-1$ instead of n makes S^2 an unbiased estimator of σ^2.

5-57. $\mu = 19.5 \qquad \sigma = 5.3 \qquad n = 100$

$$P(\bar{X} > 20) = P\left(Z > \frac{20 - 19.5}{5.3/10}\right) = P(Z > .9434) = .5 - .3273 = 0.1727$$

5-58. 95% bounds on $\bar{X}$:

$\mu \pm 1.96\sigma/\sqrt{n} = 19.5 \pm 1.96(5.3/10) = [18.4612, 20.5388]$

90% bounds on $\bar{X}$:

$19.5 \pm 1.645(5.3/10) = [18.62815, 20.37185]$

5-59. $\bar{X} \sim N(\mu, \sigma^2/n) \qquad n = 1,000$

$$P(|\bar{X} - \mu| > 0.062\sigma) = P(\bar{X} < \mu - 0.062\sigma) + P(\bar{X} > \mu + 0.062\sigma)$$

$$= P\left(Z < \frac{(\mu - 0.062\sigma) - \mu}{\sigma/\sqrt{n}}\right) + P\left(Z > \frac{(\mu + 0.062\sigma) - \mu}{\sigma/\sqrt{n}}\right)$$

$$= P\left(Z < \frac{-0.062}{1/\sqrt{1,000}}\right) + P\left(Z > \frac{0.062}{1/\sqrt{1,000}}\right)$$

$$= 2\,P(Z > 1.961) = 1 - 2\,TA(1.961) = 0.0499$$

Note that the actual value of μ is irrelevant.

5-60. $\mu = 3,324 \qquad \sigma = 500 \qquad n = 1,000$

$P(-z < Z < z) = 0.90 \qquad$ for the value $\qquad z = 1.645$

$$P(x_1 < \bar{X} < x_2) = P\left(\frac{x_1 - \mu}{\sigma/\sqrt{n}} < Z < \frac{x_2 - \mu}{\sigma/\sqrt{n}}\right) = 0.90$$

$$\frac{x_{1,2} - \mu}{\sigma/\sqrt{n}} = \pm z = \pm 1.645$$

$x_{1,2} = \mu \pm (1.645\sigma/\sqrt{n}) = 3,324 \pm (1.645)(500)/\sqrt{1,000} = [3,297.99, 3,350.01]$

5-61. $p = 0.38 \qquad n = 100$

$$P(\hat{P} > 0.30) = P\left(Z > \frac{.30 - .38}{\sqrt{(.38)(.62)/100}}\right) = P(Z > -1.648)$$

$$= .5 + .4503 = 0.9503$$

5-62. $\bar{X}$ is normal. But since σ is unknown and we use S, the quantity $(\bar{X} - \mu)/(S/\sqrt{n})$ has the $t_{(n-1)}$ distribution rather than the standard normal distribution Z.

5-63. No minimum ($n = 1$ is enough for normality).

5-64. $\bar{X}$, $\hat{P}$, S^2 are unbiased. S is the square root of an unbiased estimator of σ^2, thus it is *not* unbiased. **Proof:**

Assume $E(S) = \sigma$

then: $(E(S))^2 = \sigma^2$

and: $E(S^2) - (E(S))^2 = \sigma^2 - \sigma^2 = 0$ (since $E(S^2) = \sigma^2$).

But $E(S^2) - (E(S))^2 = V(S)$

$V(S) = 0$ means that S is not a statistical estimator. The contradiction establishes the proposition that S is biased.

5-65. This estimator is also consistent. It is more efficient than $\bar{X}$, because $\sigma^2/n^2 < \sigma^2/n$.

5-66. $df = 124 - 3 = 121$

5-67.   **a.** Normal population requires the smallest minimum n.

     b. Mound-shaped population requires the next higher minimum n.

     c. Discrete population needs the highest minimum n.

     d. Slightly skewed population: n more than for (b), less than for (c).

     e. Highly skewed population: n less than for (c), but more than for (d).

     The relative minimum required sample sizes are as follows:

$$n_a < n_b < n_d < n_e < n_c$$

5-68. Yes. $SE(\bar{X})$ decreases as n increases:

$SE(\bar{X}) = \sigma/\sqrt{n}$, which goes to 0 as n goes to ∞. Statistically, it is always good to have as large a sample as possible.

5-69. Draw repeated samples, preferably by simulation on a computer, and determine the empirical distribution of the statistic: the relative frequency distribution of its values.

5-70. $P(\hat{P} < .15) = P\left(Z < \dfrac{.15 - .20}{\sqrt{(.2)(.8)/250}}\right) = P(Z < -1.976) = .5 - .4759 = 0.0241$

5-71. $\mu = 25$ $\sigma = 2$ $n = 100$

$$P(\bar{X} < 24) = P\left(Z < \frac{24 - 25}{2/10}\right) = P(Z < -5) = 0.0000003$$

Not probable at all.

5-72. $P(|\hat{P} - 0.80| \le 0.07) = P(0.73 \le \hat{P} \le 0.87)$

$$= P\left(\frac{.73 - .80}{\sqrt{(.80)(.20)/200}} \le Z \le \frac{.87 - .80}{\sqrt{(.80)(.20)/200}}\right) = P(-2.475 \le Z \le 2.475)$$

$$= 2\,\mathrm{TA}(2.475) = 0.9866$$

5-73. $P(1.52 < \bar{X} < 1.62) = P\left(\dfrac{1.52 - 1.57}{0.4/\sqrt{200}} < Z < \dfrac{1.62 - 1.57}{0.4/\sqrt{200}}\right) = 2\,\mathrm{TA}(1.768) = 0.923$

5-74.   Inferences can only be drawn on the individual highway and city mileages, because we don't know how the 611 measured miles were divided between the two kinds of driving and among the cars selected for testing. We also don't know the sample size, i.e., how many separate cars were tested and on how many trials each. The stated results are of limited use.

Population mean and st. dev. for the 50 prices: $\mu = 25.0394$, $\sigma = 11.755$

RANDOM SAMPLES OF VARYING SIZES:

Sample size	Stocks in sample (by table entry #)	Sample mean of prices
5	9,16,26,27,48	32.902
5	7,9,12,25,36	21.376
5	5,14,19,20,50	25.352
5	27,33,39,40,42	27.376
5	8,16,18,32,46	17.902
5	21,26,31,40,47	26.554
5	20,30,34,38,44	22.828
5	11,18,21,24,42	19.702
5	7,11,37,48,49	32.702
5	2,21,38,40,48	35.552
5	3,13,16,30,38	23.378
5	3,16,23,46,48	27.126
	size-5 sample means: $\quad \bar{x} = 26.062 \qquad s = 5.487$	
15	3,6,9,12,13,18,20,21,22,24,25,27,29,35,44	21.143
15	2,5,12,13,15,16,18,20,21,33,34,37,39,45,47	27.061
15	7,8,11,12,14,15,22,29,34,38,39,41,42,44,49	20.143
15	7,10,12,13,20,22,23,31,33,36,38,44,45,49,50	20.660
15	4,5,8,13,18,20,23,24,27,30,31,38,40,48,50	25.827
15	5,8,10,15,16,23,28,29,32,35,36,38,39,40,49	23.661
15	2,6,7,13,15,16,18,19,21,23,25,29,31,33,49	22.551
15	9,14,15,18,24,28,29,30,31,33,35,42,43,44,45	24.893
15	6,7,9,10,14,18,20,22,24,26,27,31,37,41,42	21.101
15	4,9,14,15,16,18,28,30,33,34,40,41,43,45,46	25.268
15	2,8,11,18,19,20,27,28,30,31,32,37,42,46,50	26.460
15	1,3,4,6,8,10,11,12,19,21,30,31,37,40,44	21.361
	size-15 sample means: $\quad \bar{x} = 23.344 \qquad s = 2.482$	
25	1,2,3,4,5,6,7,8,9,10,16,17,18,19,22,31,32,33,37,39,44,45,46,48,49	25.057
25	1,3,6,9,10,12,16,18,20,24,25,26,27,29,30,31,34,35,37,38,39,44,45,46,50	23.392
25	2,3,6,7,10,11,12,13,14,17,18,22,25,26,27,32,33,34,36,37,38,43,44,45,48	27.982
25	1,8,9,11,12,13,16,17,18,19,21,22,24,26,27,29,30,33,36,37,41,42,44,48,49	23.678
25	1,2,4,5,7,10,12,13,14,16,18,19,22,23,24,26,27,31,32,33,36,39,42,44,46	22.347
25	4,5,6,7,8,11,12,13,20,22,23,25,26,28,29,31,32,34,36,37,39,40,42,43,45	25.942
25	2,3,5,7,10,15,18,19,20,21,22,24,29,30,33,34,35,36,37,43,45,47,48,49,50	25.527
25	5,7,8,15,16,18,19,20,26,27,28,30,33,34,37,38,39,40,43,44,46,47,48,49,50	28.357
25	1,9,10,11,13,17,18,19,20,23,24,25,26,28,32,38,39,40,41,42,43,45,46,47,48	26.182
25	1,3,6,9,13,14,17,19,20,21,22,28,29,32,33,35,37,38,39,41,42,43,44,45,49	24.812
25	2,3,4,6,7,9,10,16,17,19,23,24,25,27,31,32,33,35,36,38,40,41,45,46,48	23.706
25	1,2,5,6,12,13,14,17,19,20,23,25,27,28,31,32,34,35,38,39,41,42,44,47,48	27.592
	size-25 sample means: $\quad \bar{x} = 25.381 \qquad s = 1.926$	

35	1,2,4,6,7,8,10,12,13,14,15,17,19,22,23,24,26,27, 28,30,31,32,33,34,36,37,38,39,40,41,43,44,45,47,49	24.495
35	1,2,3,6,7,8,9,10,11,14,15,16,17,18,19,20,21,22, 27,29,30,32,35,36,37,39,40,41,42,43,45,47,48,49,50	23.595
35	2,3,4,7,9,10,12,13,14,15,17,19,20,22,24,26,28,29, 30,34,35,36,37,39,40,41,42,43,44,45,46,47,48,49,50	25.431
35	2,3,4,5,8,10,12,14,15,16,18,19,20,21,22,24,25,27, 28,29,30,31,33,34,35,36,37,38,40,41,43,46,47,48,50	25.831
35	1,3,6,7,8,9,10,11,12,15,16,17,18,19,22,23,24,25, 26,28,29,30,31,32,34,36,37,38,40,44,45,46,47,48,50	24.477
35	1,2,3,4,6,7,8,9,10,11,12,13,14,16,18,19,22,23, 24,25,27,28,29,32,35,36,37,38,39,40,43,44,45,47,50	23.613
35	2,6,7,8,9,10,11,12,13,14,16,17,18,19,20,21,26,27, 28,29,30,31,32,35,37,38,40,41,42,43,44,45,47,49,50	24.106
35	5,6,7,8,10,12,13,14,16,18,19,21,22,24,25,26,28,29, 30,31,32,33,35,37,38,40,41,43,44,45,46,47,48,49,50	25.134
35	1,2,3,4,6,8,9,10,11,14,15,18,19,20,21,23,24,26, 27,29,30,31,32,33,35,36,37,38,39,40,42,43,47,48,49	24.459
35	2,3,4,5,6,7,8,9,12,13,15,16,17,18,19,21,22,23, 24,26,28,29,32,34,36,37,38,41,42,43,44,45,46,47,50	24.116
35	1,3,4,6,7,9,10,11,12,14,15,16,18,19,21,22,23,24, 25,26,28,29,31,32,33,34,35,36,38,39,40,43,44,48,49	24.095
35	1,2,3,4,5,6,7,10,11,12,13,14,16,17,18,19,20,21, 22,26,27,28,29,31,32,33,34,36,39,40,41,42,43,44,46	24.766
	size-35 sample means: $\bar{x} = 24.510$ $s = 0.687$	
45	1,2,3,4,5,6,7,8,9,10,11,12,13,14,15,16,17,18,19,20,21,22,23, 24,25,26,27,28,29,30,31,32,33,35,36,39,40,41,42,43,45,46,47,48,50	24.907
45	1,2,3,4,6,7,8,9,10,11,12,14,15,17,18,19,20,21,22,23,24,26,27, 28,29,30,31,32,34,35,36,37,38,39,40,41,42,43,44,45,46,47,48,49,50	24.318
45	1,2,3,4,5,7,9,10,11,12,13,14,15,16,17,18,20,22,23,25,26,27,28, 29,30,31,32,33,34,35,36,37,38,39,40,41,42,43,44,45,46,47,48,49,50	25.841
45	1,2,3,4,5,6,7,9,10,11,12,13,14,15,16,17,18,19,20,21,22,23,24, 25,26,28,30,31,32,33,34,35,36,37,38,39,41,42,43,44,45,47,48,49,50	25.294
45	1,2,3,4,5,6,7,9,10,11,12,13,14,15,16,17,18,19,21,22,23,24,25, 26,27,29,30,31,32,33,34,35,36,37,38,39,40,41,42,44,46,47,48,49,50	24.224
45	1,2,3,4,5,6,7,8,9,10,11,12,13,14,15,16,17,18,19,20,21,22,23, 24,26,27,30,31,32,33,35,36,37,38,39,40,42,43,44,45,46,47,48,49,50	24.296
45	1,2,3,4,5,6,7,8,9,10,12,13,14,15,16,17,18,20,21,22,23,24,25, 26,27,28,29,30,32,34,35,36,37,39,40,41,42,43,44,45,46,47,48,49,50	25.127
45	1,2,3,4,5,6,7,8,10,11,12,14,15,16,17,18,19,20,21,22,23,24,25, 27,28,29,30,32,33,34,35,37,38,39,40,41,42,43,44,45,46,47,48,49,50	24.891
45	1,2,3,6,7,8,9,10,12,13,14,15,16,17,18,19,20,21,22,23,24,25,27, 28,29,30,31,32,33,34,35,36,37,38,39,40,41,43,44,45,46,47,48,49,50	24.535
45	1,2,3,4,5,6,7,8,9,11,12,14,15,16,17,18,19,20,21,22,23,24,25, 27,28,29,30,31,33,34,35,36,38,39,40,41,42,43,44,45,46,47,48,49,50	24.749
45	1,2,3,4,5,6,7,8,9,11,12,13,14,15,16,17,18,19,20,21,22,23,24, 25,26,27,28,29,30,31,32,34,36,37,38,39,40,42,43,44,45,46,47,48,49	25.494
45	1,2,3,5,6,7,8,9,10,11,12,13,14,15,16,17,18,19,20,21,22,23,24, 25,27,28,29,30,33,34,35,36,37,38,39,40,41,42,43,44,45,47,48,49,50	25.135
	size-45 sample means: $\bar{x} = 24.901$ $s = 0.506$	

The sample means get closer to the actual population mean as the sample size increases toward $n = 50$.

CHAPTER 6

6-1. A confidence interval is an interval of values believed to contain an unknown population parameter. It has a given level of our belief, or confidence, that the interval contains the unknown parameter.

6-2. Once the sampling has taken place, $\bar{X}$ is realized and, though unknown, it is either in the given interval, or not in the interval. Nothing is random at this point and hence we cannot talk about probabilities.

6-3. If the pre-sampling probability that the parameter will be captured in an interval is $1 - \alpha$, then $(1 - \alpha)100\%$ of the intervals that would be constructed this way would contain the unknown parameter. Hence the confidence level $(1 - \alpha)100\%$ that we attach to a given, single interval we obtain.

6-4. An expensive way of solving the problem: Buy more information. As n increases, the width of interval decreases.

Or, a cheap way to solve the problem: Lower your requried confidence level from 95% to 90% or lower. As the confidence level decreases, the interval width decreases with it.

6-5. 95% C.I.:
$$\bar{x} \pm 1.96(\sigma/\sqrt{n}) = 89{,}673.12 \pm 1.96(5{,}500/\sqrt{16})$$
$$= 89{,}673.12 \pm 2{,}695 = [86{,}978.12, \ 92{,}368.12] \text{ dollars}.$$

6-6. 99% C.I.:
$$89{,}673.12 \pm 2.576(5{,}500/\sqrt{16}) = [86{,}131.12, \ 93{,}215.12]$$
As expected, this interval is wider than the 95% C.I. based on the same results.

6-7. $\sigma = 4.6 \qquad n = 100 \qquad \bar{x} = 32$
95% C.I. for μ:
$$32 \pm 1.96(4.6/\sqrt{100}) = 32 \pm .9016 = [31.098, \ 32.902] \text{ m.p.g.}$$

6-8. We need not assume a normal population. $n = 100 > 30$, so the Central Limit Theorem applies.

6-9. $\sigma = 1.2 \qquad n = 60 \qquad \bar{x} = 9.3$

90% C.I.:

$9.3 \pm (1.645)\dfrac{1.2}{\sqrt{60}} = [9.045,\ 9.555]$ percent alcohol.

6-10. $\sigma = 32 \qquad n = 15 \qquad \bar{x} = 267$

99% C.I. (We will use $z = 2.576$):

$267 \pm 2.576\dfrac{32}{\sqrt{15}} = [245.72,\ 288.28]$ documents per day.

6-11. The findings in Problem **6-10** justify installing the machine because the manager may be 99% confident that the average number of documents that will be transmitted daily is anywhere between 245.72 and 288.28, hence over 245.

6-12. $\sigma = 2 \qquad n = 100 \qquad \bar{x} = 22$

95% C.I. for μ:

$\bar{x} \pm z_{\alpha/2}(\sigma/\sqrt{n}) = 22 \pm 1.96(2/\sqrt{100}) = 22 \pm .392 = [21.608,\ 22.392]$ minutes.

6-13. $n = 50 \qquad \bar{x} = 146.75 \qquad \sigma = 35.2$

95% C.I.: $146.75 \pm 1.96(35.2/\sqrt{50}) = [136.99,\ 156.51]$

90% C.I.: $146.75 \pm 1.645(35.2/\sqrt{50}) = [138.56,\ 154.94]$

99% C.I.: $146.75 \pm 2.576(35.2/\sqrt{50}) = [133.93,\ 159.57]$

6-14. $n = 2{,}000 \qquad \sigma = 1{,}800 \qquad \bar{x} = 8{,}562$

$\bar{x} \pm 1.96\dfrac{\sigma}{\sqrt{n}} = 8{,}562 \pm 1.96\dfrac{1{,}800}{\sqrt{2{,}000}} = [8{,}483.11,\ 8{,}640.89]$

6-15. $n = 50 \qquad \bar{x} = 20.74 \qquad \sigma = 5.0$

95% C.I.: $20.74 \pm 1.96\dfrac{5.0}{\sqrt{50}} = [19.35,\ 22.13]$

6-16. Interval width $= 2z_{\alpha/2}(\sigma/\sqrt{n})$

Consider $m = 4n$. The width of the interval is now:

$2z_{\alpha/2}(\sigma/\sqrt{4n}) = 2z_{\alpha/2}(\sigma/2\sqrt{n}) = 1/2$ of the old width.

Thus the answer is: 4 times the sample size.

6-17.
$$2(1.96\sigma/\sqrt{n}) = 10$$
$$1.96(\sigma/\sqrt{n}) = 5$$
$$\sigma/\sqrt{n} = 5/1.96 = 2.551$$

For 90% confidence, $z_{\alpha/2} = 1.645$

Width of 90% C.I. $= 2(1.645(2.551)) = 8.393$ units.

Easier way: new width $=$ (old width)$1.645/1.96 = 10(1.645)/1.96 = 8.393$

6-18. $\quad n = 50 \qquad \bar{x} = 14.5 \qquad s = 5.6$

95% C.I.: $14.5 \pm 1.96(5.6/\sqrt{50}) = [12.95, 16.05]$

90% C.I.: $14.5 \pm 1.645(5.6/\sqrt{50}) = [13.20, 15.80]$

6-19. $\quad n = 165 \qquad \bar{x} = 16{,}530 \qquad s = 5{,}542$

95% C.I.: $16{,}530 \pm 1.96(5{,}542/\sqrt{165}) = [15{,}684.37, 17{,}375.63]$

99% C.I.: $16{,}530 \pm 2.576(5{,}542/\sqrt{165}) = [15{,}418.6, 17{,}641.4]$

6-20. $\quad n = 12 \qquad \bar{x} = 34.2 \qquad s = 5.9$

95% C.I.: $\bar{x} \pm t_{.025(11)}(s/\sqrt{n}) = 34.2 \pm 2.201(5.9/\sqrt{12}) = [30.45, 37.95]$

Assume a normal population.

6-21. From the data we compute: $n = 32 \qquad \bar{x} = 30.5625 \qquad s = 5.775$

99% C.I.: $\bar{x} \pm z_{.005}(s/\sqrt{n}) = 30.5625 \pm 2.576(5.775/\sqrt{32})$

$= [27.93, 33.19]$ thousands of miles.

6-22. $\quad \bar{x} = 193 \qquad n = 500 \qquad s = 78$

95% C.I.: $\bar{x} \pm z_{.025}(s/\sqrt{n}) = 193 \pm 1.96(78/\sqrt{500}) = [186.163, 199.837]$

6-23. From the data compute: $n = 25 \qquad \bar{x} = 81.240 \qquad s = 15.447$

For df $= 24$ and $\alpha = 0.01$, we use $t_{\alpha/2} = 2.797$, so

$\bar{x} \pm t_{\alpha/2}(s/\sqrt{n}) = 81.240 \pm 2.797(15.447/5) = [72.599, 89.881]$

6-24. $\quad n = 40 \qquad \bar{x} = 42{,}539 \qquad s = 11{,}690$

90% C.I.: $42{,}539 \pm 1.645(11{,}690/\sqrt{40}) = [39{,}498.46, 45{,}579.54]$ dollars.

6-25. We must assume a normal population.

$n = 10 \qquad \bar{x} = 44.6 \qquad s = 20.59$

95% C.I.: $44.6 \pm t_{.025(9)}(s/\sqrt{n}) = 44.6 \pm 2.262(20.59/\sqrt{10}) = [29.87, 59.33]$ dollars.

6-26. $n = 400 \qquad \bar{x} = 212 \qquad s = 38$

95% C.I.: $212 \pm 1.96(38/\sqrt{400}) = [208.28, 215.72]$ calories.

98% C.I.: $212 \pm 2.326(38/\sqrt{400}) = [207.58, 216.42]$ calories.

6-27. We need to assume normality of the population.

99% C.I.: $2.6 \pm t_{.005(19)}(0.4/\sqrt{20}) = 2.6 \pm 2.861(.4/\sqrt{20}) = [2.344, 2.856]$ days.

6-28. $n = 56 \qquad \bar{x} = 258 \qquad s = 85$

95% C.I.: $258 \pm 1.96(85/\sqrt{56}) = [235.74, 280.26]$ dollars.

6-29. Assume a normal population.

$n = 13 \qquad \bar{x} = 101.23 \qquad s = 15.13$

90% C.I.: $\bar{x} \pm t_{.05(12)}(s/\sqrt{n}) = 101.23 \pm 1.782(15.13/\sqrt{13}) = [93.75, 108.71]$ sales.

6-30. $n = 225 \qquad \bar{x} = 259.6 \qquad s = 52$

95% C.I.: $259.6 \pm 1.96(52/\sqrt{225}) = [252.81, 266.39]$ dollars.

6-31. $n = 46 \qquad \bar{x} = 16.5 \qquad s = 2.2$

95% C.I.: $16.5 \pm 1.96(2.2/\sqrt{46}) = [15.86, 17.14]$ dollars.

6-32. Assume a normal population. $\qquad n = 20 \qquad \bar{x} = 5{,}139 \qquad s = 640$

95% C.I.: $\bar{x} \pm t_{.025(19)}(s/\sqrt{n}) = 5{,}139 \pm 2.093(640/\sqrt{20})$

$= [4{,}839.47, 5{,}438.52]$ dollars.

6-33. Assume a normal population.

$n = 28 \qquad \bar{x} = 6.7 \qquad s = 2.4$

99% C.I.: $\bar{x} \pm t_{.005(27)}(s/\sqrt{n}) = 6.7 \pm 2.771(2.4/\sqrt{28}) = [5.44, 7.96]$ years.

6-34. $n = 75 \qquad \bar{x} = 8.9 \qquad s = 0.5$

95% C.I.: $8.9 \pm 1.96(0.5/\sqrt{75}) = [8.79, 9.01]$ units.

6-35. Assume a normal population.

$n = 12 \qquad \bar{x} = 61.67 \qquad s = 11.22$

90% C.I.: $\bar{x} \pm t_{.05(11)}(s/\sqrt{n}) = 61.67 \pm 1.796(11.22/\sqrt{12}) = [55.85, 67.48]$ containers

6-36. $n = 100 \qquad \bar{x} = 82 \qquad s = 28$

    a. With this high an n, the t distribution is essentially normal, so for a 90% C.I. we use $t = z = 1.645$:

$$82 \pm 1.645 \frac{28}{\sqrt{100}} = [77.39,\ 86.61]$$

    b. No, 60 is not in our interval; we can be 90% confident that the national dealer average of stocks of US cars is more than 60 days' worth.

6-37. $n = 15 \qquad \bar{x} = 9.867 \qquad s = 1.685$

$\bar{x} \pm t_{.05(14)}(s/\sqrt{n}) = 9.867 \pm 1.761(1.685/\sqrt{15}) = [9.101,\ 10.633]$

We can't say for sure that the population mean μ is in this interval, merely that over repeated samplings of 15 lens locations, the calculated confidence intervals will include μ about 90% of the time.

6-38. Calculate from data: $n = 20 \qquad df = 19 \qquad \bar{x} = 11{,}123.75 \qquad s = 8761.166$

$\bar{x} \pm t_{.025(19)}(s/\sqrt{n}) = 11{,}123.75 \pm 2.093\dfrac{8761.166}{\sqrt{20}} = [7{,}023.45,\ 15{,}224.05]$

6-39. $n = 120 \qquad x = 28$

95% C.I.: $\hat{p} \pm 1.96\sqrt{\hat{p}\hat{q}/n} = \dfrac{28}{120} \pm 1.96\sqrt{\left(\dfrac{28}{120}\right)\left(\dfrac{92}{120}\right)\bigg/120}$

$= [0.1577,\ 0.3090]$

6-40. $n = 68 \qquad x = 42$

99% C.I.: $\hat{p} \pm 2.576\sqrt{\hat{p}\hat{q}/n} = \dfrac{42}{68} \pm 2.576\sqrt{\left(\dfrac{42}{68}\right)\left(\dfrac{26}{68}\right)\bigg/68}$

$= [0.4658,\ 0.7695]$

6-41. $n = 460 \qquad \hat{p} = 0.75$

95% C.I.: $.75 \pm 1.96\sqrt{(.75)(.25)/460} = [0.7104,\ 0.7896]$

6-42. $n = 80 \qquad x = 58$

90% C.I.: $\dfrac{58}{80} \pm 1.645\sqrt{\left(\dfrac{58}{80}\right)\left(\dfrac{22}{80}\right)\bigg/80} = .725 \pm 1.645\sqrt{(.725)(.275)/80}$

$= [0.6429,\ 0.8071]$

6-43. $n = 590 \qquad x = 88$

95% C.I.: $\dfrac{88}{590} \pm 1.96\sqrt{\left(\dfrac{88}{590}\right)\left(\dfrac{502}{590}\right)\big/590} = [0.1204,\ 0.1779]$

6-44. $n = 280 \qquad \hat{p} = 1/7$

90% C.I.: $\dfrac{1}{7} \pm 1.645\sqrt{\left(\dfrac{1}{7}\right)\left(\dfrac{6}{7}\right)\big/280} = [0.1085,\ 0.1773]$

6-45. $n = 2012 \qquad \hat{p} = 81/2012 = .0403 \qquad \hat{q} = .9597$

95% C.I.: $0.0403 \pm 1.96\sqrt{(0.0403)(.9597)/2012} = [0.0317,\ 0.0488]$

The reported audit rate of 0.0221 is not in this interval; the confidence interval is not based on sound statistics because this is not a random sample from among all audits nationwide. This accountant has a higher overall audit rate; perhaps she tends to make too many of the types of deductions that set off warning flags to the IRS auditors.

6-46. $n = 338 \qquad \hat{p} = .79 \qquad \hat{q} = .21 \qquad$ Use a normal approximation.

For a 99% C.I.: $.79 \pm 2.576\sqrt{(.79)(.21)/338} = [0.7329,\ 0.8471]$

6-47. $n = 52 \qquad x = 8$

98% C.I.: $\dfrac{8}{52} \pm 2.326\sqrt{\left(\dfrac{8}{52}\right)\left(\dfrac{44}{52}\right)\big/52} = [0.0375,\ 0.2702]$

6-48. $n = 250 \qquad x = 121$

99% C.I.: $0.484 \pm 2.576\sqrt{(.484)(.516)/250} = [0.4026,\ 0.5654]$

6-49. $n = 347 \qquad x = 201$

90% C.I.: $\dfrac{201}{347} \pm 1.645\sqrt{\left(\dfrac{201}{347}\right)\left(\dfrac{146}{347}\right)\big/347} = [0.5357,\ 0.6228]$

6-50. $n = 1000 \qquad \hat{p} = .81 \qquad \hat{q} = .19 \qquad$ Use a normal approximation.

For a 90% C.I.: $.81 \pm 1.645\sqrt{(.81)(.19)/1000} = [0.7896,\ 0.8304]$

6-51. $n = 5000 \qquad \hat{p} = .09 \qquad \hat{q} = 0.91 \qquad$ Use a normal approximation.

For a 95% C.I.: $.09 \pm 1.96\sqrt{(.09)(.91)/5000} = [0.0821,\ 0.0979]$

6-52. $N = 1{,}253 \qquad n = 200 \qquad \bar{x} = 648.32 \qquad s = 210$

99% C.I.: $648.32 \pm 2.576(210/\sqrt{200})\sqrt{1{,}053/1{,}252} = [613.24,\ 683.40]$

5-53. 90% C.I.: $648.32 \pm 1.645(210/\sqrt{200})\sqrt{1{,}053/1{,}252} = [625.92, 670.72]$

5-54. $\bar{x} = 50 \qquad s = 5 \qquad n = 50 \qquad N = 300$
95% C.I.: $50 \pm 1.96(5/\sqrt{50})\sqrt{250/299} = [48.73, 51.27]$ calories.

5-55. $n = 160 \qquad N = 1{,}242 \qquad x = 85 \qquad \hat{p} = 85/160$

95% C.I.: $\hat{p} \pm 1.96\sqrt{\dfrac{\hat{p}\hat{q}}{n}\left(\dfrac{N-n}{N-1}\right)} = \dfrac{85}{160} \pm 1.96\sqrt{\dfrac{(85/160)(75/160)}{160}\left(\dfrac{1{,}082}{1{,}241}\right)}$
$= [0.4590, 0.60345]$

5-56. $n = 100 \qquad N = 538 \qquad \bar{x} = 1{,}220 \qquad s = 550$
90% C.I.: $\bar{x} \pm 1.645(550/\sqrt{100})\sqrt{438/537} = [1{,}138.29, 1{,}301.71]$ candy bars.

5-57. $n = 100 \qquad N = 1{,}520 \qquad x = 12 \qquad \hat{p} = .12$
95% C.I.: $.12 \pm 1.96\sqrt{(.12)(.88)/100}\sqrt{1{,}420/1{,}519} = [0.0584, 0.1816]$

5-58. $n = 65 \qquad N = 500 \qquad x = 2 \qquad s = 0.5$
99% C.I. for μ: $2 \pm 2.576(.5/\sqrt{65})\sqrt{435/499} = [1.85, 2.15]$

5-59. $n = 20 \qquad N = 100 \qquad \bar{x} = 3.1 \qquad s = 1.8$
90% C.I.: $\bar{x} \pm 1.645(1.8/\sqrt{20})\sqrt{80/99} = [2.505, 3.695]$

5-60. $N = 1{,}000 \qquad n = 150 \qquad \hat{p} = 28/150 \qquad$ So the 99% C.I. for $\hat{p}$:

$\dfrac{28}{150} \pm 2.576\sqrt{\dfrac{(28/150)(122/150)}{150}\left(\dfrac{850}{999}\right)} = [0.111, 0.262]$

5-61. $n = 22 \qquad s^2 = 8 \qquad$ 95% C.I. for σ^2:
$\left[\dfrac{(n-1)s^2}{\chi^2}, \dfrac{(n-1)s^2}{\chi^2}\right] = [21(8)/35.48, 21(8)/10.28] = [4.74, 16.34]$

6-62. $n = 41 \qquad s^2 = 102$
99% C.I. for σ^2: $[40(102)/66.766, 40(102)/20.707] = [61.11, 197.04]$

6-63. $n = 60 \qquad s^2 = 1{,}228$
We'll use df $= 59$, approximately 60, and look in the table.
95% C.I. for σ^2: $[59(1{,}228)/83.3, 59(1{,}228)/40.5] = [869.8, 1{,}789.7]$

6-64. From Problem **6-21**: $\quad n = 32 \qquad s = 5.775$

$s^2 = (5.775)^2 = 33.35$

99% C.I. for σ^2 (using approximate df $= 30$):

$[33.35(31)/53.7,\; 33.35(31)/13.8] = [19.25,\; 74.92]$

6-65. From Problem **6-25**: $\quad n = 10 \qquad s = 20.59$

95% C.I. for σ^2 : $\quad \left[\dfrac{9(20.59)^2}{19.0228},\; \dfrac{9(20.59)^2}{2.7004} \right] = [200.58,\; 1{,}412.95]$

6-66. From Problem **6-26**: $\quad n = 400 \qquad s = 30$

Using a normal approximation to the χ^2 distribution we have: $\quad X \sim N(\text{df}, 2\text{df})$

For a 95% C.I. the critical values are:

$x_{1,2} = \mu \pm 1.96\sqrt{2(399)} = 399 \pm 1.96\sqrt{2(399)} = 343.63,\; 454.37$

95% C.I. for σ^2 : $\quad \left[\dfrac{399(38)^2}{454.37},\; \dfrac{399(38)^2}{343.63} \right] = [1{,}268.03,\; 1{,}676.68]$

6-67. From Problem **6-27**: $\quad n = 20 \qquad s = 0.4$

95% C.I. for σ^2 : $\quad \left[\dfrac{(19)(.4)^2}{32.8523},\; \dfrac{(19)(.4)^2}{8.90655} \right] = [0.0925,\; 0.3413]$

6-68. min. $n = \dfrac{z_{\alpha/2}^2 pq}{B^2} = (1.96)^2(.08)(.92)/(.05)^2 = 113.0967$

Sample at least 114 firms.

6-69. $B = 0.05 \quad$ 90% confidence. Use a guess of $p = 0.5$

$n = (1.645)^2(.5)(.5)/(.05)^2 = 270.6$

Sample at least 271 items.

6-70. $B = 5 \qquad$ 95% confidence $\qquad \sigma^2 = 100$

$n = (1.96)^2 100/2^2 = 96.04 \qquad$ Sample at least 97 runs.

6-71. $B = 2{,}000 \qquad$ 95% confidence $\qquad \sigma^2 = 40{,}000{,}000$

$n = (1.96)^2 40{,}000{,}000/(2{,}000)^2 = 38.416$

Sample at least 39 executives.

6-72. $B = 0.5 \qquad$ 95% confidence $\qquad \sigma = 2$

$n = (1.96)^2(2)^2/(.5)^2 = 61.466$

Sample at least 62 returns.

-73. An estimate of p is 0.14 $B = .05$ 90% confidence.

$n = (1.645)^2(.14)(.86)/(.05)^2 = 130.322$

Sample at least 131 people.

-74. $B = 10$ 90% confidence $\sigma = 50$

$n = (1.645)^2(50)^2/(10)^2 = 67.65$

Therefore, sample at least 68 days.

-75. $B = 0.02$ 95% confidence. Guessed $p = 0.10$

$n = (1.96)^2(.10)(.90)/(.02)^2 = 864.36$

Sample at least 865 accounts.

-76. $\bar{x} = 250$ $s = 28$ $n = 100$

90% left-hand C.I. for μ:

$[\bar{x} - z_\alpha(s/\sqrt{n}), \infty] = [250 - 1.28(28/10), \infty] = [246.42, \infty]$

-77. $n = 100$ $x = 15$ 95% upper bound for p:

$\hat{p} + z_\alpha\sqrt{\hat{p}\hat{q}/n} = .15 + 1.645\sqrt{(.15)(.85)/100} = 0.2087$

95% right-hand C.I. is $[0, 0.2087]$

-78. $n = 100$ $\bar{x} = 42$ $s = 10$ 99% lower bound for μ:

$42,000 - 2.326(10,000/\sqrt{100}) = 39,674$ miles.

$[39,674, \infty]$

-79. $n = 200$ $x = 32$ 99% lower bound for p:

$\hat{p} - 2.326\sqrt{\hat{p}\hat{q}/n} = .16 - 2.326\sqrt{(.16)(.84)/200} = 0.0997$

-80. 95% upper bound for μ. From Problem **6-18**:

$n = 50$ $\bar{x} = 14.5$ $s = 5.6$

$\bar{x} + 1.645(5.6/\sqrt{50}) = 14.5 + 1.3 = 15.80$

-81. 90% lower bound for the average amount of a claim. From Problem **6-19**:

$\bar{x} = 16,530$ $s = 5,542$ $n = 165$

$\bar{x} - 1.282(s/\sqrt{n}) = 16,530 - 1.282(5,542/\sqrt{165}) = \$15,976.9$

-82. 99% lower bound for μ. From Problem **6-30**:

$\bar{x} = 259.60$ $s = 52$ $n = 225$

$259.6 - 2.326(52/\sqrt{225}) = \$251.54$

6-83. 90% upper bound. From Problem **6-39**:

$$n = 120 \qquad x = 28$$

$$\text{Upper bound} = \frac{28}{120} + 1.28\sqrt{\left(\frac{28}{120}\right)\left(\frac{92}{120}\right)\Big/120} = 0.2828$$

6-84. Calculate from the data: $n = 16 \qquad \bar{x} = 43.625 \qquad s = 22.662$ with df $= 15$.
90% C.I.: $\bar{x} \pm t_{.05(15)}(s/\sqrt{n}) = [33.69, 53.56]$

6-85. 95% C.I. for μ:

$$n = 15 \qquad \bar{x} = 11.32 \qquad s = 4.4$$

$$11.32 \pm t_{.025(14)}(4.4/\sqrt{15}) = 11.32 \pm 2.145(1.136) = [8.883, 13.757] \text{ million dollars.}$$

6-86. $N = 1,455 \qquad n = 300 \qquad \bar{x} = 739.98 \qquad s = 312.70 \qquad$ 90% C.I. for μ:

$$739.98 \pm 1.645(312.7/\sqrt{300})\sqrt{1,155/1,454} = [713.51, 766.45] \text{ dollars.}$$

6-87. $B = 0.1 \qquad$ 95% confidence. A guess of p is 0.45:

$$n = (1.96)^2(.45)(.55)/(.1)^2 = 95.08$$

Therefore sample at least 96 people.

6-88. $n = 1,000 \qquad x = 338 \qquad$ 95% C.I. for p:

$$\hat{p} \pm 1.96\sqrt{\hat{p}\hat{q}/n} = .338 \pm 1.96\sqrt{(.338)(.662)/1,000} = [0.3087, 0.3673]$$

6-89. $n = 100 \qquad s^2 = 870,432.76$
99% C.I. for σ^2 (we'll use df $= 100$):

$$\left[\frac{(99)870,432.76}{140.1}, \frac{(99)870,432.76}{67.3}\right] = [615,081.0, \ 1,280,428.6]$$

With a linear interpolation, the interval is: $[619,948.5, \ 1,305,649.1]$

6-90. $\bar{x} = 13.2667 \qquad n = 15 \qquad s = 3.2396 \qquad$ 95% C.I. is:

$$13.2667 \pm 2.145(3.2396/\sqrt{15}) = [11.47, 15.06]$$

6-91. $n = 200 \qquad x = 54 \qquad$ 99% C.I. for p:

$$.27 \pm 2.576\sqrt{(.27)(.73)/200} = [0.1891, 0.3509]$$

6-92. $\sigma = 4.5 \qquad B = 1 \qquad$ 95% confidence:

$$n = (1.96)^2(4.5)^2/(1)^2 = 77.79$$

Therefore, sample at least 78 batteries.

6-93. From Problem **6-90**: $\qquad s^2 = (3.2396)^2 = 10.495 \qquad n = 15$

95% C.I. for σ^2:

$$\left[\frac{14(10.495)}{26.119}, \frac{14(10.495)}{5.629}\right] = [5.625, 26.102]$$

6-94. From Problem **6-91**: $\qquad x = 54 \qquad n = 200$

95% lower bound on the proportion of people who like the taste:

$$\hat{p} - 1.645\sqrt{\hat{p}\hat{q}/n} = .27 - 1.645\sqrt{(.27)(.73)/200} = 0.2184$$

6-95. $\quad n = 67 \qquad \bar{x} = 2.5 \qquad s = 1.1 \qquad$ 90% C.I. for μ:

$2.5 \pm 1.645(1.1/\sqrt{67}) = [2.279, 2.721]$ days.

6-96. From Problem **6-95**: $\qquad s^2 = (1.1)^2 = 1.21 \qquad n = 67$

90% C.I. for σ^2: df $= 66$, interpolate between 60 and 70.

$$\left[\frac{(66)(1.21)}{86}, \frac{(66)(1.21)}{48}\right] = [0.9286, 1.6638]$$

6-97. $\quad n = 2{,}000 \qquad x = 5 \qquad \hat{p} = 5/2{,}000 = .0025 \qquad$ 99% C.I. for p:

$.0025 \pm 2.576\sqrt{(.0025)(.9975)/2{,}000} = [-0.000376, 0.00538]$

Interpretation: clearly p cannot be negative, so the C.I. is $[0, 0.00538]$.

6-98. In Problem **6-97**, suppose $N = 4{,}520$. The C.I. is:

$$\hat{p} \pm 2.576\sqrt{\frac{\hat{p}\hat{q}}{n}\left(\frac{N-n}{N-1}\right)} = .0025 \pm 2.576\sqrt{\frac{(.0025)(.9975)}{2{,}000}\left(\frac{2{,}520}{4{,}519}\right)}$$

$$= [0.000352, 0.004648]$$

6-99. $\quad n = 128 \qquad \bar{x} = 356{,}080 \qquad s = 79{,}100 \qquad$ 98% C.I. for μ:

$356{,}080 \pm 2.326(79{,}100/\sqrt{128}) = [339{,}817.73, 372{,}342.27]$

6-100. $\quad n = 20 \qquad \bar{x} = 3.44 \qquad s = 2.6773 \qquad$ 95% C.I. for μ:

$3.44 \pm 2.093(2.6773/\sqrt{20}) = [2.187, 4.693]$ pounds.

6-101. In Problem **6-100**: $\qquad s^2 = (2.6773)^2 = 7.1678 \qquad n = 20$

95% C.I. for σ^2:

$$\left[\frac{(n-1)s^2}{\chi^2_{.025}}, \frac{(n-1)s^2}{\chi^2_{.975}}\right] = \left[\frac{19(7.1678)}{32.8523}, \frac{19(7.1678)}{8.90655}\right] = [4.145, 15.291]$$

6-102. In Problem **6-99**, suppose the 128 condos were selected from a population of $N = 500$ condos. Correct by using the f.p.c.f.

$$98\% \text{ C.I.}: \quad 356{,}080 \pm 2.326 \frac{79{,}100}{\sqrt{128}} \sqrt{\frac{500 - 128}{499}} = [342{,}038.86,\ 370{,}121.14]$$

6-103. Whenever we use the t or the χ^2 distributions, we need to assume a normal population distribution.

6-104. $n = 100 \qquad \bar{x} = 24{,}500 \qquad s = 2{,}500$ \qquad Using the normal approximation:

$$\bar{x} \pm z_{.005}(s/\sqrt{n}) = 24{,}500 \pm 2.576(2{,}500/10) = [23{,}856,\ 25{,}144] \text{ dollars.}$$

6-105. Using the following random sample:

year	month	FFR
91	9	5.45
82	3	14.68
83	3	8.77
93	8	3.03
91	5	5.78
86	2	7.86
91	2	6.25
88	6	7.51
87	4	6.37
94	11	5.29
88	2	6.58
88	12	8.76

calculate: $\quad n = 12 \qquad \bar{x} = 7.194 \qquad s = 2.852$

95% C.I. for μ:

$$\bar{x} \pm t_{.025(11)}(s/\sqrt{n}) = 7.194 \pm 2.201(2.852/\sqrt{12}) = [5.382,\ 9.006]$$

6-106. This is a 90% confidence interval for the population mean based on a sample of size 48, where the population standard deviation is unknown. The t distribution is therefore being used for S.E. $= s/\sqrt{n}$. But since df $= 47$, we have $t_{.05} \doteq 1.68$ which is quite close to $z_{.05} = 1.645$. The C.I. that would result from the normal distribution would be slightly narrower.

6-107. The confidence level of an interval being used to estimate a population parameter is the probability, over all possible samples of the fixed given size, that the true value of the parameter lies inside the calculated interval. Thus we need to know the probability that the true median falls between the lower and the higher of two values drawn at random from the population. This was done in Problem **2-96**: the probability is $1/2$ (so the confidence level, as a percentage, is 50%).

6-108. Same answer as for Problem **6-107**, except that the needed probability from an earlier problem is the one in Problem **2-97**: $1-(1/2)^{n-1}$. However, that probability was calculated based on the assumption that the population size is much larger than the sample size, so that the sampling could be considered as being with replacement. This limits the range of n for which this answer represents the true confidence level.

Case 6.

This is just a confidence interval using the t-distribution for the mean of a population based on a random sample. Calculating from the Equities row of the table:

$$n = 10 \qquad \bar{x} = 49.900 \qquad s = 12.627$$

Using df $= n - 1 = 9$ at the 95% confidence level, we find $t_{.025(9)} = 2.262$ from the table. So the required interval is

$$\bar{x} \pm t_{\alpha/2}\left(s/\sqrt{n}\right) = 49.900 \pm 2.262\left(12.627/\sqrt{10}\right) = [40.868, 58.932]$$

CHAPTER 7

7-1. $H_0: \mu = 31.5$ $\quad$ $H_1: \mu \neq 31.5$

$n = 100$ $\quad$ $\bar{x} = 29.8$ $\quad$ $s = 6.6$

$$z = \frac{\bar{x} - \mu_0}{s/\sqrt{n}} = \frac{29.8 - 31.5}{6.6/10} = -2.575$$

Reject H_0 at $\alpha = 0.05$ (and almost at $\alpha = .01$). The p-value is approximately 0.01

7-2. $H_0: \mu = 247$ $\quad$ $H_1: \mu \neq 247$

$n = 60$ $\quad$ $\bar{x} = 250$ $\quad$ $s = 12$ $\quad$ $\alpha = 0.05$, then also 0.01

$$z = \frac{\bar{x} - \mu_0}{s/\sqrt{n}} = \frac{250 - 247}{12/\sqrt{60}} = 1.936$$

Do not reject H_0 at $\alpha = .05$ nor at $\alpha = .01$. (p-value $= .0528$). Maybe take larger sample, or reduce your α.

7-3. $H_0: \mu = 5$ $\quad$ $H_1: \mu \neq 5$

$\alpha = .05$ $\quad$ $n = 120$ $\quad$ $\bar{x} = 2.3$ $\quad$ $s = 1.5$

$$z = \frac{2.3 - 5}{1.5/\sqrt{120}} = -19.72$$

Reject H_0 at $\alpha = .05$ and at smaller α levels. Average miles traveled per day is probably smaller than 5. Changes in service may be necessary (the p-value is very small).

7-4. $H_0: \mu = 77$ $\quad$ $H_1: \mu \neq 77$

$n = 350$ $\quad$ $\bar{x} = 84$ $\quad$ $s = 28$

$$z = \frac{84 - 77}{28/\sqrt{350}} = 4.68$$

Reject H_0 at the .01 and even smaller levels of α (the p-value is small). Customer satisfaction has probably improved.

7-5. $H_0: \mu = 11.5$ $\quad$ $H_1: \mu \neq 11.5$

$n = 50$ $\quad$ $\bar{x} = 10.8$ $\quad$ $s = 3.4$ $\quad$ $\alpha = .05$

$$z = \frac{10.8 - 11.5}{3.4/\sqrt{50}} = -1.456$$

Do not reject H_0 at any α (p-value $= 0.1454$).

7-6. H_0: $\mu = 210$ H_1: $\mu \neq 210$

$\bar{x} = 225$ $n = 120$ $s = 82$ $\alpha = 0.05, 0.01$

$$z = \frac{225 - 210}{82/\sqrt{120}} = 2.004$$

Therefore reject H_0 at $\alpha = 0.05$, but not at 0.01.

7-7. H_0: $\mu = 3.75$ H_1: $\mu \neq 3.75$

$\bar{x} = 4.15$ $n = 20$ $s = 2$

$t_{((19)} = \dfrac{4.15 - 3.75}{2/\sqrt{20}} = 0.8944$ Can not reject even at high α values; no evidence that the claimed average break-even time is wrong.

7-8. H_0: $\mu = 14.25$ H_1: $\mu \neq 14.25$

$n = 16$ $\bar{x} = 16.50$ $s = 5.8$ Use $\alpha = .05$

$$t_{(15)} = \frac{16.50 - 14.25}{5.8/\sqrt{16}} = 1.55$$

Right-hand critical point for $t_{(15)}$ and $\alpha = .05$ is 2.131 (and for $\alpha = .10$, $t = 1.753$). Do not reject H_0 (p-value $> .10$).

7-9. H_0: $\mu = 452.8$ H_1: $\mu \neq 452.8$

$n = 12$ $\bar{x} = 501.9$ $s = 65$ Use $\alpha = .05$

$$t_{(11)} = \frac{501.9 - 452.8}{65/\sqrt{12}} = 2.617$$

The right-hand critical point for $t_{(11)}$ at $\alpha = 0.05$ is 2.201, and for $\alpha = 0.02$ it is 2.718. Reject H_0 at $\alpha = .05$. The p-value is between 0.02 and 0.05.

7-10. H_0: $\mu = 0$ H_1: $\mu \neq 0$

$n = 13$ $\bar{x} = 3.1$ $s = 1$

$$t_{(12)} = \frac{3.1 - 0}{1/\sqrt{13}} = 11.177$$

The p-value is very small. Reject H_0. Inclusion in the index likely increases average stock return (at least initially).

7-11. H_0: $\mu = 102.5$ H_1: $\mu \neq 102.5$

$n = 25$ $\bar{x} = 107$ $s = 10$ Try $\alpha = .05$ and $.01$

$$t_{(24)} = \frac{107 - 102.5}{10/\sqrt{25}} = 2.25$$

The critical point at $\alpha = .05$ for $t_{(24)}$ is 2.064; the critical point at $\alpha = .01$ is 2.797. Therefore, the results are significant at $\alpha = .05$, and not significant at $\alpha = .01$. Reject H_0 at $\alpha = .05$, but not at $\alpha = .01$.

7-12. $H_0: \mu = 2.5$ $H_1: \mu \neq 2.5$

$n = 20$ $\bar{x} = 2.3$ $\sigma = 0.8$

Use z because the population is normal and σ is known.

$$z = \frac{2.3 - 2.5}{0.8/\sqrt{20}} = -1.118$$

Do not reject H_0 (p-value $= 0.2636$).

7-13. Assume random sampling from a normal population.

7-14. $H_0: \mu = 15.06$ $H_1: \mu \neq 15.06$

$n = 38$ $\bar{x} = 10.3$ $s = 5.9$

Use $\alpha = .01$; $n > 30$, so use z

$$z = \frac{10.3 - 15.06}{5.9/\sqrt{38}} = -4.9733$$

Reject H_0 (p-value is very small).

7-15. $H_0: \mu = 3.4$ $H_1: \mu \neq 3.4$

Compute: $n = 28$ $\bar{x} = 3.5$ $s = 2.134$ Use $\alpha = 0.05$

$$t = \frac{3.5 - 3.4}{2.134/\sqrt{28}} = 0.248$$

Critical point is 2.052, so do not reject H_0.

7-16. $H_0: p = .16$ $H_1: p \neq .16$

$n = 300$ $x = 51$ $\hat{p} = 51/300 = .17$ use $\alpha = .05$

$$z = \frac{\hat{p} - p_0}{\sqrt{p_0 q_0/n}} = \frac{.17 - .16}{\sqrt{(.16)(.84)/300}} = 0.472$$

Do not reject H_0 at $\alpha = .05$ (p-value $= 0.6370$).

7-17. $H_0: p = 0.42$ $H_1: p \neq 0.42$

$n = 550$ $x = 219$ $\hat{p} = 219/550 = 0.39818$ use $\alpha = .01$

$$z = \frac{.39818 - .42}{\sqrt{(.42)(.58)/550}} = -1.037$$

Do not reject H_0 (p-value $= 0.2998$).

-18. H_0: $p = 0.12$ H_1: $p \neq 0.12$

$n = 100$ $x = 17$ use $\alpha = .05$

$$z = \frac{.17 - .12}{\sqrt{(.12)(.88)/100}} = 1.539$$

Do not reject H_0 (p-value $= 0.1238$).

-19. H_0: $p = 0.35$ H_1: $p \neq 0.35$

$n = 150$ $x = 68$ $\hat{p} = 0.4533$ Use $\alpha = .05$ and $.01$

$$z = \frac{.4533 - .35}{\sqrt{(.35)(.65)/150}} = 2.653$$

Reject H_0 at both $\alpha = .05$ and $\alpha = .01$ (p-value $= 0.008$).

-20. H_0: $p = 0.56$ H_1: $p \neq 0.56$

$n = 500$ $x = 298$ $\hat{p} = 0.596$ Use $\alpha = .01$

$$z = \frac{.596 - .56}{\sqrt{(.56)(.44)/500}} = 1.622$$

Do not reject H_0 (p-value $= 0.1048$).

-21. H_0: $p = 0.31$ H_1: $p \neq 0.31$

$n = 2500$ $\hat{p} = 1201/2500 = .4804$ Use $\alpha = .05$

$$z = \frac{0.4804 - 0.31}{\sqrt{(.31)(.69)/2500}} = 18.422$$

Strongly reject H_0; p-value is very small.

-22. H_0: $p \geq .60$ H_1: $p < .60$

$n = 100$ $x = 45$

$$z = \frac{.45 - .60}{\sqrt{(.60)(.40)/100}} = -3.062$$

Reject H_0 (p-value $= 0.0011$).

-23. H_0: $\mu \geq 250$ H_1: $\mu < 250$

$n = 19$ $\bar{x} = 143$ $s = 52$

$$t_{(18)} = \frac{143 - 250}{52/\sqrt{19}} = -8.97$$

Reject H_0 (the critical point of $t_{(18)}$ for $\alpha = .01$ is -2.552). The ad is probably false (p-value is very small). Hotels on the East Coast are cheaper, on average, than claimed in the ad.

7-24. $H_0: \mu = 0$ $H_1: \mu \neq 0$

$n = 24$ $\bar{x} = 0.12$ $s = 0.2$ use $\alpha = .05$

$t_{(23)} = \dfrac{.12 - 0}{.2/\sqrt{24}} = 2.939 > 2.069$ (the critical value of $t_{(23)}$ for $\alpha = .05$, two-tailed

test). Reject H_0. This industry's stocks probably have positive excess returns in the period in question.

7-25. $H_0: \mu \leq 344$ $H_1: \mu > 344$

$n = 1,200$ $\bar{x} = 361$ $s = 110$

$z = \dfrac{361 - 344}{110/\sqrt{1,200}} = 5.354$

Reject H_0 (p-value is very small).

7-26. $H_0: \mu \leq 1.5M$ $H_1: \mu > 1.5M$

$n = 100$ $\bar{x} = 2.3M$ $s = 0.5M$

$z = \dfrac{2.3 - 1.5}{0.5/\sqrt{100}} = 16.0$

Strongly reject H_0 (p-value is very small).

7-27. $H_0: p \leq 0.17$ $H_1: p > 0.17$

$n = 2,000$ $x = 381$ $\hat{p} = 381/2,000 = 0.1905$ use $\alpha = .01$

$z = \dfrac{.1905 - .17}{\sqrt{(.17)(.83)/2,000}} = 2.44 > 2.326$

Reject H_0 (p-value $= .0073$). The reported figure of 17% is probably not correct.

7-28. $H_0: \mu \geq 125$ $H_1: \mu < 125$

$n = 100$ $\bar{x} = 121$ $s = 2$

$z = \dfrac{121 - 125}{2/\sqrt{100}} = -20$

Reject H_0 (p-value is very small). Replace all tires.

7-29. $H_0: \mu \geq 8$ $H_1: \mu < 8$

$n = 10$ $\bar{x} = 7.8$ $s = 0.4$ use $\alpha = .05$

$t_{(9)} = \dfrac{7.8 - 8}{.4/\sqrt{10}} = -1.581 > -1.833 =$ critical point of $t_{(9)}$ for $\alpha = .05$ in a left-hand

one-tailed test. We can't reject H_0 ($.05 < p$-value $< .10$). Do not reject the radar

manufacturer's claim.

7-30. H_0: $p \geq .45$ H_1: $p < .45$

$n = 125$ $\hat{p} = 49/125 = .392$

$$z = \frac{.392 - .45}{\sqrt{(.45)(.55)/125}} = -1.304$$

Do not reject H_0 (p-value $= 0.0962$). There is no strong evidence here that the program works in reducing the chance of a midlife crisis.

7-31. H_0: $p \geq 0.11$ H_1: $p < 0.11$

$n = 3,500$ $x = 421$ $\hat{p} = 421/3,500 = 0.1203$

$$z = \frac{.1203 - .11}{\sqrt{(.11)(.89)/3,500}} = +1.945$$

Since $\hat{p} = .1203 > .11$, we need not consider the test statistic value above. Do not reject H_0 (p-value $= .9741 > .5$). There is no evidence that the unemployment rate has been reduced.

7-32. H_0: $\mu \leq 2.5$ H_1: $\mu > 2.5$

$n = 100$ $\bar{x} = 5.2$ $s = 2.8$

$$z = \frac{5.2 - 2.5}{2.8/\sqrt{100}} = 9.643$$

Reject H_0 (p-value is very small). There is probable cause for action.

7-33. H_0: $\mu = -1.1$ H_1: $\mu \neq -1.1$

$n = 180$ $\bar{x} = -0.9$ $s = 0.4$

$$z = \frac{(-.9) - (-1.1)}{.4/\sqrt{180}} = 6.708$$

Reject H_0 (p-value is very small). Average world market price change for the week in question is probably greater than -1.1%.

7-34. Income: H_0: $\mu \geq 89$ H_1: $\mu < 89$

$n = 23$ $\bar{x} = 53.61$ $s = 19.33$

$$t = \frac{53.61 - 89.00}{19.33/\sqrt{23}} = -8.78 < t_{(22)}$$ at any α level; reject H_0 (p-value very close to 0).

Dining out: H_0: $\mu \geq 15.3$ H_1: $\mu < 15.3$

$n = 23$ $\bar{x} = 3.609$ $s = 2.061$

$$t = \frac{3.609 - 15.3}{2.061/\sqrt{23}} = -27.2 < t_{(22)}$$ at any α level; reject H_0 (p-value very close to 0).

7-35. Stock's value to industry execs: H_0: $\mu \geq 63.5$ H_1: $\mu < 63.5$

Compute: $n = 16$ $\bar{x} = 45.00$ $s = 11.106$

$$t = \frac{45.00 - 63.5}{11.106/\sqrt{16}} = -6.663$$

For a one-tailed test with df $= 15$, the t-value is very significant: reject H_0 (p-value extremely small).

7-36. H_0: $p = 0.11$ H_1: $p \neq 0.11$

$n = 2{,}000$ $\hat{p} = 341/2{,}000 = .1705$

$$z = \frac{.1705 - .11}{\sqrt{(0.11)(0.89)/2{,}000}} = 8.65$$

Reject H_0 (p-value very close to 0); the article probably understated British Airways' share of the market.

7-37. H_0: $p = .60$ H_1: $p \neq .60$

$n = 250$ $x = 130$ $\hat{p} = 130/250 = .52$ Two-tailed test:

$$z = \frac{\hat{p} - p_0}{\sqrt{p_0 q_0/n}} = \frac{.52 - .6}{\sqrt{(.6)(.4)/250}} = -2.582$$

p-value $= 2(.5 - .4951) = 2(.0049) = 0.0098$. Reject H_0 at $\alpha = .01$. The proportion of frequent business travelers who believe that daily service is important has probably decreased.

7-38. Standing start: H_0: $\mu \leq 5.27$ H_1: $\mu > 5.27$

$n = 100$ $\bar{x} = 5.8$ $s = 1.9$

$$z = \frac{5.8 - 5.27}{1.9/\sqrt{100}} = 2.789$$

p-value $= .5 - .4974 = 0.0026$. Reject H_0.

Braking: H_0: $\mu \leq 3.15$ H_1: $\mu > 3.15$

$n = 100$ $\bar{x} = 3.21$ $s = 0.6$

$$z = \frac{3.21 - 3.15}{0.6/\sqrt{100}} = 1.00$$

p-value $= .5 - .3413 = 0.1587$. Do not reject H_0.

7-39. H_0: $\mu = 25.2$ H_1: $\mu \neq 25.2$

$n = 115$ $\bar{x} = 26.1$ $s = 3.2$

$$z = \frac{26.1 - 25.2}{3.2/\sqrt{115}} = 3.016$$

p-value $= 2(.5 - .4987) = 0.0026$. Reject H_0. The new model probably has a higher average electric output.

-40. H_0: $p \leq .60$ H_1: $p > .60$

$n = 1{,}000$ $x = 845$ $\hat{p} = 0.845$

$$z = \frac{.845 - .6}{\sqrt{(.6)(.4)/1{,}000}} = 15.815$$

p-value = area to the right of 15.815 = very small area. Strongly reject H_0. Mandarin Orange Slice should be successful.

-41. H_0: $\mu \geq 200{,}000$ H_1: $\mu < 200{,}000$

$n = 1{,}000$ $\bar{x} = 195{,}200$ $s = 49{,}750$

$$z = \frac{195{,}200 - 200{,}000}{49{,}750/\sqrt{1{,}000}} = -3.05$$

$P(z < -3.05) = 0.0011$, so that is the p-value for this test. In other words, if the true population mean price is 200,000, the probability of finding a sample of 1,000 apartments with this sample mean or lower is about 0.0011. So for very low significance levels, as low as $\alpha = 0.0011$, we would *reject* H_0, and we can be quite confident that the stated average is upwardly inflated from the true average.

-42. All tests are two-tailed.

yield group	trading size group	z	p-value
1	1	−5.16	very small
1	2	−5.43	very small
1	3	−2.97	.003
1	4	2.51	.012
2	1	−5.90	very small
2	2	−5.41	very small
2	3	−1.91	.0562
2	4	3.17	.0016
3	1	−2.50	.0124
3	2	−0.35	.7264
3	3	0.78	.4354
3	4	7.95	very small
4	1	1.52	.1286
4	2	3.77	very small ($< .0004$)
4	3	4.28	very small ($< .00006$)
4	4	4.34	very small ($< .00006$)

Average abnormal returns probably exist in the populations of all but:

    7th down   n.s. at .05

    10th down   n.s. at .05

11th down   n.s. at .05
13th down   n.s. at .05

Also: 4th down and 9th down n.s. at .01 but sig. at .05

7-43. See the solutions to earlier problems in this chapter.

7-44. $H_0: p \leq .90$ $H_1: p > .90$
$N = 5,000$ $n = 250$ $x = 229$ $\hat{p} = 229/250 = 0.916$

$$z = \frac{\hat{p} - p_0}{\sqrt{\dfrac{p_0 q_0}{n}\left(\dfrac{N-n}{N-1}\right)}} = \frac{.016}{.018495} = 0.865$$

Do not reject H_0 (p-value = 0.1935). There is no evidence that over 90% of Britain's pubs serve Courage beers.

7-45. $H_0: \mu \leq 300$ $H_1: \mu > 300$
$N = 1,400$ $n = 400$ $\bar{x} = 521.05$ $s = 102.50$

$$z = \frac{521.05 - 300}{(102.50/\sqrt{400})\sqrt{1,000/1,399}} = 51.02$$

Reject H_0. The p-value is extremely small.
Without finite population correction: $z = 43.13$ Here, not a big difference when not using the finite population correction.

7-46. $H_0: \mu = 0$ $H_1: \mu \neq 0$
$N = 500$ $n = 45$ $\bar{x} = 0.125$ $s = 0.275$

$$z = \frac{0.125 - 0}{(0.275/\sqrt{45})\sqrt{455/499}} = 3.19$$

Reject H_0 (p-value = 0.0014). The average price change for stocks in the Fortune 500 index during the week in question was probably above zero.

7-47. $H_0: p \geq .35$ $H_1: p < .35$
$N = 155$ $n = 50$ $x = 15$ $\hat{p} = 15/50 = 0.3$

$$z = \frac{0.3 - 0.35}{\sqrt{(.35)(.65)/50}\sqrt{105/154}} = -0.898$$

Do not reject H_0 (p-value = .1846).

7-48. H_0: $p \leq .08$ H_1: $p > .08$

$N = 1,500$ $n = 100$ $x = 11$

$$z = \frac{.11 - .08}{\sqrt{(.08)(.92)/100}\sqrt{1,400/1,499}} = 1.144$$

There is no conclusive evidence to reject the shipment. The null hypothesis cannot be rejected (p-value $= 0.1263$).

7-49. H_0: $\sigma^2 \leq 25,000,000$ H_1: $\sigma^2 > 25,000,000$

$n = 25$ $s = 7,000$ Use $\alpha = .01$

$\chi^2_{(24)} = (24)(7,000)^2/25,000,000 = 47.04$

Critical point for $\chi^2_{(24)}$ ($\alpha = .01$) $= 42.98$

Critical point for $\chi^2_{(24)}$ ($\alpha = .005$) $= 45.56$

Reject H_0. p-value $< .005$.

7-50. H_0: $\sigma^2 = 10,000$ H_1: $\sigma^2 \neq 10,000$

$n = 30$ $s^2 = 13,896$

$\chi^2_{(29)} = (29)(13,896)/10,000 = 40.298$

Critical points for $\chi^2_{(29)}$ ($\alpha = .05$): 16.05 and 45.72

Therefore, we cannot reject H_0 (even at $\alpha = 0.10$).

7-51. H_0: $\sigma^2 \leq 530$ H_1: $\sigma^2 > 530$

$n = 300$ $s^2 = 544$

$\chi^2_{(299)} = (299)(544)/530 = 306.9$

Critical point for $\chi^2_{(299)}$ for $\alpha = .05$ in a right-hand one-tailed test, using a normal approximation, is:

$299 + 1.645\sqrt{598} = 339.2$

Therefore, do not reject H_0. There is no evidence that the system needs to be reworked.

7-52. H_0: $\sigma^2 \leq 1.5$ H_1: $\sigma^2 > 1.5$

$n = 60$ $s^2 = 1.8$

$\chi^2_{(59)} = (59)(1.8)/1.5 = 70.8$

We'll use approximate df $= 60$ from the table. The critical point for $\alpha = 0.10$ for χ^2 is 74.4. Do not reject H_0 (p-value > 0.10).

7-53. H_0: $\mu \leq 110$ H_1: $\mu > 110$

$\alpha = .05$ $n = 80$ $\sigma = 30$

We need the power at $\mu_1 = 120$:

$$C = \mu_0 + 1.645\sigma/\sqrt{n} = 110 + 1.645(30)/\sqrt{80} = 115.5175$$

$$\text{Power} = P(\bar{X} > C \mid \mu = 120) = P\left(Z > \frac{C - 120}{\sigma/\sqrt{n}}\right)$$

$$= P\left(Z > \frac{115.5175 - 120}{30/\sqrt{80}}\right) = P(Z > -1.336) = .4092 + .5 = 0.9092.$$

Good power at $\mu_1 = 120$.

7-54. H_0: $\mu \leq 500$ H_1: $\mu > 500$

$n = 100$ $\alpha = .05$ $\sigma^2 = 2,500$

Find the power at $\mu_1 = 520$:

$$C = 500 + 1.645(50)/\sqrt{100} = 508.225$$

Power at 520 is: $P(\bar{X} > C \mid \mu_1 = 520) = P\left(Z > \frac{508.225 - 520}{50/\sqrt{100}}\right)$

$= P(Z > -2.355) = .4908 + .5 = 0.9908$, a high power.

7-55. H_0: $\mu \leq 50$ H_1: $\mu > 50$

$n = 80$ $\alpha = .01$ $\sigma = 20$

Find the power at $\mu_1 = 60$:

$$C = 50 + 2.326(20)/\sqrt{80} = 55.201$$

$$\text{Power} = P(\bar{X} > C \mid \mu = 60) = P\left(Z > \frac{55.201 - 60}{20/\sqrt{80}}\right) = P(Z > -2.146) = 0.984$$

Power at 55: $P\left(Z > \frac{55.201 - 55}{20/\sqrt{80}}\right) = P(Z > .09) = .5 - .0359 = 0.4641$

Power at 51: $P\left(Z > \frac{55.201 - 51}{20/\sqrt{80}}\right) = P(Z > 1.88) = .5 - .4699 = 0.0301$

Power at 52: $P\left(Z > \frac{55.201 - 52}{20/\sqrt{80}}\right) = P(Z > 1.43) = 0.0764$

Power at 53 is 0.1635

Power at 54 is 0.295

Power at 55 is 0.4641

Power at 56 is 0.6406

Power at 57 is 0.7881

Power at 58 is 0.8944

Power at 59 is 0.9554

Power at 60 is 0.984

Power at 61 is 0.9952

Power Curve for Problem 7-55

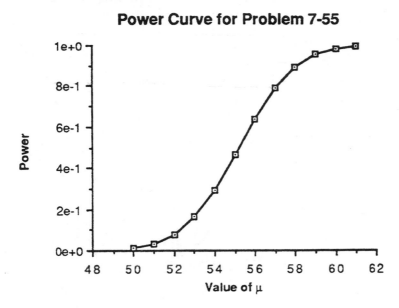

56. H_0: $p = .45$ H_1: $p \neq .45$

$n = 500$ $\alpha = .01$

$C_{1,2} = .45 \pm 2.576\sqrt{(.45)(.55)/500} = 0.507, 0.393$

The power at $p_1 = 0.5$ is: $P(\hat{P} > C_1 \mid p = 0.5)$

$$= P\left(Z > \frac{.507 - 0.5}{\sqrt{(.5)(.5)/500}}\right) = P(Z > .327) = .5 - .1282 = 0.3718$$

The power at $p_1 = 0.4$ is: $P(\hat{P} < C_2 \mid p = 0.4)$

$$= P\left(Z < \frac{.393 - 0.4}{\sqrt{(.4)(.6)/500}}\right) = P(Z < -.3338) = .5 - .1307 = 0.3693$$

Both are about 0.37.

57. H_0: $p \leq .25$ H_1: $p > .25$

$\alpha = .01$ Power at $p = 0.3$ is 0.95; assume $p = .25$

$$n = \left(\frac{z_0\sqrt{p_0 q_0} + z_1\sqrt{p_1 q_1}}{p_0 - p_1}\right)^2 = \left(\frac{2.326\sqrt{(.25)(.75)} + 1.645\sqrt{(.3)(.7)}}{.05}\right)^2$$

$= 1{,}240.47.$ Thus, sample 1,241 eleventh-graders.

7-58. H_0: $\mu \le 418$ H_1: $\mu > 418$

$\sigma = 4$ $\alpha = .05$ power at \$421 is 0.90

$n = \left[(z_0 + z_1)\sigma/(\mu_0 - \mu_1)\right]^2 = \left[(1.645 + 1.28)(4)/3\right]^2$
$= 15.21$, therefore sample 16 dealerships.

7-59. H_0: $p \le .60$ H_1: $p > .60$

$\alpha = .05$ power 0.99 at $p_1 = 0.67$

$n = \left(\dfrac{z_0\sqrt{p_0 q_0} + z_1\sqrt{p_1 q_1}}{p_0 - p_1}\right)^2 = 736.42$, therefore sample 737 shareholders.

7-60. H_0: $\mu \le 6.5$ H_1: $\mu > 6.5$

$\sigma = 2.5$ $\alpha = .01$ Power $= .95$ at $\mu = 7.0$

$n = \left[(z_0 + z_1)\sigma/(\mu_0 - \mu_1)\right]^2 = \left[(2.326 + 1.645)(2.5)/(6.5 - 7.0)\right]^2 = 394.22$

Therefore, sample 395 people.

7-61. H_0: $\mu = 3.8$ H_1: $\mu \ne 3.8$

$\sigma = 1.5$ $\alpha = .05$ Power at $\mu_1 = 4$ is to be 0.90

In a two-tailed test: $\alpha = .05$,   thus:

$C_1 = 3.8 + 1.96(1.5/\sqrt{n})$

$P(\bar{X} > C_1 \mid \mu = 4) = P\left(Z > \dfrac{C_1 - 4}{1.5/\sqrt{n}}\right) = .90$

$\dfrac{C_1 - 4}{1.5/\sqrt{n}} = -1.28$

Substituting C_1 : $\dfrac{3.8 + 1.96(1.5/\sqrt{n}) - 4}{1.5/\sqrt{n}} = -1.28$

$3.8 + 1.96(1.5/\sqrt{n}) - 4 = -1.28(1.5/\sqrt{n})$

$(1.96 + 1.28)(1.5/\sqrt{n}) = 0.2$ Therefore, $n = \left[(1.96 + 1.28)(1.5)/.2\right]^2$

$= 590.49$. Therefore, sample 591 transactions.

7-62. Slamming rate, H_0: $p_0 \le .01$ H_1: $p_0 > .10$

$n = 4000$ $\hat{p} = .07$

$z = \dfrac{\hat{p} - p_0}{\sqrt{p_0 q_0/n}} = \dfrac{.07 - .01}{\sqrt{(.01)(.99)/4000}} = 38.14$

Very small p-value; strongly reject H_0. There is ample evidence that the "slamming" rate is much higher than claimed by the phone company, and their procedures need correction.

7-63. In a two-tailed test, we are interested in detecting any deviation from the claimed value of the parameter: either above or below. In a one-tailed test, we are interested in detecting a deviation from the claimed value in a particular, given direction (upward in a right-hand tailed test, and downward in a left-hand tailed test).

7-64. At a given level α, a particular value for a parameter will be captured by a confidence interval if and only if the null hypothesis that the parameter equals this particular value is not rejected in a two-tailed test conducted using the same α.

7-65. $H_0: \mu \le .64$ $\qquad$ $H_1: \mu > .64$

$n = 100 \qquad \bar{x} = .72 \qquad s = .10$

$$z = \frac{.72 - .64}{.10/\sqrt{100}} = \frac{0.08}{.10/10} = 8$$

Reject H_0 (p-value is very small). Do not believe the advertisement.

7-66. The normal distribution with mean $df = n - 1$ and variance $2\,df = 2(n-1)$.

7-67. The "power" at the value of the parameter under H_0 is α. Power at point x is $P(\text{reject } H_0 \mid \text{parameter} = x) = P(\text{reject } H_0 \text{ when } H_0 \text{ is true if } x = \text{value of the parameter under } H_0) = \alpha$ $\quad$ [when H_0 is true].

7-68. We cannot say that the true value of the parameter is far from the value stated in H_0. We can only say that there is strong evidence to reject H_0. With large enough n (as in this case), even a small deviation from the stated value can cause rejection of the null hypothesis.

7-69. The probability of obtaining a sample result as extreme as the one obtained is 0.0002 (i.e., extremely unlikely).

7-70. $H_0: \mu \le 55 \qquad H_1: \mu > 55$

$n = 120 \qquad \bar{x} = 65.5 \qquad s = 22$

$$z = \frac{65.5 - 55}{22/\sqrt{120}} = 5.228$$

Reject H_0, p-value is very small. There is strong evidence that the campaign would increase the average charges per card.

7-71. α is the probability of rejecting H_0 when H_0 is true; β is the probability of not rejecting H_0 when H_0 is false (and should ideally have been rejected).

7-72. Power $= 1 - \beta$.

7-73. When p-value $= 0.0006$, the probability of obtaining a value of the test statistic as extreme as, or more extreme than, what we have obtained is 0.0006 *if* H_0 is true. Since we would be observing a very rare event if H_0 were true, we conclude that H_0 is actually not true.

7-74. Data snooping is cheating. Data should not be used for testing a hypothesis prompted by the same data. The power of the test is reduced by snooping.

7-75. The power is determined by:
    1. the distance of the true parameter value in H_1 from the null-hypothesized value of the parameter
    2. α
    3. σ
    4. n

7-76. The p-value is affected by
    1. the distance of the test statistic value from the hypothesized value of the parameter
    2. σ
    3. n

7-77. H_0: $\mu \geq 30$ H_1: $\mu < 30$
$n = 100$ $\bar{x} = 27$ $s = 6$
$$z = \frac{27 - 30}{6/\sqrt{100}} = -5$$
Reject H_0. p-value is very small (p-value $= .0000003$). Based on sample results, the Toshiba ad is false.

7-78. Reject H_0 because the p-value, 0.0009, is very small.

7-79. a. degrees of freedom $= n - 1 = 14$.

    b. Reject H_0, p-value is very small.

    c. The computer is not programmed to report p-values less than 0.0001. Here, p-value < 0.0001, hence listed as 0.0000.

7-80. We can increase the power without changing n by increasing the level of significance used, α.

7-81. $H_0: p = .06$ $\qquad$ $H_1: p \neq .06$

$n = 2,000$ $\qquad$ $x = 142$ $\qquad$ $\hat{p} = .071$ $\qquad$ Two-tailed test:

$$z = \frac{.071 - .06}{\sqrt{(.06)(.94)/2,000}} = 2.07$$

At $\alpha = .05$, reject H_0. The proportion is probably higher than .06. p-value $= 2(.5 - .4808) = 0.0384$

7-82. $H_0: p \leq .35$ $\qquad$ $H_1: p > .35$

$n = 3,850$ $\qquad$ $x = 1,367$ $\qquad$ $\hat{p} = 1,367/3,850 = .355$

$$z = \frac{\hat{p} - p_0}{\sqrt{p_0 q_0/n}} = .659$$

Do not reject H_0. p-value $= .5 - .2450 = 0.2550$. There is no evidence in these sampling results that the market share was higher than 35%.

7-83. $H_0: p \leq .43$ $\qquad$ $H_1: p > .43$

$n = 5,500$ $\qquad$ $x = 2,521$ $\qquad$ $\hat{p} = 0.458$

$$z = \frac{\hat{p} - p_0}{\sqrt{p_0 q_0/n}} = 4.249$$

Reject H_0. Small p-value ($< .00003$). The executive should talk about the p-value of this test. There is strong evidence that GM's market share is over 43%.

7-84. It is important to know the power of a test so that we know our probability of rejecting H_0 when it should indeed be rejected, for given values of the parameter under H_1.

7-85. The level of α is set before the test as our maximum allowed probability of a Type I error. The p-value is the *actual* significance level of the test. It is the *smallest* α at which H_0 can be rejected.

7-86. $H_0: p \leq .43$ $\qquad$ $H_1: p > .43$

Power of $p = .48$ is 0.90 and $\alpha = .01$. Find the minimum required sample size.

$$n = \left(\frac{z_0 \sqrt{p_0 q_0} + z_1 \sqrt{p_1 q_1}}{p_0 - p_1} \right)^2 = 1,283.12$$

So sample 1,284 cars.

Using $n = 1,284$, find the power at $p_1 = 0.50$:

$$C = .43 + 2.326\sqrt{\frac{(.43)(.57)}{1,284}} = 0.4621$$

Power $= P(\hat{P} > C \mid p = .50) = P(Z > -2.71) = 0.9966$

7-87. H_0: $p \geq .05$ H_1: $p < .05$

$n = 1,362$ $x = 29$ $\hat{p} = .0212922$

$$z = \frac{\hat{p} - p_0}{\sqrt{p_0 q_0 / n}} = -4.86$$

Reject H_0; very small p-value. The proportion of women in top management is probably less than 5%.

Suppose $\alpha = .05$. Find the power at $p_1 = .04$:

$$C = .05 - 1.645\sqrt{\frac{(.05)(.95)}{1,362}} = 0.0402854$$

Power $= P(Z < .0537) = .5 + .0214 = 0.5214$

7-88. H_0: $\mu \leq 78$ H_1: $\mu > 78$

$n = 24$ $\bar{x} = 83$ $s = 12$ $\alpha = .05$

$$t_{(23)} = \frac{83 - 78}{12/\sqrt{24}} = 2.04$$

At $\alpha = .05$, right-hand tailed test, the critical point is 1.714. Therefore, reject H_0. For $\alpha = .025$, the critical point is 2.069. Thus the p-value is slightly greater than .025. There is some evidence that the CRT system increases the average productivity at the bank.

7-89. H_0: $\sigma^2 \leq 156$ H_1: $\sigma^2 > 156$

$n = 25$ $s^2 = 175$ $\alpha = .05$

$$\chi^2_{(24)} = \frac{(n-1)s^2}{\sigma_0^2} = \frac{24(175)}{156} = 26.923$$

The critical point for $\alpha = .10$ is 33.1963, therefore we cannot reject H_0 and the p-value is $> .10$. There is no evidence that the variance is above 156. Maybe we need to take a larger sample.

7-90. $n = 250$ in Problem **7-89**; $s^2 = 182$. We'll use the normal distribution with mean 249 and variance 2(249). Use $\alpha = .05$:

$$\chi^2_{(249)} = \frac{(n-1)s^2}{\sigma_0^2} = \frac{249(182)}{156} = 290.5$$

At $\alpha = .05$, the critical point is: $249 + 1.645\sqrt{2(249)} = 285.71$. A better approximation: $\chi^2 = \frac{1}{2}\left(z + \sqrt{2\nu - 1}\right)^2 = \frac{1}{2}\left(1.645 + \sqrt{2(249) - 1}\right)^2 = 286.53$

Reject H_0.

7-91. H_0: $p \geq .95$ $\qquad$ H_1: $p < .95$
$n = 1,500$ $\qquad$ $x = 1,380$ $\qquad$ $\hat{p} = .92$

$$z = \frac{.92 - .95}{\sqrt{(.95)(.05)/1,500}} = -5.33$$

Reject H_0. There is evidence that the proportion of rental units decreased from 0.95 during the period in question. (The p-value is very small.)

7-92. H_0: $\mu \leq 3.1$ $\qquad$ H_1: $\mu > 3.1$
$n = 21$ $\qquad$ $\bar{x} = 4.38$ $\qquad$ $s = 5.55$

$$t_{(20)} = \frac{4.38 - 3.1}{5.55/\sqrt{21}} = 1.06$$

Do not reject H_0 even at $\alpha = 0.10$ (p-value = 0.15). No evidence that increased benefits lead to more off-time.

7-93. H_0: $p \leq .30$ $\qquad$ H_1: $p > .30$
$N = 1,000$ $\qquad$ $n = 166$ $\qquad$ $x = 59$ $\qquad$ $\alpha = .05$ $\qquad$ $\hat{p} = 59/166 = .3554$
$n/N = 166/1,000 = .166 > .05$, therefore, we need to use the f.p.c.f.

$$z = \frac{\hat{p} - p_0}{\sqrt{\dfrac{p_0 q_0}{n}\left(\dfrac{N-n}{N-1}\right)}} = \frac{.0554216}{.0324979} = 1.705$$

Reject H_0 at $\alpha = .05$; p-value $= .5 - .4559 = 0.0441$. There is *some* evidence that over 30% of the Fortune top 1,000 use the multiple scenario approach.

7-94. H_0: $\mu \geq 40$ $\qquad$ H_1: $\mu < 40$
$n = 14$ $\qquad$ $\bar{x} = 28$ $\qquad$ $s = 12$

$$t_{(13)} = \frac{28 - 40}{12/\sqrt{14}} = -3.74$$

Reject H_0. The critical point for a left-hand one-tailed test at $\alpha = .005$ for $t_{(13)}$ is -3.012. Thus, p-value $< .005$. Therefore, there is probable cause for action by the investor (assuming normality of the population of returns).

7-95. Suppose $N = 110$. Redo Problem **7-94** using the f.p.c.f.:

$$t_{(13)} = \frac{28 - 40}{(12/\sqrt{14})\left(\sqrt{(110 - 14)/109}\right)} = -3.987$$

Reject again. The p-value is even smaller (because the S.E. of $\bar{X}$ is smaller when the f.p.c.f. is used).

7-96. H_0: $\mu = 125$ $\qquad$ H_1: $\mu \neq 125$

$n = 25$ $\qquad$ $\bar{x} = 151.96$ $\qquad$ $s = 90.619$

$$t_{(24)} = \frac{151.96 - 125}{90.619/\sqrt{25}} = 1.4875$$

We cannot reject H_0 even at $\alpha = .10$. The critical points of $t_{(24)}$ are ± 1.711. There is no evidence that the average price is different from \$125 million.

7-97. H_0: $p \leq 0.25$ $\qquad$ H_1: $p > 0.25$

$n = 300$ $\qquad$ $x = 94$ $\qquad$ $\hat{p} = x/n = .31333$

$$z = \frac{\hat{p} - p_0}{\sqrt{p_0 q_0/n}} = 2.53$$

Reject H_0. There is evidence that the proportion of microcomputer owners interested in the software package is over 25%. The company should probably market the product. p-value $= .5 - .4943 = 0.0057$.

7-98. H_0: $p \geq .20$ $\qquad$ H_1: $p < .20$

$n = 5,000$ $\qquad$ $x = 876$ $\qquad$ $\hat{p} = .1752$

$$z = \frac{\hat{p} - p_0}{\sqrt{p_0 q_0/n}} = -4.38$$

The p-value is very small (p-value $< .00003$). Reject H_0. There is strong evidence that the NSF study overestimated the proportion of foreign scientists employed by American laboratories.

7-99. H_0: $\mu \leq 1,250$ $\qquad$ H_1: $\mu > 1,250$

$n = 18$ $\qquad$ $\bar{x} = 1,330$ $\qquad$ $s = 120$

$$t_{(17)} = \frac{1,330 - 1,250}{120/\sqrt{18}} = 2.828$$

The critical point for $\alpha = .01$ for $t_{(17)}$ is 2.567; therefore reject H_0. There is evidence to support the broker's claim that the average price he/she pays per ticket on this route is above the \$1,250 figure claimed by the airlines. $0.005 < p$-value < 0.01.

7-100. Use a null hypothesis that the success rate will be at least 0.90, and define "taking action" (rejection of H_0) as "not implementing the program."

Success rate: H_0: $p_0 \geq .90$ H_1: $p_0 < .90$

$n = 2{,}000$ $x = 1{,}712$ $\hat{p} = 1{,}712/2{,}000 = .856$

$z = (\hat{p} - p_0)/\sqrt{p_0 q_0/n} = -6.56$

Reject H_0, the p-value is very small, and there is excellent evidence that the success rate will not justify implementing the program.

Case 7.

Scaman's Hypothesis:

H_0: $p \geq .10$

H_1: $p < .10$ (This is what he wants to prove.)

If $p = .10$, $\text{SE}(\hat{P}) = \sqrt{(.10)(.90)/n}$

Suppose you want $\alpha = .01$ and you want a power of .99 if $p = .09$. What is the minimum required sample size?

$$n = \left(\frac{z_0\sqrt{p_0 q_0} + z_1\sqrt{p_1 q_1}}{p_1 - p_0} \right)^2$$

$$= \left(\frac{2.326\sqrt{(.10)(.90)} + 2.326\sqrt{(.09)(.91)}}{.01} \right)^2 = 18{,}590.2$$

Suppose $\alpha = .01$ and power at $p = .09$ is .95:

$$n = \left(\frac{2.326\sqrt{(.10)(.90)} + 1.645\sqrt{(.09)(.91)}}{.01} \right)^2 = 13{,}655.53$$

Suppose $\alpha = .05$, power at $p_1 = .08$ is 0.90:

$$n = \left(\frac{1.645\sqrt{(.10)(.90)} + 1.28\sqrt{(.08)(.92)}}{.02} \right)^2 = 1{,}767.17$$

For $\alpha = .05$, power of 0.90 at $p_1 = .09$:

$$n = \left(\frac{1.645\sqrt{(.10)(.90)} + 1.28\sqrt{(.09)(.91)}}{.01} \right)^2 = 7{,}392.778$$

This is manageable and within the budget. If there are 300 passengers each way: $2(300) = 600$ per week, $7{,}393/600 = 12.32$. Send people on 13 voyages throughout the summer, spaced evenly from May to September. Cost $= \$400(13) = \$5{,}200$. This leaves about $800 to cover the estimated $420 incidental expenses. The remainder can be used to get a still larger sample. Using $\alpha = 0.05$, you will have a 0.90 probability of rejecting the null hypothesis if the true proportion is 0.09. Scaman should be pleased.

CHAPTER 8

8-1. $n = 25$ $\bar{D} = 19.08$ $s_D = 30.67$

H_0: $\mu_D = 0$ H_1: $\mu_D \neq 0$

$$t_{(24)} = \frac{\bar{D} - \mu_{D_0}}{s_D/\sqrt{n}} = 3.11$$

Reject H_0 at $\alpha = 0.01$.

8-2. $n = 40$ $\bar{D} = 5$ $s_D = 2.3$

H_0: $\mu_D = 0$ H_1: $\mu_D \neq 0$

$$z = \frac{5 - 0}{2.3/\sqrt{40}} = 13.75$$

Strongly reject H_0. 95% C.I. for μ_D is $5 \pm 1.96(2.3/\sqrt{40}) = [4.29, 5.71]$.

8-3. $n = 12$ $\bar{D} = 1.29$ $s_D = 2.2$ $(D = \text{International} - \text{Domestic})$

H_0: $\mu_D = 0$ H_1: $\mu_D \neq 0$

$$t_{(11)} = \frac{\bar{D} - \mu_{D_0}}{s_D/\sqrt{n}} = 2.034$$

At $\alpha = 0.05$, we cannot reject H_0 of no difference in the average returns.

8-4. $n = 60$ $\bar{D} = 0.2$ $s_D = 1$

H_0: $\mu_D \leq 0$ H_1: $\mu_D > 0$

$$z = \frac{0.2 - 0}{1/\sqrt{60}} = 1.549. \text{ At } \alpha = 0.05, \text{ we cannot reject } H_0.$$

8-5. $n = 15$ $\bar{D} = 3.2$ $s_D = 8.436$ $D = \text{After} - \text{Before}$

H_0: $\mu_D \leq 0$ H_1: $\mu_D > 0$

$$t_{(14)} = \frac{3.2 - 0}{8.436/\sqrt{15}} = 1.469$$

There is no evidence that the shelf facings are effective.

8-6. $n = 25$ $\bar{D} = 4$ $s_D = 2$

H_0: $\mu_D \leq 0$ H_1: $\mu_D > 0$

$$t_{(24)} = \frac{4 - 0}{2/\sqrt{25}} = 10$$

Reject H_0. There is strong evidence that the average investment proportion did change in mid-October in favor of Hong Kong.

8-7. Power at $\mu_D = 0.1$ $n = 60$ $\sigma_D = 1.0$ $\alpha = .01$

H_0: $\mu_D \leq 0$ H_1: $\mu_D > 0$

$C = \mu_0 + 2.326(\sigma/\sqrt{n}) = 0.30029$ We need:

$P(\bar{D} > C \mid \mu_D = 0.1)$

$= P(\bar{D} > 0.30029 \mid \mu_D = 0.1)$

$= P\left(Z > \dfrac{0.30029 - 0.1}{1/\sqrt{60}}\right)$

$= P(Z > 1.55) = 0.0606$

8-8. $n = 20$ $\bar{D} = 1.25$ $s_D = 42.89$

H_0: $\mu_D = 0$ H_1: $\mu_D \neq 0$

$t_{(19)} = \dfrac{1.25 - 0}{42.89/\sqrt{20}} = 0.13$

Do not reject H_0; no evidence of a difference.

8-9. $n_1 = 45$ $n_2 = 32$ $\bar{x}_1 = 26$ $\bar{x}_2 = 21$ $s_1 = 8$ $s_2 = 6$

H_0: $\mu_2 - \mu_1 \geq 0$ H_1: $\mu_2 - \mu_1 < 0$

$z = \dfrac{\bar{x}_2 - \bar{x}_1 - 0}{\sqrt{(s_1^2/n_1) + (s_2^2/n_2)}} = -3.13$

Reject H_0. There is evidence that LINC reduces average programming time.

8-10. $n_1 = n_2 = 30$

H_0: $\mu_1 - \mu_2 = 0$ H_1: $\mu_1 - \mu_2 \neq 0$

Nikon (1): $\bar{x}_1 = 8.5$ $s_1 = 2.1$ Minolta (2): $\bar{x}_2 = 7.8$ $s_2 = 1.8$

$z = \dfrac{8.5 - 7.8}{\sqrt{(2.1^2/30) + (1.8^2/30)}} = 1.386$

Do not reject H_0. There is no evidence of a difference in the average ratings of the two cameras.

8-11. Bel Air (1): $n_1 = 32$ $\bar{x}_1 = 345{,}650$ $s_1 = 48{,}500$

Marin (2): $n_2 = 35$ $\bar{x}_2 = 289{,}440$ $s_2 = 87{,}090$

H_0: $\mu_1 - \mu_2 = 0$ H_1: $\mu_1 - \mu_2 \neq 0$

$z = \dfrac{\bar{x}_1 - \bar{x}_2}{\sqrt{(s_1^2/n_1) + (s_2^2/n_2)}} = 3.3$

Reject H_0. There is evidence that the average Bel Air price is higher.

8-12. British: $n_1 = 40$ $\bar{x}_1 = 12$ $s_1 = 6$

Swiss: $n_2 = 40$ $\bar{x}_2 = 20$ $s_2 = 7$

$H_0: \mu_1 - \mu_2 = 0$ $H_1: \mu_1 - \mu_2 \neq 0$

$$z = \frac{12 - 20}{\sqrt{(6^2/40) + (7^2/40)}} = -5.488$$

Reject H_0. There is strong evidence that the Swiss market has better returns. Very small p-value.

8-13. Music: $n_1 = 128$ $\bar{x}_1 = 23.5$ $s_1 = 12.2$

Verbal: $n_2 = 212$ $\bar{x}_2 = 18.0$ $s_2 = 10.5$

$H_0: \mu_1 - \mu_2 = 0$ $H_1: \mu_1 - \mu_2 \neq 0$

$$z = \frac{23.5 - 18.0}{\sqrt{(12.2^2/128) + (10.5^2/212)}} = 4.24$$

Reject H_0. Music is probably more effective.

8-14. Biomedical: $n_1 = 120$ $\bar{x}_1 = 72{,}500$ $s_1 = 5{,}000$

Chemical: $n_2 = 120$ $\bar{x}_2 = 73{,}970$ $s_2 = 6{,}500$

$H_0: \mu_1 - \mu_2 = 0$ $H_1: \mu_1 - \mu_2 \neq 0$

$$z = \frac{72{,}500 - 73{,}970}{\sqrt{(5{,}000^2/120) + (6{,}500^2/120)}} = -1.9636$$

Reject H_0 at the $\alpha = 0.05$ level; there is evidence that chemical engineers average more. p value $= 0.0496$.

8-15. Liz (1): $n_1 = 32$ $\bar{x}_1 = 4{,}238$ $s_1 = 1{,}002.5$

Calvin (2): $n_2 = 37$ $\bar{x}_2 = 3{,}888.72$ $s_2 = 876.05$

a. one-tailed: $H_0: \mu_1 - \mu_2 \leq 0$ $H_1: \mu_1 - \mu_2 > 0$

b. $z = \dfrac{4{,}238 - 3{,}888.72 - 0}{\sqrt{(1{,}002.5^2/32) + (876.05^2/37)}} = 1.53$

c. At $\alpha = .05$, the critical point is 1.645. Do not reject H_0 that Liz Claiborne models do not get more money, on the average.

d. p-value $= .5 - .437 = .063$ (It is the probability of committing a Type I error if we choose to reject and H_0 happens to be true.)

e. Redo the problem assuming the results are based on $n_1 = 10$, $n_2 = 11$:
$$t = \frac{4{,}238 - 3{,}888.72 - 0}{\sqrt{(1{,}002.5^2/10) + (876.05^2/11)}} = 0.846$$
Now df of t are approximately given by Equation (8-6):

$$df = \frac{(s_1^2/n_1 + s_2^2/n_2)^2}{\dfrac{(s_1^2/n_1)^2}{n_1 - 1} + \dfrac{(s_2^2/n_2)^2}{n_2 - 1}} = 18.010; \quad \text{approximate df} = 19.$$

Do not reject H_0.

8-16. American patents (1): $n_1 = 100$ $\bar{x}_1 = 1{,}838.69$ $s_1 = 461$
Japanese patents (2): $n_2 = 80$ $\bar{x}_2 = 1{,}050.22$ $s_2 = 560$
$H_0: \mu_1 - \mu_2 \leq 0$ $H_1: \mu_1 - \mu_2 > 0$
$$z = \frac{1{,}838.69 - 1{,}050.22}{\sqrt{(461^2/100) + (560^2/80)}} = 10.14$$
Strong evidence to reject H_0; the Japanese probably pay more in fees.

8-17. Non-research (1): $n_1 = 255$ $s_1 = 0.64$
Research (2): $n_2 = 300$ $s_2 = 0.85$
$\bar{x}_2 - \bar{x}_1 = 2.54$
95% C.I. for $\mu_2 - \mu_1$ is: $(\bar{x}_2 - \bar{x}_1) \pm z_{\alpha/2}\sqrt{(s_1^2/n_1) + (s_2^2/n_2)}$
$$= 2.54 \pm 1.96\sqrt{(.64^2/255) + (.85^2/300)} = [2.416, 2.664] \text{ percent.}$$

8-18. Audio (1): $n_1 = 25$ $\bar{x}_1 = 87$ $s_1 = 12$
Video (2): $n_2 = 20$ $\bar{x}_2 = 64$ $s_2 = 23$
$H_0: \mu_1 - \mu_2 = 0$ $H_1: \mu_1 - \mu_2 \neq 0$
$$z = \frac{\bar{x}_1 - \bar{x}_2 - 0}{\sqrt{\dfrac{(n_1 - 1)s_1^2 + (n_2 - 1)s_2^2}{n_1 + n_2 - 2}\left(\dfrac{1}{n_1} + \dfrac{1}{n_2}\right)}} = 4.326$$

Reject H_0. Audio is probably better (higher average purchase intent). Waldenbooks should concentrate in audio.

8-19. With training (1): $n_1 = 13$ $\bar{x}_1 = 55$ $s_1 = 8$
Without training (2): $n_2 = 15$ $\bar{x}_2 = 48$ $s_2 = 6$
$H_0: \mu_1 - \mu_2 \leq 4{,}000$ $H_1: \mu_1 - \mu_2 > 4{,}000$
$$t_{(26)} = \frac{(55 - 48) - 4}{\sqrt{\dfrac{(12)(8)^2 + (14)(6)^2}{26}\left(\dfrac{1}{13} + \dfrac{1}{15}\right)}} = 1.132$$

The critical value at $\alpha = .05$ for $t_{(26)}$ in a right-hand tailed test is 1.706. Since $1.132 < 1.706$, there is no evidence at $\alpha = 0.05$ that the program executives get an average of $4,000 per year more than other executives of comparable levels.

8-20. 1995 (1): $n_1 = 50$ $\bar{x}_1 = 3{,}300$ $s_1 = 1{,}000$
1991 (2): $n_2 = 50$ $\bar{x}_2 = 5{,}200$ $s_2 = 1{,}000$
H_0: $\mu_1 - \mu_2 \geq 0$ H_1: $\mu_1 - \mu_2 < 0$

$$z = \frac{3{,}300 - 5{,}200 - 0}{\sqrt{\dfrac{49(1{,}000^2 + 1{,}000^2)}{98}\left(\dfrac{1}{50} + \dfrac{1}{50}\right)}} = -9.50$$

Strongly reject H_0. There is evidence that the cost dropped; p-value very small.

8-21. 1995 (1): $n_1 = 100$ $\bar{x}_1 = 11$ $s_1 = 6$
1960 (2): $n_2 = 100$ $\bar{x}_2 = 18$ $s_2 = 6$
H_0: $\mu_1 - \mu_2 \geq 0$ H_1: $\mu_1 - \mu_2 < 0$

$$z = \frac{11 - 18 - 0}{\sqrt{\dfrac{99(6^2 + 6^2)}{198}\left(\dfrac{1}{100} + \dfrac{1}{100}\right)}} = -8.2496$$

Strongly reject H_0. There is evidence that alcohol consumption has dropped; p-value very small.

8-22. Old (1): $n_1 = 19$ $\bar{x}_1 = 8.26$ $s_1 = 1.43$
New (2): $n_2 = 23$ $\bar{x}_2 = 9.11$ $s_2 = 1.56$
H_0: $\mu_2 - \mu_1 \leq 0$ H_1: $\mu_2 - \mu_1 > 0$

$$t_{(40)} = \frac{9.11 - 8.26 - 0}{\sqrt{\dfrac{18(1.43)^2 + 22(1.56)^2}{40}\left(\dfrac{1}{19} + \dfrac{1}{23}\right)}} = 1.82$$

Some evidence to reject H_0 (p-value $= 0.038$) for the t-distribution with df $= 40$, in a one-tailed test.

8-23. New proposed route (1): $n_1 = 6$ $\bar{x}_1 = 96{,}540$ $s_1 = 12{,}522$
Alternative route (2): $n_2 = 9$ $\bar{x}_2 = 85{,}991$ $s_2 = 19{,}548$
H_0: $\mu_1 - \mu_2 \leq 0$ H_1: $\mu_1 - \mu_2 > 0$

$$t_{(13)} = \frac{96{,}540 - 85{,}991}{\sqrt{\dfrac{5(12{,}522)^2 + 8(19{,}548)^2}{13}\left(\dfrac{1}{6} + \dfrac{1}{9}\right)}} = 1.164$$

There is no evidence that the new proposed route is better than the alternative route (because for $t_{(13)}$ the critical point in a right-hand tailed test at $\alpha = 0.10$ is 1.35, which is larger).

8-24. $n_b = 18 \qquad \bar{x}_b = 7.4 \qquad s_b = 1.3$

$n_a = 23 \qquad \bar{x}_a = 8.2 \qquad s_a = 2.4$

$H_0: \mu_a - \mu_b \leq 0 \qquad H_1: \mu_a - \mu_b > 0$

$$z = \frac{8.2 - 7.4}{\sqrt{\dfrac{17(1.3)^2 + 22(2.4)^2}{39}\left(\dfrac{1}{18} + \dfrac{1}{23}\right)}} = 1.273$$

There is no evidence that management decisions increase average customer satisfaction.

8-25. "Yes" (1): $\quad n_1 = 25 \qquad \bar{x}_1 = 12 \qquad s_1 = 2.5$

"No" (2): $\quad n_2 = 25 \qquad \bar{x}_2 = 13.5 \qquad s_2 = 1$

Assume independent random sampling from normal populations with equal population variances.

$H_0: \mu_2 - \mu_1 \leq 0 \qquad H_1: \mu_2 - \mu_1 > 0$

$$z = \frac{13.5 - 12}{\sqrt{\dfrac{24(2.5)^2 + 24(1)^2}{48}\left(\dfrac{1}{25} + \dfrac{1}{25}\right)}} = 2.785$$

At $\alpha = 0.05$, reject H_0. Also reject at $\alpha = 0.01$. p-value $= 0.0026$.

8-26. $H_0: \mu_1 - \mu_2 = 0 \qquad H_1: \mu_1 - \mu_2 \neq 0$

$$z = \frac{.1331 - .105 - 0}{\sqrt{\dfrac{20(.09)^2 + 27(.122)^2}{47}\left(\dfrac{1}{21} + \dfrac{1}{28}\right)}} = 0.8887$$

Do not reject H_0. There is no evidence of a difference in average stock returns for the two periods.

8-27. Public sources (1): $\quad n_1 = 12 \qquad \bar{x}_1 = 12{,}500 \qquad s_1 = 3{,}400$

Private sources (2): $\quad n_2 = 18 \qquad \bar{x}_2 = 21{,}000 \qquad s_2 = 5{,}000$

$$t_{(28)} = \frac{21{,}000 - 12{,}500}{\sqrt{\dfrac{11(3{,}400)^2 + 17(5{,}000)^2}{28}\left(\dfrac{1}{12} + \dfrac{1}{18}\right)}} = 5.136$$

There is strong evidence that private sources lend more, on the average.

8-28. From Problem **8-25**:

$$n_1 = n_2 = 25 \qquad \bar{x}_1 = 12 \qquad \bar{x}_2 = 13.5 \qquad s_1 = 2.5 \qquad s_2 = 1$$

We want a 95% C.I. for $\mu_2 - \mu_1$:

$$(\bar{x}_2 - \bar{x}_1) \pm 1.96 \sqrt{\frac{(n_1 - 1)s_1^2 + (n_2 - 1)s_2^2}{n_1 + n_2 - 2}\left(\frac{1}{n_1} + \frac{1}{n_2}\right)}$$

$$= (13.5 - 12) \pm 1.96 \sqrt{\frac{24(2.5)^2 + 24(1)^2}{48}\left(\frac{1}{25} + \frac{1}{25}\right)}$$

$$= [0.4445, 2.555] \text{ percent.}$$

8-29. Before (1): $x_1 = 85 \qquad n_1 = 100$

After (2): $x_2 = 68 \qquad n_2 = 100$

$H_0\colon p_1 - p_2 \le 0 \qquad H_1\colon p_1 - p_2 > 0$

$$z = \frac{\hat{p}_1 - \hat{p}_2}{\sqrt{\hat{p}(1 - \hat{p})\left(\frac{1}{n_1} + \frac{1}{n_2}\right)}} = \frac{.85 - .68}{\sqrt{(.765)(.235)\left(\frac{1}{100} + \frac{1}{100}\right)}} = 2.835$$

Reject H_0. On-time departure percentage has probably declined after NW's merger with Republic. p-value $= 0.0023$.

8-30. Small towns (1): $n_1 = 1{,}000 \qquad x_1 = 850$

Big cities (2): $n_2 = 2{,}500 \qquad x_2 = 1{,}950$

$H_0\colon p_1 - p_2 \le 0 \qquad H_1\colon p_1 - p_2 > 0$

$$z = \frac{\dfrac{850}{1{,}000} - \dfrac{1{,}950}{2{,}500}}{\sqrt{\left(\dfrac{850 + 1{,}950}{3{,}500}\right)\left(1 - \dfrac{2{,}800}{3{,}500}\right)\left(\dfrac{1}{1{,}000} + \dfrac{1}{2{,}500}\right)}} = 4.677$$

Reject H_0. There is strong evidence that the percentage of word-of-mouth recommendations in small towns is greater than it is in large metropolitan areas.

8-31. $n_1 = 31 \qquad x_1 = 11 \qquad n_2 = 50 \qquad x_2 = 19$

$H_0\colon p_1 - p_2 = 0 \qquad H_1\colon p_1 - p_2 \ne 0$

$$z = \frac{\hat{p}_1 - \hat{p}_2}{\sqrt{\hat{p}(1 - \hat{p})\left(\frac{1}{n_1} + \frac{1}{n_2}\right)}} = -0.228$$

Do not reject H_0. There is no evidence that one corporate raider is more successful than the other.

8-32. Before campaign (1): $n_1 = 2{,}060$ $\quad \hat{p}_1 = 0.13$

After campaign (2): $\quad n_2 = 5{,}000$ $\quad \hat{p}_2 = 0.19$

$H_0: p_2 - p_1 \leq .05$ $\qquad H_1: p_2 - p_1 > .05$

$$z = \frac{\hat{p}_2 - \hat{p}_1 - D}{\sqrt{\dfrac{\hat{p}_1(1 - \hat{p}_1)}{n_1} + \dfrac{\hat{p}_2(1 - \hat{p}_2)}{n_2}}} = \frac{0.19 - 0.13 - .05}{\sqrt{\dfrac{(.13)(.87)}{2{,}060} + \dfrac{(.19)(.81)}{5{,}000}}} = 1.08$$

No evidence to reject H_0; cannot conclude that the campaign has increased the proportion of people who prefer California wines by over 0.05.

8-33. 95% C.I. for $p_2 - p_1$: $\qquad (\hat{p}_2 - \hat{p}_1) \pm 1.96 \sqrt{\dfrac{\hat{p}_1(1 - \hat{p}_1)}{n_1} + \dfrac{\hat{p}_2(1 - \hat{p}_2)}{n_2}}$

$$= .06 \pm 1.96 \sqrt{\frac{(.13)(.87)}{2{,}060} + \frac{(.19)(.81)}{5{,}000}} = [0.0419,\, 0.0781]$$

We are 95% confident that the increase in the proportion of the population preferring California wines is anywhere from 4.19% to 7.81%.

8-34. The statement to be tested must be hypothesized before looking at the data:

Chase Man. (1): $\quad n_1 = 650$ $\qquad x_1 = 48$

Manuf. Han. (2): $\quad n_2 = 480$ $\qquad x_2 = 20$

$H_0: p_1 - p_2 \leq 0$ $\qquad H_1: p_1 - p_2 > 0$

$$z = \frac{\hat{p}_1 - \hat{p}_2}{\sqrt{\hat{p}(1 - \hat{p})\left(\dfrac{1}{n_1} + \dfrac{1}{n_2}\right)}} = 2.248$$

Reject H_0. p-value $= 0.0122$.

8-35. American execs (1): $\quad n_1 = 120$ $\qquad x_1 = 34$

European execs (2): $\quad n_2 = 200$ $\qquad x_2 = 41$

$H_0: p_1 - p_2 \leq 0$ $\qquad H_1: p_1 - p_2 > 0$

$$z = \frac{.283 - .205}{\sqrt{(.234)(1 - .234)\left(\dfrac{1}{120} + \dfrac{1}{200}\right)}} = 1.601$$

At $\alpha = 0.05$, there is no evidence to conclude that the proportion of American executives who prefer the A320 is greater than that of European executives. (p-value $= 0.0547$.)

8-36. Cleveland (1): $n_1 = 1{,}000$ $\quad x_1 = 75$ $\quad \hat{p}_1 = .075$

Chicago (2): $\quad n_2 = 1{,}000$ $\quad x_2 = 72$ $\quad \hat{p}_2 = .072$

H_0: $p_1 - p_2 = 0$ $\qquad H_1$: $p_1 - p_2 \neq 0$ $\qquad \hat{p} = (72 + 75)/2{,}000 = .0735$

$$z = \frac{\hat{p}_1 - \hat{p}_2}{\sqrt{\hat{p}(1 - \hat{p})\left(\dfrac{1}{n_1} + \dfrac{1}{n_2}\right)}} = 0.257$$

We cannot reject H_0.

8-37. 99% C.I. for difference in the unemployment rate between Cleveland and Chicago:

$$(\hat{p}_1 - \hat{p}_2) \pm 2.576\sqrt{\frac{\hat{p}_1(1 - \hat{p}_1)}{n_1} + \frac{\hat{p}_2(1 - \hat{p}_2)}{n_2}}$$

$$= .003 \pm 2.576\sqrt{\frac{(.075)(.925)}{1{,}000} + \frac{(.072)(.928)}{1{,}000}} = [-0.027, 0.033]$$

This confidence interval contains zero as expected from our non-rejection of H_0 in Problem **8-36**.

8-38. California (1): $\quad n_1 = 1{,}000$ $\quad x_1 = 285$ $\quad p_1 = .285$

New York (2): $\quad n_2 = 1{,}500$ $\quad x_2 = 452$ $\quad p_2 = .301$

H_0: $p_2 - p_1 = 0$ $\qquad H_1$: $p_2 - p_1 \neq 0$ $\qquad \hat{p} = (285 + 452)/2{,}500 = .295$

$$z = \frac{.301 - .285}{\sqrt{(.295)(1 - .295)\left(\dfrac{1}{1{,}000} + \dfrac{1}{1{,}500}\right)}} = 0.877$$

Do not reject H_0; no evidence to suggest the market shares are different in the two areas.

8-39. Motorola (1): $\quad n_1 = 120$ $\quad x_1 = 101$ $\quad p_1 = .842$

Blaupunkt (2): $\quad n_2 = 200$ $\quad x_2 = 110$ $\quad p_2 = .550$

H_0: $p_1 \leq p_2$ $\qquad H_1$: $p_1 > p_2$ $\qquad \hat{p} = (101 + 110)/320 = .659$

$$z = \frac{.842 - .550}{\sqrt{(.659)(1 - .659)\left(\dfrac{1}{120} + \dfrac{1}{200}\right)}} = 5.33$$

Strongly reject H_0; Motorola's system is superior (p-value is very small).

8-40. Old method (1): $n_1 = 40$ $s_1^2 = 1{,}288$
New method (2): $n_2 = 15$ $s_2^2 = 1{,}112$
H_0: $\sigma_1^2 \leq \sigma_2^2$ H_1: $\sigma_1^2 > \sigma_2^2$ Use $\alpha = .05$

$F_{(39,14)} = s_1^2/s_2^2 = 1{,}288/1{,}112 = 1.158$

The critical point at $\alpha = 0.05$ is $F_{(39,14)} = 2.27$ (using approximate df in the table). Do not reject H_0. There is no evidence that the variance of the new production method is smaller.

8-41. Test the equal-variance assumption of Problem **8-27**:
H_0: $\sigma_1^2 = \sigma_2^2$ H_1: $\sigma_1^2 \neq \sigma_2^2$

$F_{(17,11)} = (5{,}000)^2/(3{,}400)^2 = 2.16$

Do not reject H_0 at $\alpha = 0.10$. (The approximate critical point is 2.7.)

8-42. "Yes" (1): $n_1 = 25$ $s_1 = 2.5$
"No" (2): $n_2 = 25$ $s_2 = 1$
H_0: $\sigma_1^2 = \sigma_2^2$ H_1: $\sigma_1^2 \neq \sigma_2^2$
Put the larger s^2 in the numerator and use 2α:

$F_{(24,24)} = s_1^2/s_2^2 = (2.5)^2/(1)^2 = 6.25$

From the F table using $\alpha = .01$, the critical point is $F_{(24,24)} = 2.66$. Therefore, reject H_0. The population variances are not equal at $\alpha = 2(.01) = 0.02$.

90% C.I. for the ratio of the two population variances:

C.I. of $(1 - 2\alpha)100\%$: $\left[\dfrac{s_1^2/s_2^2}{F_{(\alpha)}}, \dfrac{s_1^2/s_2^2}{F_{(1-\alpha)}} \right] = \left[\dfrac{6.25}{1.98}, \dfrac{6.25}{.505} \right] = [3.157, \ 12.376]$

(because $F_{.05(24,24)} = 1.98$ and the left-hand critical point is obtained as:
$F_{.95} = 1/F_{.05(24,24)} = 1/1.98 = 0.505$)

8-43. $n_1 = 21$ $s_1 = .09$ $n_2 = 28$ $s_2 = .122$
$F_{(27,20)} = (.122)^2/(.09)^2 = 1.838$

At $\alpha = .10$, we cannot reject H_0 because the critical point for $\alpha = .05$ from the table with df's $= 30, 20$ is 2.04 and for df's $24, 20$ it is 2.08. 98% C.I. for the ratio of the two population variances (interpolating for df's $30, 20$ and $24, 20$ to get $F = 2.82$, and $1/F_{.01(20,27)} = 1/2.63 = 0.38$), is found as follows: $[1.838/2.82, 1.838/.38] = [0.652, 4.837]$. The C.I. contains the value 1.00. We did not reject H_0 at $\alpha = .10$ so we would also not reject it at $\alpha = .02$. Hence this particular C.I. contains the value 1.00.

8-44. Before (1): $n_1 = 12$ $s_1^2 = 16,390.545$

After (2): $n_2 = 11$ $s_2^2 = 86,845.764$

$H_0: \sigma_1^2 = \sigma_2^2$ $H_1: \sigma_1^2 \neq \sigma_2^2$

$F_{(10,11)} = 5.298$

The critical point from the table, using $\alpha = 0.01$, is $F_{(10,11)} = 4.54$. Therefore, reject H_0. The population variances are probably not equal. p-value $< .02$ (double the α).

8-45. $n_1 = 25$ $s_1 = 2.5$ $n_2 = 25$ $s_2 = 3.1$

$H_0: \sigma_1^2 = \sigma_2^2$ $H_1: \sigma_1^2 \neq \sigma_2^2$ $\alpha = .02$

$F_{(24,24)} = (3.1)^2/(2.5)^2 = 1.538$

From the table: $F_{.01(24,24)} = 2.66$. Do not reject H_0. There is no evidence that the variances in the two waiting lines are unequal.

8-46. $n_A = 25$ $s_A^2 = 6.52$ $n_B = 22$ $s_B^2 = 3.47$

$H_0: \sigma_A^2 \leq \sigma_B^2$ $H_1: \sigma_A^2 > \sigma_B^2$ $\alpha = .01$

$F_{(24,21)} = 6.52/3.47 = 1.879$

The critical point for $\alpha = .01$ is $F_{(24,21)} = 2.80$. Do not reject H_0. There is no evidence that stock A is riskier than stock B.

8-47. The assumptions we need are: independent random sampling from the populations in question, and normal population distributions. The normality assumption is not terribly crucial as long as no serious violations of this assumption exist. In time series data, the assumption of random sampling is often violated when the observations are dependent on each other through time. We must be careful.

8-48. Savannah (1): $n_1 = 17$ $\bar{x}_1 = 6.8235294$ $s_1 = 1.4677915$

Kingston (2): $n_2 = 9$ $\bar{x}_2 = 8.2222222$ $s_2 = 2.3333333$

$H_0: \mu_1 - \mu_2 = 0$ $H_1: \mu_1 - \mu_2 \neq 0$

$$t_{(24)} = \frac{\bar{x}_1 - \bar{x}_2 - 0}{\sqrt{\dfrac{(n_1 - 1)s_1^2 + (n_2 - 1)s_2^2}{n_1 + n_2 - 2}\left(\dfrac{1}{n_1} + \dfrac{1}{n_2}\right)}}$$

$$= \frac{1.3986928}{\sqrt{\dfrac{34.47059 + 43.555556}{24}\left(\dfrac{1}{17} + \dfrac{1}{9}\right)}} = 1.88$$

Critical point: $t_{.025(24)} = 2.064$. At $\alpha = 0.05$ there is no evidence that one port demands, on the average, more containers than the other. (If we wanted to prove $\mu_2 > \mu_1$, the answer would have been yes, because $t_{.05(24)} = 1.711 < 1.88$).

8-49. 99% C.I. for $\mu_s - \mu_k$:

$$(\bar{x}_1 - \bar{x}_2) \pm t_{.005(24)}\sqrt{\frac{(n_1 - 1)s_1^2 + (n_2 - 1)s_2^2}{n_1 + n_2 - 2}\left(\frac{1}{n_1} + \frac{1}{n_2}\right)}$$

$= (6.8235294 - 8.2222222) \pm 2.797(.743285) = [-3.4776612, 0.6802753]$

The C.I. contains zero as expected from the results of Problem **8-48**.

8-50. Japanese (1): $\quad x_1 = 85 \quad\quad n_1 = 500$
American (2): $\quad x_2 = 312 \quad\quad n_2 = 800$
H_0: $p_1 - p_2 = 0 \quad\quad H_1$: $p_1 - p_2 \neq 0$

$$\hat{p}_1 = 85/500 = .170 \quad\quad \hat{p}_2 = 312/800.390 \quad\quad \hat{p} = \frac{85 + 312}{500 + 800} = .305$$

$$z = \frac{\hat{p}_1 - \hat{p}_2}{\sqrt{\hat{p}(1 - \hat{p})\left(\dfrac{1}{n_1} + \dfrac{1}{n_2}\right)}} = \frac{.170 - .390}{\sqrt{(.305)(.695)\left(\dfrac{1}{500} + \dfrac{1}{800}\right)}} = -8.379$$

Strongly reject H_0; the two rates of casual wear are different. p-value is very small.

8-51. 95% C.I. for the difference between rates of casual wear in Problem **8-50**:

$$(\hat{p}_1 - \hat{p}_2) \pm 1.96\sqrt{\frac{\hat{p}_1(1 - \hat{p}_1)}{n_1} + \frac{\hat{p}_2(1 - \hat{p}_2)}{n_2}}$$

$$= .170 - .390 \pm 1.96\sqrt{\frac{.170(.830)}{500} + \frac{.390(.610)}{800}} = [-0.267, -0.173]$$

8-52. Chrysler (1): $\quad n_1 = 25 \quad\quad \bar{x}_1 = 9,500 \quad\quad s_1 = 1,500$
GM (2): $\quad\quad n_2 = 25 \quad\quad \bar{x}_2 = 9,780 \quad\quad s_2 = 1,500$
H_0: $\mu_2 - \mu_1 \leq 0 \quad\quad H_1$: $\mu_2 - \mu_1 > 0$

$$z = \frac{9,780 - 9,500}{\sqrt{\dfrac{24(1,500)^2 + 24(1,500)^2}{48}\left(\dfrac{1}{25} + \dfrac{1}{25}\right)}} = 0.66$$

Do not reject H_0. There is no evidence that a GM car costs more on the average.

8-53. 99% C.I. for the difference between the average cost for GM and the average cost for Chrysler:

$$(\bar{x}_1 - \bar{x}_2) \pm 2.576\sqrt{\frac{24(1{,}500)^2 + 24(1{,}500)^2}{48}\left(\frac{1}{25} + \frac{1}{25}\right)}$$

$$= 280 \pm 2.576(424.26) = [-812.9, 1{,}372.9]$$

The C.I. contains zero, as expected.

8-54. Using the method of Section 8-3 is easier and does not require the assumption of equal population variances. Redo using $n_1 = n_2 = 100$:

$$z = \frac{\bar{x}_2 - \bar{x}_1}{\sqrt{(s_1^2/n_1) + (s_2^2/n_2)}} = \frac{280}{\sqrt{(1{,}500^2/100) + (1{,}500^2/100)}} = 1.32$$

We still cannot reject H_0 (p-value $= 0.0934$).

8-55. $x_1 = 60 \qquad n_1 = 80 \qquad x_2 = 65 \qquad n_2 = 100 \qquad \hat{p} = 125/180 = .6944$

$H_0: p_1 - p_2 = 0 \qquad H_1: p_1 - p_2 \neq 0$

$$z = \frac{\hat{p}_1 - \hat{p}_2 - 0}{\sqrt{\hat{p}(1 - \hat{p})\left(\dfrac{1}{n_1} + \dfrac{1}{n_2}\right)}} = \frac{.75 - .65}{\sqrt{(.6944)(1 - .6944)\left(\dfrac{1}{80} + \dfrac{1}{100}\right)}} = 1.447$$

Do not reject H_0. There is no evidence that one movie will be more successful than the other (p-value $= 0.1478$).

8-56. 95% C.I. for the difference between the two population proportions:

$$(\hat{p}_1 - \hat{p}_2) \pm 1.96\sqrt{\frac{\hat{p}_1(1 - \hat{p}_1)}{n_1} + \frac{\hat{p}_2(1 - \hat{p}_2)}{n_2}}$$

$$= 0.10 \pm 1.96\sqrt{\frac{(.75)(.25)}{80} + \frac{(.65)(.35)}{100}} = [-0.0332, 0.2332]$$

Yes, 0 is in the C.I., as expected from the results of Problem **8-55**.

8-57. K: $\qquad n_K = 12 \qquad \bar{x}_K = 12.55 \qquad s_K = .7342281$

L: $\qquad n_L = 12 \qquad \bar{x}_L = 11.925 \qquad s_L = .3078517$

$H_0: \mu_K - \mu_L = 0 \qquad H_1: \mu_K - \mu_L \neq 0$

$$t_{(22)} = \frac{12.55 - 11.925}{\sqrt{\dfrac{11(.7342281)^2 + 11(.3078517)^2}{22}\left(\dfrac{1}{12} + \dfrac{1}{12}\right)}} = 2.719$$

Reject H_0. The critical points for $t_{(22)}$ at $\alpha = .02$ are ± 2.508. Critical points for $t_{(22)}$ at $\alpha = .01$ are ± 2.819. So $.01 < p$-value $< .02$. The L-boat is probably faster.

8-58. Do Problem **8-57** with the data being paired. The differences $K - L$ are:

$$0.2 \quad 1.0 \quad -0.2 \quad 1.0 \quad 2.2 \quad -0.2 \quad 0.8 \quad 0.9 \quad 1.0 \quad 0.2 \quad -0.6 \quad 1.2$$

$n = 12 \qquad \bar{D} = .625 \qquad s_D = .7723929$

$$t_{(11)} = \frac{.625 - 0}{.7723929/\sqrt{12}} = 2.803$$

$2.718 < 2.803 < 3.106$ (between the critical points of $t_{(11)}$ for $\alpha = .01$ and $.02$). Hence, $.01 < p$-value $< .02$, which is as before, in Problem **8-57** (the pairing did not help much here—we reach the same conclusion).

8-59. The variables Relationship Quality, Distributive Fairness, and Environmental Uncertainty all showed non-significant differences (the tests for differing sample means did not have low enough p-values to permit rejection of the null hypothesis of equal means). The remaining variables all showed very significant differences: the p-values are quite low. You can't deduce the difference results just from the means shown in the table because we also need to know the standard deviations of each sample.

8-60. IIT (1): $\qquad n_1 = 100 \qquad \hat{p}_1 = 0.94$

Competitor (2): $n_2 = 125 \qquad \hat{p}_2 = 0.92$

H_0: $p_1 - p_2 = 0 \qquad H_1$: $p_1 - p_2 \neq 0 \qquad \hat{p} = .92888$

$$z = \frac{.02}{\sqrt{(.9288)(1 - .9288)\left(\dfrac{1}{100} + \dfrac{1}{125}\right)}} = 0.58$$

There is no evidence that one program is more successful than the other.

8-61. Design (1): $\quad n_1 = 15 \qquad \bar{x}_1 = 2.17333 \qquad s_1 = .3750555$

Design (2): $\quad n_2 = 13 \qquad \bar{x}_2 = 2.5153846 \qquad s_2 = .3508232$

H_0: $\mu_1 - \mu_2 = 0 \qquad H_1$: $\mu_1 - \mu_2 \neq 0$

$$t_{(26)} = \frac{2.5153846 - 2.173333}{\sqrt{\dfrac{14(.3750555)^2 + 12(.3508232)^2}{26}\left(\dfrac{1}{15} + \dfrac{1}{13}\right)}} = 2.479$$

p-value $= .02$. Reject H_0. Design 1 is probably faster.

8-62. H_0: $\sigma_1^2 = \sigma_2^2 \qquad H_1$: $\sigma_1^2 \neq \sigma_2^2$

$$F_{(14,12)} = s_1^2/s_2^2 = (.3750555)^2/(.3508232)^2 = 1.143$$

Do not reject H_0 at $\alpha = 0.10$. (Since $1.143 < 2.62$. Also < 2.10, so the p-value > 0.20.) The solution of Problem **8-61** is valid from the equal-variance requirement.

8-63. A = After: $n_A = 16$ $\bar{x}_A = 91.75$ $s_A = 5.0265959$

B = Before: $n_B = 15$ $\bar{x}_B = 84.7333$ $s_B = 5.3514573$

H_0: $\mu_A - \mu_B \leq 5$ H_1: $\mu_A - \mu_B > 5$

$$t_{(29)} = \frac{91.75 - 84.733 - 5}{\sqrt{\dfrac{15(5.0265959)^2 + 14(5.3514573)^2}{29}\left(\dfrac{1}{16} + \dfrac{1}{15}\right)}} = 1.08$$

Do not reject H_0. There is no evidence that advertising is effective.

8-64. H_0: $\sigma_1^2 = \sigma_2^2$ H_1: $\sigma_1^2 \neq \sigma_2^2$

$F_{(14,15)} = (5.3514573)^2/(5.0265959)^2 = 1.133$

Do not reject H_0 at $\alpha = 0.10$. There is no evidence that the population variances are not equal.

8-65. Savannah (1): $n_1 = 17$ $s_1 = 1.4677915$

Kingston (2): $n_2 = 9$ $s_2 = 2.333333$

H_0: $\sigma_1^2 \leq \sigma_2^2$ H_1: $\sigma_1^2 > \sigma_2^2$

Since $s_1^2 < s_2^2$, do not reject H_0.

8-66. H_0: $\sigma_K^2 = \sigma_L^2$ H_1: $\sigma_K^2 \neq \sigma_L^2$

$F_{(11,11)} = (.7342281)^2/(.3078517)^2 = 5.688$

Critical point for $\alpha = 0.02$ is about 4.5. Therefore, reject H_0. Thus the analysis in Problem **8-57** is not valid. We need to use the other test. The other test also gives $t = 2.719$ but the df are obtained using Equation (8-6):

$$\text{df} = \frac{\left(s_1^2/n_1 + s_2^2/n_2\right)^2}{\dfrac{(s_1^2/n_1)^2}{n_1 - 1} + \dfrac{(s_2^2/n_2)^2}{n_2 - 1}} = \text{approximately 14 (rounded downward).}$$

$t_{.02(14)} = 2.624 < 2.719 < 2.977 = t_{.01(14)}$, hence $0.01 < p$-value < 0.02. Reject H_0.

8-67. Differences $A - B$:

   -11 -3 3 14 -8 -10 -5 -7 2 -2 -12 6 -5 10 -22 12

$\bar{D} = -2.375$ $s_D = 9.7425185$ $n = 16$

$$t_{(15)} = \frac{-2.375 - 0}{9.7425185/\sqrt{16}} = -0.9751$$

Do not reject H_0. There is no evidence that one package is better liked than the other.

8-68.

Supplier A: $n_A = 200$ $x_A = 12$

Supplier B: $n_B = 250$ $x_B = 38$

H_0: $p_A - p_B = 0$ H_1: $p_A - p_B \neq 0$ $\hat{p} = (12 + 38)/450 = .1111$

$$z = \frac{\hat{p}_A - \hat{p}_B - 0}{\sqrt{\hat{p}(1 - \hat{p})\left(\dfrac{1}{n_1} + \dfrac{1}{n_2}\right)}} = \frac{.06 - .152}{\sqrt{(.1111)(.8888)\left(\dfrac{1}{200} + \dfrac{1}{250}\right)}} = -3.086$$

Reject H_0. p-value $= .002$. Supplier A is probably more reliable as the proportion of defective components is lower.

8-69. 95% C.I. for the difference in the proportion of defective items for the two suppliers:

$$(\hat{p}_B - \hat{p}_A) \pm 1.96\sqrt{\frac{\hat{p}_A(1 - \hat{p}_A)}{n_A} + \frac{\hat{p}_B(1 - \hat{p}_B)}{n_B}}$$

$$= .092 \pm 1.96(.0282415) = [0.0366, 0.1474].$$

8-70. 90% C.I. for the difference in average occupancy rate at the Westin Plaza Hotel before and after the advertising:

$$(\bar{x}_B - \bar{x}_A) \pm 1.699\sqrt{\frac{15(5.0265959)^2 + 14(5.3514573)^2}{29}\left(\frac{1}{15} + \frac{1}{16}\right)}$$

$$= 7.016667 \pm 3.1666375 = [3.85, 10.18] \text{ percent occupancy.}$$

8-71.

Machine A: $n_A = 25$ $s_A^2 = 561$

Machine B: $n_B = 18$ $s_B^2 = 386$

H_0: $\sigma_A^2 = \sigma_B^2$ H_1: $\sigma_A^2 \neq \sigma_B^2$

$F_{(24,17)} = 561/386 = 1.453$

Critical point at $\alpha = .05$ for $F_{(24,17)}$ is 2.19. Therefore, do not reject H_0 at $\alpha = 0.10$.

8-72. $F_{(k_1,k_2)} = \dfrac{\chi_{(k_1)}^2/k_1}{\chi_{(k_2)}^2/k_2}$ where $\chi_{(k_1)}^2$ is independent of $\chi_{(k_2)}^2$.

8-73. 99% C.I. for the difference in mean time to complete a computation using the two methods in Problem **8-61**:

$$(2.5153846 - 2.173333) \pm 2.779\sqrt{\frac{14(.3750555)^2 + 12(.3508232)^2}{29}\left(\frac{1}{15} + \frac{1}{13}\right)}$$

$= [-0.0413, 0.7254].$ The C.I. contains zero (because H_0 in Problem **8-61** would not have been rejected at $\alpha = 0.01$).

8-74.
USA (1): $p_1 = .395$ $n_1 = 1,000$ $x_1 = 395$
USSR (2): $p_2 = .429$ $n_2 = 1,000$ $x_2 = 429$
H_0: $p_1 - p_2 = 0$ H_1: $p_1 - p_2 \neq 0$ $\hat{p} = (395 + 429)/2,000 = .412$

$$z = \frac{.395 - .429}{\sqrt{.412(1 - .412)\left(\dfrac{1}{1,000} + \dfrac{1}{1,000}\right)}} = -1.545$$

Do not reject H_0; no evidence to believe the two proportions are significantly different.

8-75. This is a t-test for H_0: $\mu_1 \leq \mu_2$ vs. H_1: $\mu_1 > \mu_2$ of two independent samples of sizes 16, 17 respectively. The p-value $= 0.85$ resulting from $t_{(27)} = -1.05$ shows that H_0 cannot be rejected, and $[-2.62, 0.85]$ is the 95% confidence interval for $\mu_1 - \mu_2$.

8-76. This is a t-test using a pooled estimate of the population variance, for H_0: $\mu_1 = \mu_2$ vs. H_1: $\mu_1 \neq \mu_2$ of two independent samples of sizes 16, 17 respectively. The p-value < 0.0000 resulting from the statistic $t_{(31)} = 11.07$ indicates strong rejection of H_0, i.e., good evidence that the two population means differ, also evidenced by the 95% C.I. for $\mu_1 - \mu_2 = [8.00, 11.61]$ which does not contain 0.

Case 8.

Assume the two groups are *independent* random samples of Dow-Jones price changes. Also assume normal populations of changes. The groups are:

No-test period (NT): Jan. 5–Jan. 14, and Jan. 25 (9 data points)

Test period (T): Jan. 15–Jan. 22 (6 data points)

We want to test whether there is higher volatility—higher variance—when there is program trading (as during the No-test period):

H_0: $\sigma_{NT}^2 \leq \sigma_T^2$ H_1: $\sigma_{NT}^2 > \sigma_T^2$

Compute the sample variances:

$S_{NT}^2 = 3,514.0775$ $S_T^2 = 1,083.436$

$F_{(8,5)} = 3,514.0775/1,083.436 = 3.243 < 4.82$, the critical point $F_{(8,5)}$ at $\alpha = 0.05$. Using the $\alpha = 0.10$ table we find the critical point at $\alpha = 0.10$: $F_{(8,5)} = 3.34$. Therefore, there is no evidence (p-value $> .10$) for the hypothesis that program trading increases volatility of Dow-Jones price changes. Since we get a high $F = 3.243$, I would recommend that NYSE ask its member firms to refrain from program trading for a longer test period, and see what happens. Also, not all program traders refrained from program trading during the test period (only member firms did so), and this weakened the test.

CHAPTER 9

9-1. H_0:   X X X X $\mu_1 = \mu_2 = \mu_3 = \mu_4$

H_1:   X X X X   All 4 are different

X X X X   2 equal; 2 different

X X X X   3 equal; 1 different

X X X X   2 equal; other 2 equal but different from first 2

9-2.   ANOVA assumptions: normal populations with equal variance. Independent random sampling from the r populations.

9-3.   Series of paired t-tests are *dependent* on each other. There is no control over the probability of a Type I error for the joint *series* of tests.

9-4. $r = 5$ $n_1 = n_2 = \ldots = n_5 = 21$ $n = 105$
df's of F are 4 and 100. Computed $F = 3.6$. The p-value is close to 0.01. Reject H_0. There is evidence that not all 5 plants have equal average output.

9-5. $r = 4$ $n_1 = 52$ $n_2 = 38$ $n_3 = 43$ $n_4 = 47$
Computed $F = 12.53$. Reject H_0. The average price per lot is not equal at all 4 cities. Feel very strongly about rejecting the null hypothesis as the critical point of $F_{(3,176)}$ for $\alpha = .01$ is approximately 3.8.

9-6.   Treatment deviation = deviation of a sample mean from the grand mean.
Error deviation = deviation of a data point from its sample mean.

9-7.   Because the sum of all the deviations from a mean is equal to 0.

9-8.   Total deviation $= x_{ij} - \bar{\bar{x}} = (\bar{x}_i - \bar{\bar{x}}) + (x_{ij} - \bar{x}_i)$
$$= \text{treatment deviation} + \text{error deviation}.$$

9-9.   The sum of squares principle says that the sum of the squared total deviations of all the data points is equal to the sum of the squared treatment deviations plus the sum of all squared error deviations in the data.

9-10. An error is any deviation from a sample mean that is not explained by differences among populations. An error may be due to a host of factors not studied in the experiment.

9-11. Both MSTR and MSE are *sample statistics* given to natural variation about their own means. (If $\bar{x} > \mu_0$ we cannot immediately reject H_0 in a single-sample case either.)

9-12. The main principle of ANOVA is that if the r population means are not all equal then it is likely that the variation of the data points about their sample means will be small compared to the variation of the sample means about the grand mean.

9-13. Distances among population means manifest themselves in treatment deviations that are large relative to error deviations. When these deviations are squared, added, and then divided by df's, they give two variances. When the treatment variance is (significantly) greater than the error variance, population mean differences are likely to exist.

9-14. Within: error (data point − sample mean)
Between (among): treatment (sample mean − grand mean)
Unexplained: error
Explained: treatment

9-15. SSTO = SSTR + SSE, but MSTO $\neq$ MSTR + MSE. A counterexample:
Let $n = 21$ $r = 6$ SSTO = 100   SSTR = 85   SSE = 15
(So SSTO = SSTR + SSE).   But:
$$\text{MSTR} + \text{MSE} = \frac{\text{SSTR}}{r-1} + \frac{\text{SSE}}{n-r} = \frac{85}{5} + \frac{15}{15} = 18 \neq 5 = \frac{\text{SSTO}}{n-1} = \text{MSTO}$$

9-16. When the null hypothesis of ANOVA is false, the ratio MSTR/MSE is not the ratio of two independent, unbiased estimators of the common population variance σ^2, hence this ratio does not follow an F distribution.

9-17. For each observation x_{ij}, we know that

$$(\text{tot.}) = (\text{treat.}) + (\text{error}): \qquad x_{ij} - \bar{\bar{x}} = (\bar{x}_i - \bar{\bar{x}}) + (x_{ij} - \bar{x}_i)$$

Squaring both sides of the equation:

$$(x_{ij} - \bar{\bar{x}})^2 = (\bar{x}_i - \bar{\bar{x}})^2 + 2(\bar{x}_i - \bar{\bar{x}})(x_{ij} - \bar{x}_i) + (x_{ij} - \bar{x}_i)^2$$

Now sum this over all observations (all treatments $i = 1, \ldots, r$; and within treatment i, all observations $j = 1, \ldots, n_i$):

$$\sum_{i=1}^{r}\sum_{j=1}^{n_i}(x_{ij} - \bar{\bar{x}})^2 = \sum_{i=1}^{r}\sum_{j=1}^{n_i}(\bar{x}_i - \bar{\bar{x}})^2 + \sum_{i=1}^{r}\sum_{j=1}^{n_i}2(\bar{x}_i - \bar{\bar{x}})(x_{ij} - \bar{x}_i) + \sum_{i=1}^{r}\sum_{j=1}^{n_i}(x_{ij} - \bar{x}_i)^2$$

Notice that the first sum of the R.H.S. here equals $\displaystyle\sum_{i=1}^{r} n_i(\bar{x}_i - \bar{\bar{x}})^2$ since for each i the summand doesn't vary over each of the n_i values of j. Similarly the second sum is $2\displaystyle\sum_{i=1}^{r}\left[(\bar{x}_i - \bar{\bar{x}})\sum_{j=1}^{n_i}(x_{ij} - \bar{x}_i)\right]$. But for each fixed i, $\displaystyle\sum_{j=1}^{n_i}(x_{ij} - \bar{x}_i) = 0$ since this is just the sum of all deviations from the mean within treatment i. Thus the whole second sum in the long R.H.S. above is 0, and the equation is now

$$\sum_{i=1}^{r}\sum_{j=1}^{n_i}(x_{ij} - \bar{\bar{x}})^2 = \sum_{i=1}^{r} n_i(\bar{x}_i - \bar{\bar{x}})^2 + \sum_{i=1}^{r}\sum_{j=1}^{n_i}(x_{ij} - \bar{x}_i)^2$$

which is precisely Equation (9-12).

9-18. (From Minitab):

Source	df	SS	MS	F
Treatment	2	381127	190563	20.71
Error	27	248460	9202	
Total	29	629587		

The critical point for $F_{(2,27)}$ at $\alpha = 0.01$ is 5.49. Therefore, reject H_0. The average range of the 3 prototype planes is probably not equal.

9-19. (From Minitab):

Source	df	SS	MS	F
Treatment	3	0.1152	0.0384	1.47
Error	28	0.7315	0.0261	
Total	31	0.8467		

Critical point $F_{(3,28)}$ for $\alpha = 0.01$ is 2.29. Therefore we cannot reject H_0. There is no evidence of differences in the average price per barrel of oil from the four sources. The Rotterdam oil market may be efficient. The conclusion is valid only for Rotterdam, and only for Arabian Light. Also, non-rejection of a null hypothesis is a *weak* conclusion. We need to assume *independent random samples* from these populations, normal populations with equal population variance. Observations are time-dependent (days during February), thus the assumptions could be violated. This is a limitation of the study. Another limitation is that February may be different from other months.

9-20. $n_1 = 20$ $n_2 = 18$ $n_3 = 21$ SSE = 1,240   SSTR = 740

Source	df	SS	MS	F
Treatment	2	740	370.00	16.71
Error	56	1240	22.14	
Total	58	1980		

$16.71 > F_{(2,56)}$ for $\alpha = 0.01$, which is about 4.98. Therefore reject H_0. Not all sweater types last the same time, on average.

9-21.   The null hypothesis that all four means (of brand effectiveness) are equal could not be rejected, because the F-ratio was well within a normal range given the data. So these four particular firms probably do not differ much in their effectiveness in developing and managing social brands (or if they do, the samples used do not provide the evidence for it).

9-22. $n_1 = 50$ $n_2 = 32$ $n_3 = 28$ SSE = 22,399.8   SSTO = 32,156.1

Source	df	SS	MS	F
Treatment	2	9756.3	4848.15	23.3
Error	107	22399.8	209.34	
Total	109	32156.1		

$23.3 > F_{.01(2,107)} = 4.82$. Therefore, reject H_0. Differences in average annualized returns do exist. Manager should shift proportions of the fund.

9-23. $r = 8$ $n_i = 100$ for all $i = 1, \ldots, 8$ $n = 800$
SSTR = 45,210   SSTO = 92,340

Source	df	SS	MS	F
Treatment	7	45210	6458.57	108.53
Error	792	47130	59.51	
Total	799	92340		

108.53 is much greater than the value of $F_{.01(7,792)}$, which is approximately 2.66. Reject H_0. There is evidence that not all 8 brands have equal average consumer quality ratings.

9-24. 95% C.I.'s for the mean responses:

Martinique: $\bar{x}_2 \pm t_{\alpha/2}\sqrt{\text{MSE}/n_2} = 75 \pm 1.96\sqrt{504.4/40} = [68.04, 81.96]$

Eleuthera: $73 \pm 1.96\sqrt{\text{MSE}/n_3} = [66.04, 79.96]$

Paradise Island: $91 \pm 1.96\sqrt{\text{MSE}/n_4} = [84.04, 97.96]$

St. Lucia: $85 \pm 1.96\sqrt{\text{MSE}/n_5} = [78.04, 91.96]$

9-25. Where do differences exist in the circle-square-triangle populations from Table 9-1, using Tukey? From the text: $\quad$ MSE $= 2.125$

triangles: $n_1 = 4 \quad \bar{x}_1 = 6$

squares: $\quad n_2 = 4 \quad \bar{x}_2 = 11.5$

circles: $\quad n_3 = 3 \quad \bar{x}_3 = 2$

For $\alpha = 0.01$, $q_{\alpha(r,n-r)} = q_{0.01(3,8)} = 5.63$. Smallest n_i is 3:
$T = q_\alpha\sqrt{\text{MSE}/3} = 5.63\sqrt{2.125/3} = 4.738$

$|\bar{x}_1 - \bar{x}_2| = 5.5 > 4.738 \qquad$ sig.

$|\bar{x}_2 - \bar{x}_3| = 9.5 > 4.738 \qquad$ sig.

$|\bar{x}_1 - \bar{x}_3| = 4.0 < 4.738 \qquad$ n.s.

Thus: "1 = 3"; "2 > 1"; "2 > 3"

9-26. Find which prototype planes are different in Problem 9-18:

MSE $= 9{,}202 \qquad n_i = 10$ for all $i \qquad \bar{x}_A = 4{,}407 \qquad \bar{x}_B = 4{,}230 \qquad \bar{x}_C = 4{,}135$

For $\alpha = 0.05$, $q_{\alpha(3,27)} =$ approximately 3.51. $T = 3.51\sqrt{9{,}202/10} = 106.475$

$|\bar{x}_A - \bar{x}_B| = 177 > 106.475 \qquad$ sig.

$|\bar{x}_B - \bar{x}_C| = 95 < 106.475 \qquad$ n.s.

$|\bar{x}_A - \bar{x}_C| = 272 > 106.475 \qquad$ sig.

Prototype A is shown to have higher average range than both B and C. Prototypes B and C have no significant difference in average range (all conclusions are at $\alpha = 0.05$).

9-27. Since H_0 was not rejected in Problem **9-19**, there are no significant differences. (Let's try anyway.) $T = q_{0.05(4,28)}\sqrt{.0261/8} = 0.22$

$|17.996 - 17.984| = 0.012$

$|17.996 - 18.136| = 0.140$

$|17.996 - 18.048| = 0.052$

$|17.984 - 18.136| = 0.152$

$|17.984 - 18.048| = 0.064$

$|18.136 - 18.048| = 0.088$

All are < 0.22, thus not significant—as expected.

9-28. $\bar{x}_{\text{Irish}} = 6.4 \qquad \bar{x}_{\text{Peruvian}} = 2.5 \qquad \bar{x}_{\text{Shetland}} = 4.9 \qquad \text{MSE} = 22.14$

$q_{0.05(3,56)} = 3.4 \qquad T = 3.4\sqrt{22.14/18} = 3.77$

I,P: $|6.4 - 2.5| = 3.9 > 3.77$

I,S: $|6.4 - 4.9| = 1.5 < 3.77$

P,S: $|2.5 - 4.9| = 2.4 < 3.77$

Only significant difference at 0.05 is I,P. There is evidence that $\mu_{\text{Irish}} > \mu_{\text{Peruvian}}$, but I,S and P,S are not significantly different.

9-29. $\text{MSE} = 59.51 \qquad n_i = 100$ for all $i \qquad \alpha = 0.01$

$q_{.01(8,792)} = 4.99 \qquad T = 4.99\sqrt{59.51/100} = 3.85$

Absolute differences (the starred ones denoting that the difference is greater than 3.85, thus significant at $\alpha = 0.01$):

$|M - G| = 1$, $|M - P| = 5^*$, $|M - Z| = 17^*$, $|M - S| = 11^*$, $|M - Ph| = 12^*$, $|M - Sl| = 13^*$, $|M - R| = 10^*$, $|G - P| = 4^*$, $|G - Z| = 16^*$, $|G - S| = 10^*$, $|G - Ph| = 11^*$, $|G - Sl| = 12^*$, $|G - R| = 9^*$, $|P - Z| = 12^*$, $|P - S| = 6^*$, $|P - Ph| = 7^*$, $|P - Sl| = 8^*$, $|P - R| = 5^*$, $|Z - S| = 6^*$, $|Z - Ph| = 5^*$, $|Z - Sl| = 4^*$, $|Z - R| = 7^*$, $|S - Ph| = 1$, $|S - Sl| = 2$, $|S - R| = 1$, $|Ph - R| = 2$, $|Ph - Sl| = 1$, $|Sl - R| = 3$. Thus the significant differences are shown below (a circle around two or more brands implies no significant difference in average ratings at $\alpha = 0.01$):

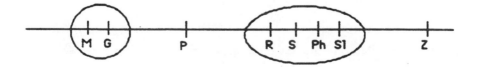

9-30. $\alpha = 0.05$ $n_i = 31$ for all i MSE $= 49.5$

$\bar{x}_1 = 18$ $\bar{x}_2 = 11$ $\bar{x}_3 = 15$ $\bar{x}_4 = 14$

$T = q_{0.05(4,120)} \sqrt{49.5/31} = 3.68 \sqrt{49.5/31} = 4.65$

Only investments 1 and 2 have significantly different annualized average returns, at $\alpha = 0.05$. $|\bar{x}_1 - \bar{x}_2| = 18 - 11 = 7 > 4.65$

9-31. We cannot extend the results to planes built after the analysis. We used fixed effects here, not random effects. The 3 prototypes were not randomly chosen from a population of levels as would be required for the random effects model.

9-32. A randomized complete block design is a design with restricted randomization. Each block of experimental units is assigned to treatments with randomization of treatments within the block.

9-33. Fly all 3 planes on the same route every time. The route (flown by the 3 planes) is the block.

9-34. Look at the residuals. If the spread of the residuals is not equal, we probably have unequal σ^2, the assumption of equal variances is violated. A histogram of the residuals will reveal normality violations. If there are violations of the ANOVA assumptions, use the Kruskal-Wallis test instead of ANOVA.

9-35. Otherwise you are not randomly sampling from a population of treatments, and inference is not valid for the entire "population."

9-36. No. Rotterdam (and Arabian Light) was not randomly chosen.

9-37. If the locations and the artists are chosen randomly, we have a random effects model.

9-38. 1. Testing for possible interactions among factor levels.
2. Efficiency.

9-39. Limitations and problems: (1) We don't know the overall significance level of the 3 tests; (2) If we have 1 observation per cell then there are 0 degrees of freedom for error. Also, for a fixed sample size there is a reduction of the df for error.

9-40.   1. As more factors are included, df for error decreases.

2. As more factors are included, we lose the control on α, and the probability of at least one Type I error increases.

9-41.   Table entry with the nearest denominator is $F_{(4,150)} = 3.44$ at $\alpha = 0.01$. Hence we can reject H_0 (no interaction) at a p-value < 0.01—good evidence.

9-42.   At $\alpha = 0.05$:

Location: $F = 50.6$, significant

Job type: $F = 50.18$, significant

Interaction: $F = 2.14$, n.s.

9-43.

	ABC	CBS	NBC	Source	SS	df	MS	F
Morning	50	50	50	Network	145	2	72.5	5.16
Evening	50	50	50	Newstime	160	2	80	5.69
Late Night	50	50	50	Interaction	240	4	60	4.27
				Error	6200	441	14.06	
				Total	6745	449		

From table: $F_{0.01(4,400)} = 3.36$ $F_{0.01(2,400)} = 4.66$

Therefore, all are significant at $\alpha = 0.01$. There are interactions. There are Network main effects averaged over Newstime levels. There are Newstime main effects averaged over Network levels.

9-44.   **a.** Levels of task difficulty: $a - 1 = 1$; therefore $a - 2$

b. Levels of effort: $b - 1 = 1$; therefore $b = 2$

c. There are no task difficulty main effects because p-value $= 0.5357$

d. There are effort main effects because p-value < 0.0001

e. There are no significant interactions, as p-value $= 0.1649$.

9-45. **a.** Explained is "Treatment":   Treat $=$ Factor A $+$ Factor B $+$ (AB)

b. Levels of exercise price: $a - 1 = 2$; therefore $a = 3$

c. Levels of time of expiration: $b - 1 = 1$; therefore $b = 2$

d. $ab(n - 1) = 144$, $a = 3$, $b = 2$; therefore $n - 1 = 24$, $n = 25$, $N = 25 \cdot 6 = 150$

e. $n = 25$

f. There are no exercise-price main effects ($F = 0.42 < 1$).

g. There are time-of-expiration main effects at $\alpha = 0.05$ but not at $\alpha = 0.01$ because $F_{(1,144)} = 4.845$. From the F table, for df's $= 1, 150$: critical point for $\alpha = 0.05$ is 3.91 and for $\alpha = 0.01$ it is 6.81.

h. There are no interactions: $F = .193 < 1$

i. There is some evidence for time-of-expiration main effects. There is no evidence for exercise-price main effects or interaction effects.

j. For time-of-expiration main effects, $.01 < p\text{-value} < .05$. For the other two tests, the p-values are very high.

k. We could use a t-test for time-of-expiration effects: $t^2_{(144)} = F_{(1,144)}$

9-46. All Outcome variables except YL are highly significant, as are the Group variables Y and YL. None of the others, including interactions, are significant.

9-47. Advantages: reduced experimental errors and great economy of sample size. Disadvantages: restrictive, because it requires that number of treatments $=$ number of rows $=$ number of columns.

9-48. Use blocking by firm, to reduce the error contributions arising from differences between firms.

9-49. We could have a Latin square: 4 observations, UK, Mexico, UAE, Oman at 4 locations and 4 different dates.

9-50. Block by firm, in a randomized complete blocking design.

9-51. Yes. Have people of the same occupation/age/demographics use sweaters of the 3 kinds under study. Each group of 3 people are a block.

9-52. Repeated measures design: have every person evaluate all 8 kinds of color television set.

9-53. We could group the executives into blocks according to some choice of common characteristics such as age, sex, years employed at current firm, etc. The different blocks for the chosen attribute would then form a third variable beyond Location and Type to use in a 3-way ANOVA.

9-54. We must assume no block-factor interactions.

9-55. SSTR = 3,233   SSE = 12,386 $n = 100$ blocks

df error $= (n-1)(r-1) = 99(2) = 198$ df treatment $= r - 1 = 2$

$F = \text{MSTR/MSE} = \dfrac{3,233/2}{12,386/198} = 25.84$

Reject H_0. p-value is very small. There are differences among the 3 sweeteners. Should be very confident of results. Blocking reduces experimental error here, as people of the same weight/age/sex will tend to behave homogeneously with respect to losing weight.

9-56. $n = 70$ $r = 4$

SSTR = 9,875   SSBL = 1,445   SSTO = 22,364

SSE $= 22,364 - 1,445 - 9,875 = 11,044$

MSE $= \dfrac{11,044}{(69)(3)} = 53.35$ MSTR $= \dfrac{9,875}{3} = 3,291.67$

$F_{(3,207)} = \text{MSTR/MSE} = 61.7$

Reject H_0. p-value is very small. Not all of the four methods are equally effective.

9-57. SSTR = 7,102   SSE = 10,511 $r = 8$ $n_i = 20$ for all i

MSTR $= \text{SSTR}/(r-1) = 7,102/7 = 1,014.57$

MSE $= \text{SSE}/(n-r) = 10,511/(160-8) = 69.15$

$F_{(7,152)} = 14.67 > 2.76$ (crit. point for $\alpha = 0.01$). Therefore, reject H_0. Not all tapes are equally appealing. p-value is very small.

9-58. $n_1 = 32$ $n_2 = 30$ $n_3 = 38$ $n_4 = 41$ $n = 141$
MSTR = SSTR$/(r - 1) = 4{,}537/3 = 1{,}512.33$
$F_{(3,137)}$ = MSTR/MSE = $1{,}512.33/412 = 3.67$
(at $\alpha = 0.05$) $2.67 < 3.67 < 3.92$ (at $\alpha = 0.01$)

We can reject H$_0$ at $\alpha = 0.05$. There is some evidence that the four names are not all equally well liked.

9-59. At $\alpha = 0.05$, using the nearest table entry: $F_{(1,40)} = 4.08$, we find evidence of a taste cue positioning effect, a gender effect, and an interaction. Thus the differences due to taste cue positioning are averaged over gender, and *vice versa*.

9-60. Software packages: 3   Computers: 4
SS software = 77,645
SS computer = 54,521
SS int. = 88,699
SSE = 434,557
$n = 60$

Source	SS	df	MS	F
software	77,645	2	38,822.5	63.25
computer	54,521	3	18,173.667	29.60
interaction	88,699	6	14,783.167	24.09
error	434,557	708	613.78	
Total	655,422	719		

Both main effects and the interactions are highly significant.

9-61.

Source	SS	df	MS	F
process	165.644	2	82.822	14.252
film	1,363.378	2	681.689	117.308
interaction	247.022	4	61.756	10.627
error	209.200	36	5.811	

Film and Process effects are highly significant and so are the interactions.

9-62. At $\alpha = 0.05$, only the following effects are significant:

For RDIFF: METH, METH $\times$ UNIQ, METH $\times$ SE, UNIQ $\times$ P.
For BIAS: METH, METH $\times$ UNIQ, SE $\times$ P.
For BE: UNIQ, UNIQ $\times$ P, SE $\times$ P.

9-63.

Source	SS	df	MS	F
pet	22,245	3	7,415	1.93
location	34,551	3	11,517	2.99
interaction	31,778	9	3,530.89	0.92
error	554,398	144	3,849.99	
Total	642,972	159		

There are no interactions. There are no pet main effects.

$(\alpha = 0.05)$ $2.68 < 2.99 < 3.95$ $(\alpha = 0.01)$

Thus there are location main effects at $\alpha = 0.05$.

9-64. F-ratio $= 4.5471$ p-value $= .0138$ (using a computer). At $\alpha = 0.05$, only groups 1 and 3 are significantly different from each other. Drug group is significantly different from the No Treatment group.

9-65. **a.** Blocking (repeated measures) is more efficient as every person is his/her own control. Reductions in errors. Limitations? Maybe carryover effects from trial to trial.

b. SSTR $= 44,572$ SSE $= 112,672$ $r = 3$ $n = 30$

MSTR $= 44,572/2 = 22,286$

MSE $= 112,672/(29)(2) = 1,942.62$

$F_{(2,58)} = 11.47$.   Reject H_0.

9-66. $n_1 = n_2 = n_3 = 15$ $r = 3$ A one-way ANOVA gives an F-value of 22.21, which is significant even at $\alpha < 0.001$, hence we reject the hypothesis of no differences among the three models. MSE $= 48.1$, so at $\alpha = 0.01$ we use the critical point $q_\alpha = 4.37$ (closest to the required value for df's $= 3, 42$), giving the Tukey criterion $T = q_\alpha \sqrt{MSE}/\sqrt{n_i} = 7.83$. Observed means:

$\bar{x}_{GI} = 124.73$ $\bar{x}_P = 121.40$ $\bar{x}_Z = 108.73$

So: $|\bar{x}_{GI} - \bar{x}_P| = 3.33$ $|\bar{x}_{GI} - \bar{x}_Z| = 16.00\,^*$ $|\bar{x}_P - \bar{x}_Z| = 12.67\,^*$

Using $T = 7.83$, we reject the hypothesis of $\bar{x}_{GI} = \bar{x}_Z$ and also $\bar{x}_P = \bar{x}_Z$ (at the 0.01 level of significance), but not the $\bar{x}_{GI} = \bar{x}_P$ hypothesis.

9-67. $n = 50$ $r = 3$

SSTR $= 128,899$ SSE $= 42,223.987$

$$F_{(2,98)} = \frac{128,899/2}{42,223.987/98} = 0.14958$$

Do not reject the null hypothesis.

9-68. $t^2_{(df)} = F_{(1,df)}$

9-69. Rents are equal on average. There is no evidence of differences among the four cities.

9-70. This is a test of three hypotheses: that mean toy-awareness level among the English speakers is the same as among the French speakers; that the mean level is the same among low-income subjects as among higher-income ones; and that there are no interactions between the two kinds of factors. The F-statistics give very strong evidence against the first two hypotheses; both language and income *do* have an effect on the awareness level. Furthermore, there appears to be no interaction between the two factors.

9-71. A one-way ANOVA strongly rejecting H_0. For the three levels of Store, 95% confidence intervals are calculated for the means, as shown, which don't overlap at all.

Case 9.

Assume normal populations. Use block design ANOVA:

$$\sum x^2 = 9{,}382 \qquad \sum x = 406 \qquad \sum_{i=1}^{n} x_i^2 \Big/ r = 8{,}600 \qquad \sum_{j=1}^{r} x_j^2 \Big/ n = 6{,}370$$

$SSE = 9{,}382 - 8{,}600 - 6{,}370 + 406^2/27 = 517.03$

$SSTR = 6{,}370 - 406^2/27 = 264.96$

$$F_{(2,16)} = \frac{264.96/2}{517.03/16} = 4.1 > 3.63$$

$0.01 < p\text{-value} < 0.05$. There is some evidence of differences.

Advantages: blocking reduces experimental error. Limitations: small samples.

CHAPTER 10

10-1. A statistical model is a set of mathematical formulas and assumptions that describe some real-world situation.

10-2. Steps in statistical model building: 1) Hypothesize a statistical model; 2) Estimate the model parameters; 3) Test the validity of the model; and 4) Use the model.

10-3. Assumptions of the simple linear regression model: 1) A straight-line relationship between X and Y; 2) The values of X are fixed; 3) The regression errors, ε, are identically normally distributed random variables, uncorrelated with each other through time.

10-4. β_0 is the Y-intercept of the regression line, and β_1 is the slope of the line.

10-5. The conditional mean of Y, $E(Y \mid X)$, is the population regression line.

10-6. The regression model is used for understanding the relationship between the two variables, X and Y; for prediction of Y for given values of X; and for possible control of the variable Y, using the variable X.

10-7. The error term captures the randomness in the process. Since X is assumed non-random, the addition of ε makes the result (Y) a random variable. The error term captures the effects on Y of a host of unknown random components not accounted for by the simple linear regression model.

10-8. Advertising versus sales (over a limited range of values; use: control and prediction); an accounting ratio versus firm profitability (use: understanding); return on a stock versus return on the market as a whole (use: understanding).

10-9. The least-squares procedure produces the best estimated regression line in the sense that the line lies "inside" the data set. The line is the best unbiased linear estimator of the true regression line as the estimators β_0 and β_1 have smallest variance of all linear unbiased estimators of the line parameters. Least-squares line is obtained by minimizing the sum of the squared deviations of the data points from the line.

10-10. Least squares is less useful when outliers exist. Outliers tend to have a greater influence on the determination of the estimators of the line parameters because the procedure is based on minimizing the squared distances from the line. Since outliers have large squared distances they exert undue influence on the line. A more robust procedure may be appropriate when outliers exist.

10-11. Regression output using SYSTAT:

```
DEP VAR: PLR   N: 15  MULTIPLE R: .976  SQUARED MULTIPLE R: .952
ADJUSTED SQUARED MULTIPLE R:   .948
STANDARD ERROR OF ESTIMATE:  0.184

VARIABLE  COEFFICIENT STD ERROR  STD COEF TOLERANCE    T     P(2 TAIL)


CONSTANT    -0.847       0.538       0.000          -1.573    0.140
FFR          1.352       0.084     0.976 .100E+01    16.008   0.000
```

ANALYSIS OF VARIANCE

```
   SOURCE    SUM-OF-SQUARES    DF  MEAN-SQUARE    F-RATIO      P

 REGRESSION      8.701          1     8.701       256.269    0.000
 RESIDUAL        0.441         13     0.034
```

$b_1 = 1.35$ $b_0 = -0.847$ (The rest of the results above will be used in the solution of some following problems.)

10-12. $SS_X = 4.760$ $SS_Y = 9.143$ $SS_{XY} = 6.436$ (These were actually obtained from the output above: SST, SSR, SSE, b_1, using relations, e.g. Equation (10-31), given throughout the chapter.)

10-13. $b_1 = SS_{XY}/SS_X = 934.49/765.98 = 1.22$

10-14. Using SYSTAT:

```
DEP VAR: Y   N: 13  MULTIPLE R:  .960  SQUARED MULTIPLE R:  .922
ADJUSTED SQUARED MULTIPLE R:   .915
STANDARD ERROR OF ESTIMATE:  0.995
```

VARIABLE	COEFFICIENT	STD ERROR	STD COEF	TOLERANCE	T	P(2 TAIL)
CONSTANT	-3.057	0.971		0.000	-3.148	0.009
X	0.187	0.016	0.960	.100E+01	11.381	0.000

ANALYSIS OF VARIANCE

SOURCE	SUM-OF-SQUARES	DF	MEAN-SQUARE	F-RATIO	P
REGRESSION	128.332	1	128.332	129.525	0.000
RESIDUAL	10.899	11	0.991		

Thus, $b_0 = -3.057 \qquad b_1 = 0.187$

10-15. $b_1 = \text{SS}_{XY}/\text{SS}_X = 2.11$

$b_0 = \bar{y} - b_1\bar{x} = 165.3 - (2.11)(88.9) = -22.279$

10-16. From SYSTAT:

DEP VAR: COST N:11 MULTIPLE R: .929 SQUARED MULTIPLE R: .864
ADJUSTED SQUARED MULTIPLE R: .848
STANDARD ERROR OF ESTIMATE: 168.036

VARIABLE	COEFFICIENT	STD ERROR	STD COEF	TOLERANCE	T	P(2 TAIL)
CONSTANT	2260.7	108.7		0.000	20.79	0.000
DAYS	153.60	20.35	0.929	.100E+01	7.55	0.000

ANALYSIS OF VARIANCE

SOURCE	SUM-OF-SQUARES	DF	MEAN-SQUARE	F-RATIO	P
REGRESSION	1608527.128	1	1608527.128	56.967	0.000
RESIDUAL	254124.508	9	28236.056		

Equation of the estimated regression line: Cost $= 2260.7 + 153.60\,\text{Days} + e$

10-17. From MINITAB:

```
The regression equation is
Salary = 6.11 + 0.160 Stock

Predictor        Coef       Stdev     t-ratio        p
Constant       6.1102      0.8052       7.59     0.002
Stock         0.15961     0.04104       3.89     0.018

s = 1.938       R-sq = 79.1%     R-sq(adj) = 73.9%

Analysis of Variance

SOURCE          DF          SS          MS         F        p
Regression       1      56.776      56.776     15.12    0.018
Error            4      15.017       3.754
Total            5      71.793
```

So $\beta_1 = 0.160$ $\beta_0 = 6.11$

10-18. $SSE = \sum(y - b_0 - b_1 x)^2$ Take partial derivatives with respect to b_0 and b_1:

$$\partial/\partial b_0 \left[\sum(y - b_0 - b_1 x)^2\right] = -2\sum(y - b_0 - b_1 x)$$

$$\partial/\partial b_1 \left[\sum(y - b_0 - b_1 x)^2\right] = -2\sum x(y - b_0 - b_1 x)$$

Setting the two partial derivatives to zero and simplifying, we get:

$$\sum(y - b_0 - b_1 x) = 0 \quad \text{and} \quad \sum x(y - b_0 - b_1 x) = 0. \quad \text{Expanding, we get:}$$

$$\left(\sum y\right) - n b_0 - \left(\sum x\right) b_1 = 0 \quad \text{and} \quad \left(\sum xy\right) - \left(\sum x\right) b_0 - \left(\sum x^2\right) b_1 = 0$$

Solving the above two equations simultaneously for b_0 and b_1 gives the required results.

10-19. 99% C.I. for β_1: $1.25533 \pm 2.807(0.04972) = [1.1158, 1.3949]$.
The confidence interval does not contain zero.

10-20. $MSE = 0.034$

10-21. $s(b_0) = 0.538$ $s(b_1) = 0.084$

10-22. 95% C.I. for b_0: $b_0 \pm t_{.025(13)} s(b_0) = -.847 \pm 2.16(.538) = [-2.009, 0.315]$
(contains zero);
for b_1: $b_1 \pm t_{.025(13)} s(b_1) = 1.352 \pm 2.16(.084) = [1.171, 1.533]$
(does not contain zero).

10-23. $s(b_0) = 0.971$ $s(b_1) = 0.016$;   estimate of the error variance is MSE $= 0.991$.
95% C.I. for β_1: $0.187 \pm 2.201(0.016) = [0.1518, 0.2222]$. Zero is not a plausible value at $\alpha = 0.05$.

10-24. Reading from the "Stdev" column in the MINITAB output shown in the solution to Problem **10-17**: $s(b_0) = 0.805$ $s(b_1) = 0.041$; estimate of the error variance is MSE $= 3.754$ (the "MS" column in the MINITAB output).
95% C.I. for β_1:   We use $t_{(.025,4)} = 2.776$: $0.1596 \pm 2.776(0.0410) = [0.0457, 0.2735]$ (does not contain zero)

10-25. s^2 gives us information about the variation of the data points about the computed regression line.

10-26. In correlation analysis the two variables, X and Y, are viewed in a symmetric way, where no one of them is "dependent" and the other "independent," as is the case in regression analysis. In correlation analysis we are interested in the relation between two random variables, both assumed normally distributed.

10-27. $r = 0.976$

10-28. $r = 0.960$

10-29. $t_{(9)} = \dfrac{r}{\sqrt{(1 - r^2)/(n - 2)}} = \dfrac{0.929}{\sqrt{0.0152}} = 7.53$. Reject the null hypothesis of a zero correlation in favor of the alternative that the two variables are correlated (p-value is very small).

10-30. Yes. For example, suppose $n = 5$ and $r = .51$; then:
$t = \dfrac{r}{\sqrt{(1 - r^2)/(n - 2)}} = 1.02$ and we do not reject H_0. But if we take $n = 10,000$ and $r = 0.04$, giving $t = 14.28$, this leads to strong rejection of H_0.

10-31. We have: $r = 0.875$ and $n = 10$. Conducting the test:
$t_{(8)} = \dfrac{r}{\sqrt{(1 - r^2)/(n - 2)}} = \dfrac{.875}{\sqrt{(1 - .875^2)/8}} = 5.11$
There is statistical evidence of a correlation between the prices of gold and of copper. Limitations: data are time-series data, hence not independent random samples. Also, data set contains only 10 points.

10-34. $n = 65$ $r = 0.37$ $t_{(63)} = \dfrac{.37}{\sqrt{(1 - .37^2)/63}} = 3.16$

Yes. Significant. There is a correlation between the two variables.

10-35. $z' = \dfrac{1}{2} \ln\left[(1 + r)/(1 - r)\right] = \dfrac{1}{2} \ln(1.37/0.63) = 0.3884$

$\mu' = \dfrac{1}{2} \ln\left[(1 + \rho)/(1 - \rho)\right] = \dfrac{1}{2} \ln(1.22/0.78) = 0.2237$

$\sigma' = 1/\sqrt{n - 3} = 1/\sqrt{62} = 0.127$

$z = (z' - \mu')/\sigma' = (0.3884 - 0.2237)/0.127 = 1.297.$ Cannot reject H_0.

10-36. $t_{(10)} = b_1/s(b_1) = 2.435/1.567 = 1.554.$

Do not reject H_0. There is no evidence of a linear relationship even at $\alpha = 0.10$.

10-37. $t_{(16)} = b_1/s(b_1) = 3.1/2.89 = 1.0727.$

Do not reject H_0. There is no evidence of a linear relationship using *any* α. (Why would the journal report such a non-finding?)

10-38. $b_1/s(b_1) = 1.35/.084 = 16.1$

Yes, reject H_0. There is evidence of a linear relationship between the two variables.

10-39. $t_{(11)} = b_1/s(b_1) = 0.187/0.016 = 11.69$

Reject H_0. There is strong evidence of a linear relationship between the two variables.

10-40. Test for linear relationship (Problem **10-16**):

$t_{(9)} = b_1/s(b_1) = 153.6/20.35 = 7.548$

Therefore, reject H_0: there is evidence of a linear relationship.

10-41. $t_{(58)} = b_1/s(b_1) = 1.24/0.21 = 5.90$

Yes, there is evidence of a linear relationship.

10-42. $t_{(21)} = b_1/s(b_1) = 3.467/0.775 = 4.474$

Yes, there is evidence of a linear relationship.

10-43. $t_{(211)} = z = b_1/s(b_1) = 0.68/12.03 = 0.0565$

Do not reject H_0. There is no evidence of a linear relationship using *any* α. (Why report such results?)

10-44. $b_1 = 5.49$ $s(b_1) = 1.21$ $t_{(26)} = 4.537$
Yes, there is evidence of a linear relationship.

10-45. No surprise, since there is no evidence of a linear relatinship between the two variables in Problem **10-37**.

10-46. a. The model should not be used for prediction purposes because only 0.2% of the variation in pension funding is explained by its relationship with firm profitability.

b. The model explains virtually nothing.

c. Probably not. The model explains too little.

10-47. In Problem **10-11**, $r^2 = 0.952$. Thus, 95.2% of the variation in the dependent variable is explained by the regression relationship.

10-48. In Problem **10-14**, $r^2 = 0.922$. Thus, 92.2% of the variation in the dependent variable is explained by the regression relationship.

10-49. r^2 in Problem **10-16**: $r^2 = 0.864$

10-50. Reading directly from the MINITAB output: $r^2 = 0.791$

10-51. $r^2 = \dfrac{SSR}{SST} = \dfrac{SSR}{SSR + SSE} = 0.873$. Thus, 87.3% of the variation in the dependent variable is explained by the regression relationship. Yes, the regression model should therefore be useful in predicting sales based on advertising expenditure.

10-52. No linear relations in evidence for any of the firms.

10-53. $SST = SS_Y = 12,500$
$SSR = (SS_{XY})^2/SS_X = (4,502.53)^2/2,133.9$
$r^2 = SSR/SST = 0.76$

10-54. $\sum(y - \bar{y})^2 = \sum\left[(\hat{y} - \bar{y}) + (y - \hat{y})\right]^2 = \sum\left[(\hat{y} - \bar{y})^2 + 2(\hat{y} - \bar{y})(y - \hat{y}) + (y - \hat{y})^2\right]$

$= \sum(\hat{y} - \bar{y})^2 + 2\sum(\hat{y} - \bar{y})(y - \hat{y}) + \sum(y - \hat{y})^2$

But: $2\sum(\hat{y} - \bar{y})(y - \hat{y}) = 2\sum\hat{y}(y - \hat{y}) - 2\bar{y}\sum(y - \hat{y}) = 0$ because the first term on the right is the sum of the weighted regression residuals, which sum to zero. The second term is the sum of the residuals, which is also zero. This establishes the result: $\sum(y - \bar{y})^2 = \sum(\hat{y} - \bar{y})^2 + \sum(y - \hat{y})^2$.

10-55. From Equation (10-10): $b_1 = SS_{XY}/SS_X$.   From Equation (10-31):

$SSR = b_1 SS_{XY}$.   Hence, $SSR = (SS_{XY}/SS_X)SS_{XY} = (SS_{XY})^2/SS_X$

10-56. $MSR = 8.701$ $MSE = 0.034$ $F_{(1,13)} = 256.269$ p-value very close to 0.

10-57. $F_{(1,11)} = 129.525$ $t_{(11)} = 11.381$ $t^2 = 11.381^2 = $ the F-statistic value already calculated.

10-58. $F_{(1,4)} = 15.12$ $t_{(9)} = 3.89$ $t^2 = 3.89^2 = $ the F-statistic value already calculated.

10-59. $F_{(1,n-2)} = MSR/MSE = \dfrac{SSR/1}{SSE/43} = \dfrac{9{,}500.34}{(12{,}500 - 9{,}500.34)/43} = 136.19$

Strongly reject H_0.

10-60. $F_{(1,102)} = MSR/MSE = \dfrac{87{,}691/1}{12{,}745/102} = 701.8$ There is extremely strong evidence of a linear relationship between the two variables.

10-61. $t_{(k)}^2 = F_{(1,k)}$.   Thus, $F_{(1,20)} = [b_1/s(b_1)]^2 = (2.556/4.122)^2 = 0.3845$

Do not reject H_0. There is no evidence of a linear relationship.

10-62. $t_{(k)}^2 = [b_1/s(b_1)]^2 = \left(\dfrac{SS_{XY}/SS_X}{s/\sqrt{SS_X}}\right)^2$

[using Equations (10-10) and (10-15) for b_1 and $s(b_1)$, respectively]

$= \left(\dfrac{SS_{XY}/SS_X}{\sqrt{MSE}/\sqrt{SS_X}}\right)^2 = \dfrac{(SS_{XY}/SS_X)^2}{MSE/SS_X}$

$= \dfrac{SS_{XY}^2/SS_X}{MSE} = \dfrac{SSR/1}{MSE} = \dfrac{MSR}{MSE} = F_{(1,k)}$

[because $SS_{XY}^2/SS_X = SSR$ by Equations (10-31) and (10 10)].

10-63. **a.** Heteroscedasticity.

     b. No apparent inadequacy.

     c. Data display curvature, not a straight-line relationship.

10-64. **a.** No apparent inadequacy.

     b. A pattern of increase with time.

10-65. **a.** No serious inadequacy.

     b. Yes. A deviation from the normal-distribution assumption is apparent.

10-66. Residuals plotted against the independent variable of Problem **10-11**:

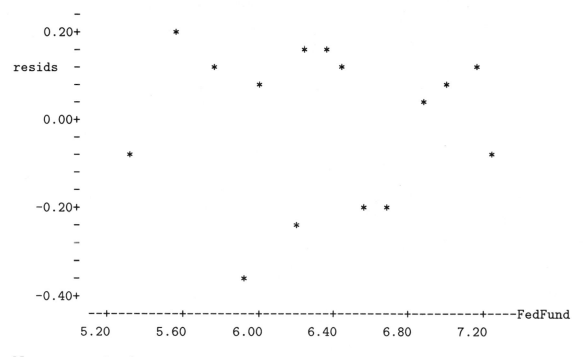

No apparent inadequacy.

10-67. Residuals plotted against the independent variable of Problem **10-14**:

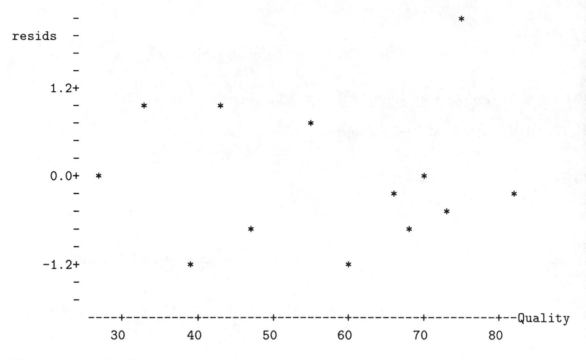

No apparent inadequacy.

10-68. Residuals plotted against the independent variable of Problem **10-16**:

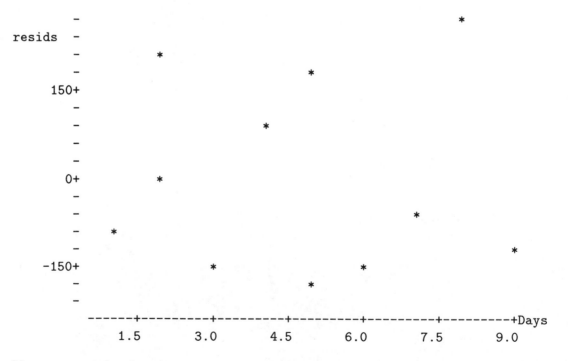

No apparent inadequacy.

10-69. In the American Express example, give a 95% prediction interval for $x = 5,000$:

$\hat{y} = 274.85 + 1.2553(5,000) = 6,551.35$

$$\text{P.I.} = 6,551.35 \pm (2.069)(318.16)\sqrt{1 + \frac{1}{25} + \frac{(5,000 - 3,177.92)^2}{40,947,557.84}}$$

$= [5,854.4,\ 7,248.3]$

10-70. 95% C.I. for $E(Y \mid x = 5,000)$ is:

$$\text{C.I.} = 6,551.35 \pm (2.069)(318.16)\sqrt{\frac{1}{25} + \frac{(5,000 - 3,177.92)^2}{40,947,557.84}}$$

$= [6,322.3,\ 6,780.4]$

10-71. For 99% P.I.: $\quad t_{.005(23)} = 2.807$

$$6,551.35 \pm (2.807)(318.16)\sqrt{1 + \frac{1}{25} + \frac{(5,000 - 3,177.92)^2}{40,947,557.84}}$$

$= [5,605.75,\ 7,496.95]$

10-72. For 99% P.I.: $\quad t_{.005(13)} = 3.012$

Point prediction: $\quad \hat{y} = -.847 + 1.352(6.5) = 7.941$

$$\text{P.I.} = 7.941 \pm (3.012)(0.184)\sqrt{1 + \frac{1}{15} + \frac{(6.5 - 6.348)^2}{4.819}} = [7.367,\ 8.515]$$

10-73. $SS_X = 4.819 \qquad SS_{XY} = 6.4278 \qquad SSR = 8.6795$

99% C.I. for average PLR when FFR $= 6.5$: $\qquad -.847 + 1.352(6.5) = 7.941$

$$\text{C.I.} = 7.941 \pm t_{.005(13)}(s)\sqrt{\frac{1}{n} + \frac{(x - \bar{x})^2}{SS_X}}$$

$$= 7.941 \pm 3.012(.184)\sqrt{\frac{1}{15} + \frac{(6.5 - 6.348)^2}{4.819}}$$

$= [7.793,\ 8.089]$

10-74. In Problem **10-16**, 95% C.I. for $E(Y \mid x = 5)$

$n = 11 \qquad \bar{x} = 4.7272 \qquad SS_X = 68.1818 \qquad s = 168.035$

$\hat{y}$ (for $x = 5$) $= 2,260.7 + 153.6(5) = 3,028.7$

95% C.I.: $\quad 3,028.7 \pm t_{.025(9)}(168.035)\sqrt{\dfrac{1}{11} + \dfrac{(5 - 4.7272)^2}{68.1818}} = [2,913.4,\ 3,144.00]$

10-75. In Problem **10-16**, 95% P.I. for:

$x = 5$ $n = 11$ $\bar{x} = 4.7272$ $SS_X = 68.1818$ $s = 168.035$

$\hat{y}$ (for $x = 5$) $= 2{,}260.7 + 153.6(5) = 3{,}028.7$

95% P.I.: $3{,}028.7 \pm t_{.025(9)}(168.035)\sqrt{1 + \dfrac{1}{11} + \dfrac{(5 - 4.7272)^2}{68.1818}}$

$= [2{,}631.5,\ 3{,}425.9]$

10-76. Referring to the data in Problem **10-17**:

$\hat{y} = 6.110 + 0.160x$ So for $x = 20$, $\hat{y} = 9.302$ is the point prediction (units are millions of dollars, as in the original problem).

Calculate: $\bar{x} = -3.667$ $SS_X = 2{,}228.67$. The MINITAB results include $s = 1.9376$. $t_{(.05,4)} = 2.132$, so we want:

90% C.I.: $9.302 \pm (2.132)(1.9376)\sqrt{\dfrac{1}{6} + \dfrac{(20 - (-3.667))^2}{2{,}228.67}} = [6.632,\ 11.973]$

10-77. $F = \dfrac{45{,}678/1}{3{,}343/126} = 1{,}721.64$ Yes, there is strong evidence of a linear relationship.

$r^2 = SSR/(SSR + SSE) = 0.93$ A strong relationship.

10-78. Model 1: $r^2 = 0.7628$ Model 2: $r^2 = 0.502$

Thus Model 1 is better.

10-79. $F = MSR/MSE = \dfrac{(87{,}695.98 - 5{,}432.87)/1}{5{,}432.87/21} = 317.98$

Yes, there is strong evidence of a linear relationship.

10-80. $SS_X = .0101996$ $SS_Y = .07165$ $SS_{XY} = -.008239$

$b_1 = SS_{XY}/SS_X = -0.808$ $b_0 = \bar{y} - b_1\bar{x} = 0.0086$

$SSE = SS_Y - b_1 SS_{XY} = 0.065$ $SSR = b_1 SS_{XY} = 0.00666$

$F_{(1,58)} = MSR/MSE = \dfrac{.00666}{.065/58} = 5.94$ Significant at $\alpha = 0.05$.

$r^2 = SSR/SST = 0.093$. Weak regression, low r^2. Do not use for prediction; limited use in explaining the relationship between the two variables.

10-81. $t_{(14)} = b_1/s(b_1) = -3.453/.987 = -3.498$ At $\alpha = 0.01$, there is evidence of a linear relationship. $F_{(1,14)} = t_{(14)}^2 = 12.24$ (also significant at $\alpha = 0.01$).

10-82. $H_0: \rho = 0 \qquad H_1: \rho \neq 0$

$$t_{(14)} = \frac{r}{\sqrt{(1 - r^2)/(n - 2)}} = 0.16/\sqrt{.0696} = 0.606 \qquad \text{Do not reject } H_0. \text{ There is}$$

no evidence of a correlation between the two variables.

10-83. 95% C.I. for β_0: $\quad 12.43 \pm t_{.025(19)}s(b_0) = [-16.14, 41.00]$

95% C.I. for β_1: $\quad 1.076 \pm t_{.025(19)}s(b_1) = [0.90228, 1.250]$

95% C.I. for the average Y when $x = 10{,}000$:

$$\hat{y} = 12.43 + 1.076(10{,}000) = 10{,}772.43 \qquad s = \sqrt{\text{MSE}} = \sqrt{1{,}076.11/19} = 7.526$$

$$\text{C.I.:} \quad 10{,}772.43 \pm 2.093(7.526)\sqrt{\frac{1}{21} + \frac{(10{,}000 - 12{,}453)^2}{72.641}} = [6{,}238.86,\ 15{,}306.00]$$

95% Prediction interval:

$$\text{P.I.:} \quad 10{,}772.43 \pm 2.093(7.526)\sqrt{1 + \frac{1}{21} + \frac{(10{,}000 - 12{,}453)^2}{72.641}}$$

$$= [6{,}238.83,\ 15{,}306.03]$$

10-84. From SYSTAT:

```
DEP VAR: OCCPCY  N:14   MULTIPLE R: .944
SQUARED MULTIPLE R: .890
ADJUSTED SQUARED MULTIPLE R: .881
STANDARD ERROR OF ESTIMATE: 2.642
```

VARIABLE	COEFFICIENT	STD ERROR	STD COEF	TOLERANCE	T	P(2 TAIL)
CONSTANT	98.252	1.536	0.000		63.978	0.000
MILES	-25.477	2.580	-0.944	.100E+01	-9.874	0.000

ANALYSIS OF VARIANCE

SOURCE	SUM-OF-SQUARES	DF	MEAN-SQUARE	F-RATIO	P
REGRESSION	680.596	1	680.596	97.505	0.000
RESIDUAL	83.762	12	6.980		

For 75% occupancy: $\quad \hat{y} = 75 = 98.252 + (-25.477)x$

Thus, $x = (98.252 - 75)/25.477 = 0.913$. The hotel should be built at a distance no greater than 0.913 miles from the beach. (One can also use prediction or confidence bounds in this problem, for a given required confidence that occupancy rate will be at least 75%.)

10-85. $b_0 = 1.195238$ $b_1 = 1.928571$ $t_{(13)} = 18.512$

Evidence of a linear relationship. $r^2 = 0.96345$

$\hat{y}$ (for $x = 13$) $= 1.195238 + 1.928571(13) = \$26.27$

10-86. The sample size here is very large. Thus the observed statistical significance of the regression ($F = 12.56$) may not have much practical significance. We reject the null hypothesis that the true regression slope is *identically* zero; however, the true slope may be very *close to zero*. The regression relationship is still extremely weak, as evidenced by the minuscule r^2. This problem demonstrates the usual difficulty with two-tailed tests: that with a large enough sample we may reject virtually any null hypothesis.

10-87. Entertainment $= -81.04 + 0.7183 \,(\text{S\&P})$

$R^2 = 0.942$ $F = 374.6$ (*p*-value very close to 0). Excellent linear relationship.

10-88. From a computer regression: GNP $= 1.78 + 0.391 \text{Production}$

Case 10.

The following results are obtained using SYSTAT:

```
DEP VAR: YEAR  N: 38     MULTIPLE R: .613    SQUARED MULTIPLE R:  .376
ADJUSTED SQUARED MULTIPLE R: .359
STANDARD ERROR OF ESTIMATE: 13.166
```

VARIABLE	COEFFICIENT	STD ERROR	STD COEF	TOLERANCE	T	P(2 TAIL)
CONSTANT	5.707	2.224	0.000		2.566	0.015
JANUARY	1.925	0.413	0.613	.100E+01	4.658	0.000

ANALYSIS OF VARIANCE

SOURCE	SUM-OF-SQUARES	DF	MEAN-SQUARE	F-RATIO	P
REGRESSION	3760.892	1	3760.892	21.696	0.000
RESIDUAL	6240.428	36	173.345		

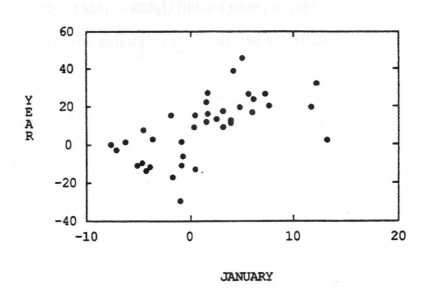

As seen from the plot above, severe hetcroscedasticity is evident. There is, however, strong evidence of a linear relationship between the January change and the yearly change. While the r^2 is relatively small, it might be interesting to try and use the model for predicting the change in the stock index value for the year.

CHAPTER 11

11-1. The assumptions of the multiple regression model are that the errors are normally and independently distributed with mean zero and common variance σ^2. We also assume that the X_i are fixed quantities rather than random variables; at any rate, they are independent of the error terms. The assumption of normality of the errors is needed for conducting tests about the regression model.

11-2. Holding age *constant*, the job performance measure increases by 1.34 units, on the average, per increase of 1 unit in the experience variable.

11-3. In a correlational analysis, we are interested in the relationships among the variables. On the other hand, in a regression analysis with k independent variables, we are interested in the effects of the k variables (considered fixed quantities) on the dependent variable only (and not on one another).

11-4. A response surface is a generalization to higher dimensions of the regression line of simple linear regression. For example, when 2 independent variables are used, each in the first order only, the response surface is a plane in 3-dimensional euclidean space. When 7 independent variables are used, each in the first order, the response surface is a 7-dimensional hyperplane in 8-dimensional euclidean space.

11-5. 8 equations.

11-6. The least-squares estimators of the parameters of the multiple regression model, obtained as solutions of the normal equations.

11-7.
$$\sum Y = nb_0 + b_1 \sum X_1 + b_2 \sum X_2$$
$$\sum X_1 Y = b_0 \sum X_1 + b_1 \sum X_1^2 + b_2 \sum X_1 X_2$$
$$\sum X_2 Y = b_0 \sum X_2 + b_1 \sum X_1 X_2 + b_2 \sum X_2^2$$

$852 = 100b_0 + 155b_1 + 88b_2$
$11{,}423 = 155b_0 + 2{,}125b_1 + 1{,}055b_2$
$8{,}320 = 88b_0 + 1{,}055b_1 + 768b_2$

$b_0 = (852 - 155b_1 - 88b_2)/100$
$11{,}423 = 155(852 - 155b_1 - 88b_2)/100 + 2{,}125b_1 + 1{,}055b_2$

$$8{,}320 = 88(852 - 155b_1 - 88b_2)/100 + 1{,}055b_1 + 768b_2$$

Continue solving the equations to obtain the solutions:
$$b_0 = -1.1454469 \qquad b_1 = 0.0487011 \qquad b_2 = 10.897682$$

11-8. Using SYSTAT:

```
DEP VAR: VALUE  N: 9  MULTIPLE R: .909   SQUARED MULTIPLE R: .826
ADJUSTED SQUARED MULTIPLE R:   .769
STANDARD ERROR OF ESTIMATE:  59.477
```

VARIABLE	COEFFICIENT	STD ERROR	STD COEF	TOLERANCE	T	P(2 TAIL)
CONSTANT	-9.800	80.763	0.000		-0.121	0.907
SIZE	0.173	0.040	0.753	0.9614430	4.343	0.005
DISTANCE	31.094	14.132	0.382	0.9614430	2.200	0.070

ANALYSIS OF VARIANCE

SOURCE	SUM-OF-SQUARES	DF	MEAN-SQUARE	F-RATIO	P
REGRESSION	101032.867	2	50516.433	14.280	0.005
RESIDUAL	21225.133	6	3537.522		

11-9. With no advertising and no spending on in-store displays, sales are $b_0 = 47.165$ (thousands) on the average. Per each unit (thousand) increase in advertising expenditure, keeping in-store display expenditure constant, there is an average increase in sales of $b_1 = 1.599$ (thousand). Similarly, for each unit (thousand) increase in in-store display expenditure, keeping advertising constant, there is an average increase in sales of $b_2 = 1.149$ (thousand).

11-10. We test whether there is a linear relationship between Y and *any* of the X_i variables (that is, with at least one of the X_i). If the null hypothesis is not rejected, there is nothing more to do since there is no evidence of a regression relationship. If H_0 is rejected, we need to conduct further analyses to determine which of the variables have a linear relationship with Y and which do not, and we need to develop the regression model.

11-11. Degrees of freedom for error $= n - 13$.

11-12. $k = 4$ $n = 120$ $SSE = 4{,}560$ $SSR = 562$

$$F_{(4,115)} = \frac{562/4}{4{,}560/115} = 3.54 > 3.51 = \text{crit. pt. for } \alpha = .01.$$

Reject H_0. Yes, there is evidence of a linear regression relationship.

11-13. $F_{(4,40)} = MSR/MSE = \dfrac{7{,}768/4}{(15{,}673 - 7{,}768)/40} = 1{,}942/197.625 = 9.827$

Yes, there is evidence of a linear regression relationship between Y and at least one of the independent variables.

11-14.

Source	SS	df	MS	F
Regression	7,474.0	3	2,491.33	48.16
Error	672.5	13	51.73	
Total	8,146.5	16		

Since the F-ratio is highly significant, there is evidence of a linear regression relationship between overall appeal score and at least one of the three variables prestige, comfort, and economy.

11-15. When the sample size is small; when the degrees of freedom for error are relatively small—when adding a variable and thus losing a degree of freedom for error is substantial.

11-16. $R^2 = SSR/SST$. As we add a variable, SSR cannot decrease. Since SST is constant, R^2 cannot decrease.

11-17. No. The adjusted coefficient is used in evaluating the importance of new variables in the presence of old ones. It does not apply in the case where all we consider is a single independent variable.

11-18. By the definition of the adjusted coefficient of determination, Equation (11-13):

$$\bar{R}^2 = 1 - \frac{SSE/(n - k - 1)}{SST/(n - 1)} = 1 - (SSE/SST)\frac{n - 1}{n - k - 1}$$

But: $SSE/SST = 1 - R^2$, so the above is equal to:

$$1 - (1 - R^2)\frac{n - 1}{n - (k + 1)} \qquad \text{which is Equation (11-14).}$$

11-19. The mean square error gives a good indication of the variation of the errors in regression. However, other measures such as the coefficient of multiple determination and the adjusted coefficient of multiple determination are useful in evaluating the *proportion* of the variation in the dependent variable explained by the regression—thus giving us a more meaningful measure of the regression fit.

11-20.

Source	df	SS	MS	F
Regression	3	11,778	3,926.0	22.5
Error	40	6,980	174.5	
Total	43	18,758		

$R^2 = 11,778/18,758 = 0.6279 \qquad s = \sqrt{\text{MSE}} = 13.21$

$\bar{R}^2 = 1 - (1 - 0.6279)(43/40) = 0.60$

11-21. $R^2 = 7,474.0/8,146.5 = 0.9174 \qquad$ A good regression.

$\bar{R}^2 = 1 - (1 - 0.9174)(16/13) = 0.8983 \qquad s = \sqrt{\text{MSE}} = \sqrt{51.73} = 7.192$

11-22. $F_{(1,101)} = 2.53 < 3.92$ (the approximate critical point for $\alpha = 0.05$). Hence no evidence of a linear regression relationship.

$\bar{R}^2 = 1 - (1 - 0.67)(102/100) = 0.6634$

11-23. $\bar{R}^2 = 1 - (1 - R^2)\dfrac{n-1}{n-(k+1)} = 1 - (1 - 0.918)(16/12) = 0.8907$

Since $\bar{R}^2$ has decreased, do not include the new variable.

11-24. $\bar{R}^2 = 1 - (1 - R^2)\dfrac{n-1}{n-(k+1)} = 1 - (1 - 0.61)(102/101) = 0.6061$

Since $\bar{R}^2$ has decreased, add the variable back into the equation.

11-25. **a.** The regression expresses stock returns as a plane in space, with firm size ranking and stock price ranking as the two horizontal axes:

RETURN $= 0.484 - 0.030(\text{SIZRNK}) - 0.017(\text{PRCRNK})$

The *t*-test for a linear relationship between returns and firm size ranking is highly significant, but not for returns against stock price ranking.

b. We know that $\bar{R}^2 = 0.093$ and $n = 50$, $k = 2$. Using Equation (11-14) we calculate:

$(1 - R^2)\left(\dfrac{n-1}{n-(k+1)}\right) = 1 - \bar{R}^2$

$$R^2 = 1 - (1 - \bar{R}^2) \left(\frac{n - (k+1)}{n-1} \right) = 1 - (1 - 0.093)(47/49) = 0.130$$

Thus, 13% of the variation is due to the two independent variables.

c. The adjusted R^2 is quite low, indicating that the regression on both variables is not a good model. They should try regressing on size alone.

11-26. $\bar{R}^2 = 1 - (1 - R^2) \dfrac{n-1}{n - (k+1)} = 1 - (1 - 0.72)(712/710) = 0.719$

Based solely on this information, this is not a bad regression model.

11-27. $k = 6 \qquad n = 250 \qquad SSE = 5{,}445 \qquad SST = 22{,}679$

$MSE = 5{,}445/243 = 22.407$

$$F_{(6,243)} = MSR/MSE = \frac{(22{,}679 - 5{,}445)/6}{5{,}445/243} = 2{,}872.33/22.407 = 128.19$$

Reject H_0. There is strong evidence of a linear regression relationship.

$R^2 = SSR/SST = 0.7599 \qquad \bar{R}^2 = 1 - \dfrac{SSE/[n - (k+1)]}{SST/(n-1)} = 0.75398$

11-28. A joint confidence region for both parameters is a set of *pairs* of likely values of β_1 and β_2 at 95%. This region accounts for the mutual dependency of the estimators and hence is elliptical rather than rectangular. This is why the region may not contain a bivariate point included in the separate univariate confidence intervals for the two parameters.

11-29. Due to the dependency between the two independent variables (i.e., multicollinearity), the estimate of the slope for the first variable changed as the second variable was added. And, more importantly, the first variable now appears to be *not significant* once the second variable is in the equation.

11-30. 1. The usual caution about the possibility of a Type I error.

2. Multicollinearity may make the tests unreliable.

3. Autocorrelation in the errors may make the tests unreliaible.

11-31. 95% C.I.'s for β_2 through β_5:

β_2 : $5.6 \pm 1.96(1.3) = [3.052, 8.148]$

β_3 : $10.35 \pm 1.96(6.88) = [-3.135, 23.835]$

β_4 : $3.45 \pm 1.96(2.7) = [-1.842, 8.742]$

β_5 : $-4.25 \pm 1.96(0.38) = [-4.995, -3.505]$

11-32.   **1.** The variable may be insignificant, i.e., lacking in explanatory power with respect to the dependent variable.

       2. The variable may be significant, but collinear with one or both of the other variables in the equation.

To determine which is the case, drop one of the remaining two variables, one at a time, from the equation and see what happens to the "insignificant" variable.

11-33. Yes. Considering the joint confidence region for both slope parameters is equivalent to conducting an F test for the existence of a linear regression relationship. Since $(0, 0)$ is not in the joint 95% region, this is equivalent to rejecting the null hypothesis of the F test at $\alpha = 0.05$.

11-34. Prestige is not significant (or at least appears so, pending further analysis). Comfort and Economy are significant (Comfort only at the 0.05 level). The regression should be rerun with variables deleted.

11-35. Variable Lend seems insignificant because of collinearity with M_1 or Price.

11-36.   **a.** As Price is dropped, Lend becomes significant: there is, apparently, a collinearity between Lend and Price.

     b.,c. The best model so far is the one in Table 11-9, with M_1 and Price only. The adjusted R^2 for that model is higher than for the other regressions.

      d. For the model in this problem, MINITAB reports $F = 114.09$. Highly significant. For the model in Table 11-9: $F = 150.67$. Highly significant.

      e. $s = 0.3697$. For Problem **11-35**: $s = 0.3332$. As a variable is deleted, s (and its square, MSE) increases.

      f. In Problem **11-35**: MSE $= s^2 = (0.3332)^2 = 0.111$.

11-37. Autocorrelation of the regression errors may cause this.

11-38. "Bidder Q is large" is not significant; the R^2 is very low.

11-39. All variables except "Store feature" have significant t-ratios for a linear relationship with consideration function, but this report does not give an R^2 result, so we cannot conclude much about the power of the regression model. It appears that a better model may be obtainable by omitting "Store feature".

11-40. The residual plot exhibits both heteroscedasticity and a curvature apparently not accounted for in the model.

11-41. The residuals do not appear to be normally distributed.

11-42. An outlier is an observation far from the others.

11-43. A plot of the data or a plot of the residuals will reveal outliers. Also, most computer packages (e.g., MINITAB) will automatically report all outliers and suspected outliers.

11-44. Outliers, unless they are due to errors in recording the data, may contain important information about the process under study and should not be blindly discarded. The relationship of the true data may well be nonlinear.

11-45. An outlier tends to "tilt" the regression surface toward it, because of the high influence of a large squared deviation in the least-squares formula, thus creating a possible bias in the results.

11-46. An influential observation is one that exerts relatively strong influence on the regression surface. For example, if all the data lie in one region in X-space and one observation lies far away in X, it may exert strong influence on the estimates of the regression parameters.

11-47. This creates a bias. In any case, there is no reason to force the regression surface to go through the origin.

11-48. The residual plot in Figure 11-15 exhibits strong heteroscedasticity.

11-49. The regression relationship may be quite different in a region where we have no observations from what it is in the estimation-data region. Thus predicting outside the range of available data may create large errors.

11-50. $\hat{y} = 47.165 + 1.599(8) + 1.149(12) = 73.745$ (thousands), i.e., \$73,745.

11-51. In Problem **11-8**: X_2 (distance) is not a significant variable, but we use the complete original regression relationship given in that problem anyway (since this problem calls for it):

$\hat{y} = -9.800 + 0.173X_1 + 31.094X_2$
$\hat{y}(1800, 2.0) = -9.800 + (.173)1800 + (31.094)2.0 = 363.78$

11-52. Using the regression coefficients reported in Problem **11-25**:
$\hat{Y} = 0.484 - 0.030\text{Sizrnk} - 0.017\text{Prcrnk} = 0.484 - 0.030(5.0) - 0.017(6.0) = 0.232$

11-53. Estimated $\text{SE}(\hat{Y})$ is obtained as: $(5.3530 - 3.9885)/4 = 0.341$.
Estimated $\text{SE}(E(Y \mid x))$ is obtained as: $(4.8412 - 4.5003)/4 = 0.085$.

11-54. From MINITAB:
Fit: 73.742   St Dev Fit: 2.765
95% C.I. [67.203, 80.281]   95% P.I. [65.793, 81.692]
(all numbers are in thousands)

11-55. The estimators are the same although their standard errors are different.

11-56. A prediction interval reflects more variation than a confidence interval for the conditional mean of Y. The additional variation is the variation of the *actual* predicted value about the conditional mean of Y (the estimator of which is itself a random variable).

11-57. This is a regression with one continuous variable and one dummy variable. Both variables are significant. Thus there are two distinct regression lines. The coefficient of determination is respectably high. During times of restricted trade with the Orient, the company sells 26,540 more units per month, on average.

11-58. Should not use such a model. Use two dummy variables.

11-59. Two-way ANOVA.

11-60. Use analysis of covariance. Run it as a regression—Length of Stay is the concomitant variable.

11-61. Early investment is not statistically significant (or may be collinear with another variable). Rerun the regression without it. The dummy variables are both significant—there is a distinct line (or plane if you do include the insignificant variable) for each type of firm.

11-62. This is a second-order regression model in three independent variables with cross-terms.

11-63. The STEPWISE routine chooses Price and M_1*Price as the best set of explanatory variables. This gives the estimated regression relationship:

$$\text{Exports} = -1.39 + 0.0229\text{Price} + 0.00248 M_1 * \text{Price}$$

The t-statistics are: -2.36, 4.57, 9.08, respectively. $R^2 = 0.822$

11-64. The STEPWISE routine chooses the three original variables: Prod, Prom, and Book, with no squares. Thus the original regression model of Example 11-3 is better than a model with squared terms.

11-65. 1) The usual reason for parsimony, as in the example in the beginning of the chapter. 2) The danger of multicollinearity, which increases with the number of power terms of a variable that are used in the regression.

11-66. The squared X_1 variable and the cross-product term appear not significant. Drop the least significant term first, i.e., the squared X_1, and rerun the regression. See what happens to the cross-product term now.

11-67. Try a quadratic regression (you should get a negative estimated x^2 coefficient).

11-68. Try a quadratic regression (you should get a positive estimated x^2 coefficient). Also try a cubic polynomial.

11-69. Linearizing a model; finding a more parsimonious model than is possible without a transformation; stabilizing the variance.

11-70. A transformed model may be more parsimonious, when the model describes the process well.

11-71. Try the transformation $\log Y$.

11-72. A good model is $\log(\text{Exports})$ versus $\log(M_1)$ and $\log(\text{Price})$. This model has $R^2 = 0.8652$. This implies a multiplicative relation.

11-73. A logarithmic model.

11-74. This dataset fits an exponential model, so use a logarithmic transformation to linearize it.

11-75. A multiplicative relation (Equation (11-26)) with multiplicative errors. The reported error term, ε, is the logarithm of the original multiplicative error term. The transformed error term is assumed to satisfy the usual model assumptions.

11-76. An exponential model $Y = (e^{\beta_0 + \beta_1 x_1 + \beta_2 x_2})\varepsilon$

11-77. No. We cannot find a transformation that will linearize this model.

11-78. Take logs of both sides of the equation, giving:
$\log Q = \log \beta_0 + \beta_1 \log C + \beta_2 \log K + \beta_3 \log L + \log \varepsilon$

11-79. Taking reciprocals of both sides of the equation.

11-80. The square-root transformation $Y' = \sqrt{Y}$

11-81. No. They minimize the sum of the squared deviations relevant to the estimated, transformed model.

11-82. A logarithmic model.

11-83.

	Earn	Prod	Prom
Prod	.867		
Prom	.882	.638	
Book	.547	.402	.319

As evidenced by the relatively low correlations between the *independent* variables, multicollinearity does not seem to be serious here.

11-84. The VIFs are: 1.82, 1.70, 1.20. No severe multicollinearity is present.

11-85. The sample correlation is 0.740.

11-86. A good intuitive explanation may include the ideas of directions in space, as discussed in the text. Students with background in linear algebra should be able to give deeper explanations involving linear dependencies of vectors.

11-87. Artificially high variances of regression coefficient estimators; unexpected magnitudes of some coefficient estimates; sometimes wrong signs of these coefficients. Large changes in coefficient estimates and standard errors as a variable or a data point is added or deleted.

11-88. Perfect collinearity exists when at least one variable is a linear combination of other variables. This causes the determinant of the $\mathbf{X'X}$ matrix to be zero and thus the matrix non-invertible. The estimation procedure breaks down in such cases. (Other, less technical, explanations based on the text will suffice.)

11-89. Not true. Predictions may be good when carried out within the same region of the multicollinearity as used in the estimation procedure.

11-90. No. There are probably no relationships between Y and any of the two independent variables.

11-91. X_2 and X_3 are probably collinear.

11-92. Delete one of the variables X_2, X_3, X_4 to check for multicollinearity among a subset of these three variables, or whether they are all insignificant.

11-93. Drop some of the other variables one at a time and see what happens to the suspected sign of the estimate.

11-94. The purpose of the test is to check for a possible violation of the assumption that the regression errors are uncorrelated with each other.

11-95. Autocorrelation is correlation of a variable with itself, lagged back in time. Third-order autocorrelation is a correlation of a variable with itself lagged 3 periods back in time.

11-96. First-order autocorrelation is a correlation of a variable with itself lagged one period back in time. Not necessarily: a partial fifth-order autocorrelation may exist without a first-order autocorrelation.

11-97. 1) The test checks only for first-order autocorrelation. 2) The test may not be conclusive. 3) The usual limitations of a statistical test owing to the two possible types of errors.

11-98. $DW = 0.93$ $n - 21$ $k = 2$
$d_L = 1.13$ $d_U = 1.54$ $4 - d_L = 2.87$ $4 - d_U = 2.46$
At the 0.10 level, there is some evidence of a positive first-order autocorrelation.

11-99. $DW = 2.13$ $n = 20$ $k = 3$
$d_L = 1.00$ $d_U = 1.68$ $4 - d_L = 3.00$ $4 - d_U = 2.32$
At the 0.10 level, there is no evidence of a first-order autocorrelation.

11-100. $DW = 1.79$ $n = 10$ $k = 2$ Since the table does not list values for $n = 10$, we will use the closest table values, those for $n = 15$ and $k = 2$:
$d_L = 0.95$ $d_U = 1.54$ $4 - d_L = 3.05$ $4 - d_U = 2.46$
At the 0.10 level, there is no evidence of a first-order autocorrelation. Note that the table values decrease as n decreases, and thus our conclusion would probably also hold if we knew the actual critical points for $n = 10$ and used them.

11-101. Suppose that we have time-series data and that it is known that, if the data are autocorrelated, by the nature of the variables the correlation can only be positive. In such cases, where the hypothesis is made before looking at the actual data, a one-sided DW test may be appropriate. (And similarly for a negative autocorrelation.)

11-102. Using $\alpha = 0.005$ and the $n = 100$ row of the table, regressors (1) and (2) both have DW statistics $< d_L$, indicating positive autocorrelation. For (3) and (4), DW $> 4 - d_L$, indicating negative correlation.

11-103. $F_{(r,\,n-(k+1))} = \dfrac{(\text{SSE}_R - \text{SSE}_F)/r}{\text{MSE}_F} = \dfrac{(6.996 - 6.9898)/2}{0.1127} = 0.0275$

Cannot reject H_0. The two variables should definitely be dropped—they add nothing to the mo   del.

11-104. $Y = 47.16 + 1.599X_1 + 1.1149X_2$ The STEPWISE regression routine selects both variables for the equation. $R^2 = 0.961$.

11-105. The STEPWISE procedure selects all three variables. $R^2 = 0.9667$.

11-106. All possible regressions is the best procedure because it evaluates every possibility. It is expensive in computer time; however, as computing power and speed increase, this becomes a very viable option. Forward selection is limited by the fact that once a variable is in, there is no way it can come out once it becomes insignificant in the presence of new variables. Backward elimination is similarly limited. Stepwise regression is an excellent method that enjoys very wide use and that has stood the test of time. It has the advantages of both the forward and the backward methods, without their limitations.

11-107. Because a variable may lose explanatory power and become insignificant once other variables are added to the model.

11-108. Highest adjusted R^2; lowest MSE; highest R^2 for a given number of variables and the assessment of the increase in R^2 as we increase the number of variables; Mallows's C_p.

11-109. No. There may be several different "best" models. A model may be best using one criterion, and not the best using another criterion.

11-110. Using stepwise regression of V(alue) and also of V^2 against the nine variables: the independent variables S(ales), P(rofits), A(ssets), and all possible second-order cross-terms from those three, yields the best result:

$V^2 = -1.08 \times 10^9 + (1.305 \times 10^6)P - 0.335 S * A + 4.89 P * A$

with $R^2 = 0.754$.

11-111. All variables except Power distance and Collectivism in section B are significant.

11-112. Neither variable is significant in the equation as it is.

11-113. These data do not fit a linear model well, even after various transformations. After removing the 1991 data as an outlier, a plot of the six remaining Near Collisions numbers versus Flights looks a lot like a cubic curve. A least-squares fit gives:

$$NC = 3.32F^3 - 54.12F^2 + 291.73F - 518.52$$

11-114. STEPWISE chooses only Number of Bedrooms and Assessed Value.
$$b_0 = 910 \qquad b_1 = 78.5 \qquad b_2 = 0.234 \qquad R^2 = 0.591$$

11-115. Only for WC Benefit is there any evidence of a linear relationship. The sample size may have been too small.

Case 11.

The estimated regression equation is:

$$\text{Lines} = 258.2 - 1.047\,\text{Installation} - 3.269\,\text{Monthly} - 3.008\,\text{CallWaiting}$$

All three variables are significant at the 0.05 level.

$R^2 = 0.983$. Adjusted $R^2 = 0.980$.

Predicting the demand by the 62 businesses when all types of charges are highest:

$$\text{Lines} = 258.2 - 1.047(37.10) - 3.269(34.00) - 3.008(4.50) = 94.674$$

Now, to predict total demand for lines by the population of 1,317 new businesses, we expand the prediction as follows:

$$\text{Total Lines} = (\text{Lines})\frac{1{,}317}{62} = 94.674\frac{1{,}317}{62} = 2{,}011.07,$$

or about 2,011 lines. The results, of course, cannot be directly applied to other populations.

CHAPTER 12

12-1.   Trend analysis is a quick method of determining in which general direction the data are moving through time. The method lacks, however, the theoretical justification of regression analysis because of the inherent autocorrelations and the intended use of the method in extrapolation beyond the estimation data set.

12-2.   A regression on the data gives:
$\hat{Z} = 21.33 + 0.4917t$
Since we used $t = -7, -5, \ldots, 7$ for the time data, predicting the next year's assets requires $t = 9$: $21.33 + 0.4917(9) = 25.75$.

12-3.   A regression gives:
$b_0 = -4.58 \qquad b_1 = 0.1137 \qquad r^2 = .992$
$\hat{y}\,(1996) = 226{,}399 \qquad \hat{y}\,(1997) = 253{,}660$

12-4.   A regression gives:
$b_0 = 119.36 \qquad b_1 = -1.118 \qquad r^2 = .846$
$\hat{y}\,(1996) = 111.54$

12-5.   No, because of the seasonality.

12-6.   No. Cyclicity is not well modeled by trend analysis.

12-7.   The term 'seasonal variation' is reserved for variation with a cycle of one year.

12-8.   There will be too few degrees of freedom for error.

12-9.   The weather, for one thing, changes from year to year. Thus sales of winter clothing, as an example, would have a variable seasonal component.

12-10. Beer sales at a local establishment, as an example: high during weekend nights, low at other times.

12-11. Using a computer:

Linear regression trend line: Zhat(t) = 372.876 + 0.8896 t

t (mon.)	data: Z(t)	trend: Zhat(t)	Centered Moving Average	C(t)= CMA/ Zhat(t)	Ratio Moving Average	Seasonal Index S	[Deseasoned] Z(t)/S%
1 (Jun)	375.00	373.77				99.52	376.83
2 (Jul)	370.00	374.66				98.87	374.22
3 (Aug)	374.00	375.54				99.25	376.82
4 (Sep)	378.00	376.43				99.74	378.97
5 (Oct)	376.00	377.32				99.78	376.82
6 (Nov)	380.00	378.21				100.48	378.20
7 (Dec)	384.00	379.10	378.62	0.999	101.42	102.33	375.26
8 (Jan)	380.00	379.99	379.37	0.998	100.16	100.95	376.43
9 (Feb)	378.00	380.88	380.29	0.998	99.40	99.84	378.62
10 (Mar)	380.00	381.77	381.12	0.998	99.70	99.39	382.31
11 (Apr)	382.00	382.66	382.08	0.998	99.98	100.09	381.64
12 (May)	383.00	383.55	383.17	0.999	99.96	99.76	383.92
13 (Jun)	382.00	384.44	384.46	1.000	99.36	99.52	383.86
14 (Jul)	381.00	385.33	386.00	1.002	98.70	98.87	385.35
15 (Aug)	385.00	386.22	387.37	1.003	99.39	99.25	387.91
16 (Sep)	387.00	387.11	388.37	1.003	99.65	99.74	387.99
17 (Oct)	390.00	388.00	389.25	1.003	100.19	99.78	390.85
18 (Nov)	392.00	388.89	390.12	1.003	100.48	100.48	390.14
19 (Dec)	403.00	389.78	390.96	1.003	103.08	102.33	393.82
20 (Jan)	398.00	390.67	391.83	1.003	101.57	100.95	394.26
21 (Feb)	393.00	391.56	392.54	1.003	100.12	99.84	393.65
22 (Mar)	389.00	392.45	393.21	1.002	98.93	99.39	391.37
23 (Apr)	394.00	393.34	393.79	1.001	100.05	100.09	393.63
24 (May)	392.00	394.23	394.33	1.000	99.41	99.76	392.94
25 (Jun)	393.00	395.12	394.92	0.999	99.51	99.52	394.91
26 (Jul)	391.00	396.01	395.42	0.999	98.88	98.87	395.46
27 (Aug)	392.00	396.89	396.12	0.998	98.96	99.25	394.96
28 (Sep)	396.00	397.78	397.25	0.999	99.69	99.74	397.02
29 (Oct)	395.00	398.67	398.12	0.999	99.22	99.78	395.86
30 (Nov)	400.00	399.56	398.75	0.998	100.31	100.48	398.11
31 (Dec)	409.00	400.45				102.33	399.69
32 (Jan)	404.00	401.34				100.95	400.21
33 (Feb)	404.00	402.23				99.84	404.67
34 (Mar)	405.00	403.12				99.39	407.47
35 (Apr)	399.00	404.01				100.09	398.63
36 (May)	402.00	404.90				99.76	402.97

-------------FORECAST-------------

37 (Jun) (Zhat = 405.79)(S = 99.52)/100 = 403.82

12-12. Using a computer:

Linear regression trend line: Zhat(t) = 7.2043 - 0.0194 t

t (mon.)	data: Z(t)	trend: Zhat(t)	Centered Moving Average	C(t)= CMA/ Zhat(t)	Ratio Moving Average	Seasonal Index S	[Deseasoned] Z(t)/S%
1 (Jul)	7.40	7.18				95.68	7.73
2 (Aug)	6.80	7.17				92.25	7.37
3 (Sep)	6.40	7.15				90.57	7.07
4 (Oct)	6.60	7.13				97.57	6.76
5 (Nov)	6.50	7.11				95.96	6.77
6 (Dec)	6.00	7.09				92.22	6.51
7 (Jan)	7.00	7.07	7.02	0.993	99.76	102.47	6.83
8 (Feb)	6.70	7.05	7.01	0.995	95.54	98.21	6.82
9 (Mar)	8.20	7.03	7.05	1.002	116.38	114.41	7.17
10 (Apr)	7.80	7.01	7.10	1.012	109.92	110.59	7.05
11 (May)	7.70	6.99	7.15	1.022	107.76	109.60	7.03
12 (Jun)	7.30	6.97	7.20	1.032	101.45	100.45	7.27
13 (Jul)	7.00	6.95	7.25	1.043	96.55	95.68	7.32
14 (Aug)	7.10	6.93	7.30	1.052	97.32	92.25	7.70
15 (Sep)	6.90	6.91	7.30	1.057	94.47	90.57	7.62
16 (Oct)	7.30	6.89	7.29	1.057	100.17	97.57	7.48
17 (Nov)	7.00	6.87	7.28	1.059	96.16	95.96	7.29
18 (Dec)	6.70	6.86	7.25	1.058	92.41	92.22	7.27
19 (Jan)	7.60	6.84	7.20	1.053	105.62	102.47	7.42
20 (Feb)	7.20	6.82	7.11	1.043	101.29	98.21	7.33
21 (Mar)	7.90	6.80	7.00	1.029	112.92	114.41	6.90
22 (Apr)	7.70	6.78	6.89	1.017	111.73	110.59	6.96
23 (May)	7.60	6.76	6.79	1.005	111.90	109.60	6.93
24 (Jun)	6.70	6.74	6.71	0.996	99.88	100.45	6.67
25 (Jul)	6.30	6.72	6.62	0.985	95.21	95.68	6.58
26 (Aug)	5.70	6.70	6.51	0.971	87.58	92.25	6.18
27 (Sep)	5.60	6.68	6.43	0.963	87.05	90.57	6.18
28 (Oct)	6.10	6.66	6.40	0.960	95.37	97.57	6.25
29 (Nov)	5.80	6.64				95.96	6.04
30 (Dec)	5.90	6.62				92.22	6.40
31 (Jan)	6.20	6.60				102.47	6.05
32 (Feb)	6.00	6.58				98.21	6.11
33 (Mar)	7.30	6.56				114.41	6.38
34 (Apr)	7.40	6.54				110.59	6.69

------------FORECAST------------

35 (May) (Zhat = 6.525)(S = 109.60)/100 = 7.15

12-13. Simple regression on the raw data give next quarter's rate = 1,596.37; moving averages give adjusted seasonal factor for second quarter = 99.138%. So the forecast is 1,582.61.

12-14. Using a computer:

Linear regression trend line: Zhat(t) = 27.047 + 0.6044 t

t (mon.)	data: Z(t)	trend: Zhat(t)	Centered Moving Average	C(t)= CMA/ Zhat(t)	Ratio Moving Average	Seasonal Index S	[Deseasoned] Z(t)/S%
1 (Jan)	21.00	27.65				73.29	28.65
2 (Feb)	23.00	28.26				78.36	29.35
3 (Mar)	20.00	28.86				68.76	29.09
4 (Apr)	24.00	29.46				82.24	29.18
5 (May)	33.00	30.07				108.05	30.54
6 (Jun)	41.00	30.67				125.72	32.61
7 (Jul)	45.00	31.28	31.67	1.012	142.11	139.40	32.28
8 (Aug)	50.00	31.88	32.00	1.004	156.25	151.97	32.90
9 (Sep)	42.00	32.49	32.33	0.995	129.90	131.69	31.89
10 (Oct)	28.00	33.09	32.75	0.990	85.50	86.40	32.41
11 (Nov)	25.00	33.70	33.63	0.998	74.35	76.12	32.84
12 (Dec)	26.00	34.30	34.75	1.013	74.82	78.00	33.33
13 (Jan)	25.00	34.90	35.79	1.025	69.85	73.29	34.11
14 (Feb)	27.00	35.51	36.83	1.037	73.30	78.36	34.46
15 (Mar)	24.00	36.11	37.88	1.049	63.37	68.76	34.90
16 (Apr)	30.00	36.72	38.58	1.051	77.75	82.24	36.48
17 (May)	48.00	37.32	38.96	1.044	123.21	108.05	44.42
18 (Jun)	53.00	37.93	39.42	1.039	134.46	125.72	42.16
19 (Jul)	58.00	38.53	39.83	1.034	145.61	139.40	41.61
20 (Aug)	62.00	39.13	40.21	1.027	154.20	151.97	40.80
21 (Sep)	55.00	39.74	40.58	1.021	135.52	131.69	41.76
22 (Oct)	32.00	40.34	40.96	1.015	78.13	86.40	37.04
23 (Nov)	30.00	40.95	40.71	0.994	73.69	76.12	39.41
24 (Dec)	32.00	41.55	40.13	0.966	79.75	78.00	41.03
25 (Jan)	29.00	42.16	40.00	0.949	72.50	73.29	39.57
26 (Feb)	32.00	42.76	40.17	0.939	79.67	78.36	40.84
27 (Mar)	28.00	43.37	40.54	0.935	69.06	68.76	40.72
28 (Apr)	35.00	43.97	41.29	0.939	84.76	82.24	42.56
29 (May)	37.00	44.57	42.21	0.947	87.66	108.05	34.24
30 (Jun)	50.00	45.18	42.92	0.950	116.50	125.72	39.77
31 (Jul)	58.00	45.78	43.71	0.955	132.70	139.40	41.61
32 (Aug)	66.00	46.39	44.63	0.962	147.90	151.97	43.43
33 (Sep)	60.00	46.99	45.54	0.969	131.75	131.69	45.56
34 (Oct)	45.00	47.60	46.42	0.975	96.95	86.40	52.08
35 (Nov)	39.00	48.20	47.83	0.992	81.53	76.12	51.23
36 (Dec)	40.00	48.80	49.58	1.016	80.67	78.00	51.28

37 (Jan)	40.00	49.41	50.83	1.029	78.69	73.29	54.58
38 (Feb)	43.00	50.01	51.58	1.031	83.36	78.36	54.87
39 (Mar)	39.00	50.62	52.04	1.028	74.94	68.76	56.72
40 (Apr)	45.00	51.22	52.63	1.027	85.51	82.24	54.72
41 (May)	61.00	51.83	53.04	1.023	115.00	108.05	56.46
42 (Jun)	68.00	52.43	53.04	1.012	128.20	125.72	54.09
43 (Jul)	70.00	53.04				139.40	50.22
44 (Aug)	72.00	53.64				151.97	47.38
45 (Sep)	65.00	54.24				131.69	49.36
46 (Oct)	54.00	54.85				86.40	62.50
47 (Nov)	40.00	55.45				76.12	52.55
48 (Dec)	39.00	56.06				78.00	50.00

```
------------FORECAST-------------
49 (Jan)  (Zhat = 56.66)(S = 73.29)/100  =  41.53
```

12-15. Using a computer:
Linear regression trend line: $\hat{Z}(t) = 23.1121 - 0.2035\ t$

t (mon.)	data: Z(t)	trend: $\hat{Z}(t)$	Centered Moving Average	C(t)= CMA/ $\hat{Z}(t)$	Ratio Moving Average	Seasonal Index S	[Deseasoned] Z(t)/S%
1 (Q1)	21.60	22.91				102.16	21.14
2 (Q2)	23.00	22.71				96.98	23.72
3 (Q3)	22.90	22.50	23.06	1.025	99.30	97.17	23.57
4 (Q4)	24.00	22.30	23.09	1.035	103.95	103.69	23.15
5 (Q1)	23.10	22.09	22.70	1.027	101.76	102.16	22.61
6 (Q2)	21.70	21.89	22.05	1.007	98.41	96.98	22.38
7 (Q3)	21.10	21.69	21.39	0.986	98.66	97.17	21.71
8 (Q4)	20.60	21.48	20.91	0.973	98.51	103.69	19.87
9 (Q1)	21.20	21.28	20.61	0.969	102.85	102.16	20.75
10 (Q2)	19.80	21.08	20.73	0.983	95.54	96.98	20.42
11 (Q3)	20.60	20.87	20.89	1.001	98.62	97.17	21.20
12 (Q4)	22.00	20.67	20.85	1.009	105.52	103.69	21.22
13 (Q1)	21.10	20.47	20.55	1.004	102.68	102.16	20.65
14 (Q2)	19.60	20.26	20.16	0.995	97.21	96.98	20.21
15 (Q3)	18.40	20.06	19.91	0.993	92.40	97.17	18.94
16 (Q4)	21.10	19.86	19.70	0.992	107.11	103.69	20.35
17 (Q1)	20.00	19.65	19.68	1.001	101.65	102.16	19.58
18 (Q2)	19.00	19.45	19.58	1.007	97.06	96.98	19.59
19 (Q3)	18.80	19.24				97.17	19.35
20 (Q4)	19.90	19.04				103.69	19.19

```
------------FORECAST-------------
21 ( Q1)  (Zhat = 18.839)(S = 102.16)/100  =  19.24
```

12-16. Using a computer:

```
w = 0.6        Zhat(1) = Z(1) = 142

Zhat( 2): 0.6(142.00) + 0.4(142.00) = 142.00
Zhat( 3): 0.6(137.00) + 0.4(142.00) = 139.00
Zhat( 4): 0.6(143.00) + 0.4(139.00) = 141.40
Zhat( 5): 0.6(142.00) + 0.4(141.40) = 141.76
Zhat( 6): 0.6(149.00) + 0.4(141.76) = 146.10
Zhat( 7): 0.6(143.00) + 0.4(146.10) = 144.24
Zhat( 8): 0.6(151.00) + 0.4(144.24) = 148.30
Zhat( 9): 0.6(150.00) + 0.4(148.30) = 149.32
Zhat(10): 0.6(151.00) + 0.4(149.32) = 150.33
Zhat(11): 0.6(146.00) + 0.4(150.33) = 147.73
Zhat(12): 0.6(144.00) + 0.4(147.73) = 145.49
Zhat(13): 0.6(145.00) + 0.4(145.49) = 145.20
-------------FORECAST-------------
Zhat(14): 0.6(147.00) + 0.4(145.20) = 146.28
```

By experimenting, we find that lower values of w in this case produce $\hat{Z}$ values that agree more closely with the raw data at the end of the series.

12-17. Using a computer:

```
w = 0.3        Zhat(1) = Z(1) = 57                    w = 0.8

Zhat( 2): 0.3(57.00) + 0.7(57.00) = 57.00  0.8(57.00) + 0.2(57.00) = 57.00
Zhat( 3): 0.3(58.00) + 0.7(57.00) = 57.30  0.8(58.00) + 0.2(57.00) = 57.80
Zhat( 4): 0.3(60.00) + 0.7(57.30) = 58.11  0.8(60.00) + 0.2(57.80) = 59.56
Zhat( 5): 0.3(54.00) + 0.7(58.11) = 56.88  0.8(54.00) + 0.2(59.56) = 55.11
Zhat( 6): 0.3(56.00) + 0.7(56.88) = 56.61  0.8(56.00) + 0.2(55.11) = 55.82
Zhat( 7): 0.3(53.00) + 0.7(56.61) = 55.53  0.8(53.00) + 0.2(55.82) = 53.56
Zhat( 8): 0.3(55.00) + 0.7(55.53) = 55.37  0.8(55.00) + 0.2(53.56) = 54.71
Zhat( 9): 0.3(59.00) + 0.7(55.37) = 56.46  0.8(59.00) + 0.2(54.71) = 58.14
Zhat(10): 0.3(62.00) + 0.7(56.46) = 58.12  0.8(62.00) + 0.2(58.14) = 61.23
Zhat(11): 0.3(57.00) + 0.7(58.12) = 57.79  0.8(57.00) + 0.2(61.23) = 57.85
Zhat(12): 0.3(50.00) + 0.7(57.79) = 55.45  0.8(50.00) + 0.2(57.85) = 51.57
Zhat(13): 0.3(48.00) + 0.7(55.45) = 53.21  0.8(48.00) + 0.2(51.57) = 48.71
Zhat(14): 0.3(52.00) + 0.7(53.21) = 52.85  0.8(52.00) + 0.2(48.71) = 51.34
Zhat(15): 0.3(55.00) + 0.7(52.85) = 53.50  0.8(55.00) + 0.2(51.34) = 54.27
Zhat(16): 0.3(58.00) + 0.7(53.50) = 54.85  0.8(58.00) + 0.2(54.27) = 57.25
Zhat(17): 0.3(61.00) + 0.7(54.85) = 56.69  0.8(61.00) + 0.2(57.25) = 60.25
```

The $w = .8$ forecasts follow the raw data much more closely. This makes sense because the raw data jump back and forth fairly abruptly, so we need a high w for the forecasts to respond to those oscillations sooner.

12-18. Using a computer:

```
w = 0.7        Zhat(1) = Z(1) = 195

Zhat( 2): 0.7(195.00) + 0.3(195.00) = 195.00
Zhat( 3): 0.7(193.00) + 0.3(195.00) = 193.60
Zhat( 4): 0.7(190.00) + 0.3(193.60) = 191.08
Zhat( 5): 0.7(185.00) + 0.3(191.08) = 186.82
Zhat( 6): 0.7(180.00) + 0.3(186.82) = 182.05
Zhat( 7): 0.7(190.00) + 0.3(182.05) = 187.61
Zhat( 8): 0.7(185.00) + 0.3(187.61) = 185.78
Zhat( 9): 0.7(186.00) + 0.3(185.78) = 185.94
Zhat(10): 0.7(184.00) + 0.3(185.94) = 184.58
Zhat(11): 0.7(185.00) + 0.3(184.58) = 184.87
Zhat(12): 0.7(198.00) + 0.3(184.87) = 194.06
Zhat(13): 0.7(199.00) + 0.3(194.06) = 197.52
Zhat(14): 0.7(200.00) + 0.3(197.52) = 199.26
Zhat(15): 0.7(201.00) + 0.3(199.26) = 200.48
Zhat(16): 0.7(199.00) + 0.3(200.48) = 199.44
Zhat(17): 0.7(187.00) + 0.3(199.44) = 190.73
Zhat(18): 0.7(186.00) + 0.3(190.73) = 187.42
Zhat(19): 0.7(191.00) + 0.3(187.42) = 189.93
Zhat(20): 0.7(195.00) + 0.3(189.93) = 193.48
Zhat(21): 0.7(200.00) + 0.3(193.48) = 198.04
Zhat(22): 0.7(200.00) + 0.3(198.04) = 199.41
Zhat(23): 0.7(190.00) + 0.3(199.41) = 192.82
Zhat(24): 0.7(186.00) + 0.3(192.82) = 188.05
Zhat(25): 0.7(196.00) + 0.3(188.05) = 193.61
Zhat(26): 0.7(198.00) + 0.3(193.61) = 196.68
Zhat(27): 0.7(200.00) + 0.3(196.68) = 199.01
------------FORECAST------------
Zhat(28): 0.7(200.00) + 0.3(199.01) = 199.70
```

12-19. Using a computer:

```
w = 0.6        Zhat(1) = Z(1) = 16.4

Zhat( 2): 0.6(16.40) + 0.4(16.40) = 16.40
Zhat( 3): 0.6(17.10) + 0.4(16.40) = 16.82
Zhat( 4): 0.6(16.90) + 0.4(16.82) = 16.87
Zhat( 5): 0.6(17.30) + 0.4(16.87) = 17.13
Zhat( 6): 0.6(17.50) + 0.4(17.13) = 17.35
Zhat( 7): 0.6(17.20) + 0.4(17.35) = 17.26
Zhat( 8): 0.6(17.30) + 0.4(17.26) = 17.28
Zhat( 9): 0.6(17.10) + 0.4(17.28) = 17.17
Zhat(10): 0.6(16.90) + 0.4(17.17) = 17.01
Zhat(11): 0.6(17.00) + 0.4(17.01) = 17.00
Zhat(12): 0.6(17.10) + 0.4(17.00) = 17.06
```

```
------------FORECAST------------
Zhat(13): 0.6(17.20) + 0.4(17.06) = 17.14
```

12-21. Equation (12-11):
$$\hat{Z}_{t+1} = wZ_t + w(1-w)Z_{t-1} + w(1-w)^2 Z_{t-2} + w(1-w)^3 Z_{t-3} + \ldots$$
The same equation for $\hat{Z}_t$ (shifting all subscripts back by 1):
$$\hat{Z}_t = wZ_{t-1} + w(1-w)Z_{t-2} + w(1-w)^2 Z_{t-3} + w(1-w)^3 Z_{t-4} + \ldots$$
Now multiplying this second equation throughout by $(1-w)$ gives:
$$(1-w)\hat{Z}_t = w(1-w)Z_{t-1} + w(1-w)^2 Z_{t-2} + w(1-w)^3 Z_{t-3} + w(1-w)^4 Z_{t-4} + \ldots$$
Now note that all the terms on the right side of the equation above are identical to all the terms in Equation (12-11) on the top, after the term wZ_t. Hence we can substitute in Equation (12-11) the left hand side of our last equation, $(1-w)\hat{Z}_t$, for all the terms past the first. This gives us:
$$\hat{Z}_{t+1} = wZ_t + (1-w)\hat{Z}_t$$
which is Equation (12-12).

12-22. Equation (12-13) is: $\hat{Z}_{t+1} = Z_t + (1-w)(\hat{Z}_t - Z_t)$ Multiplying out we get:
$\hat{Z}_{t+1} = Z_t + (1-w)\hat{Z}_t - (1-w)Z_t = Z_t + (1-w)\hat{Z}_t - Z_t + wZ_t = wZ_t + (1-w)\hat{Z}_t$,
which is Equation (12-12).

12-23. Simply divide each CPI by $\dfrac{289.1}{100}$; thus:

year	old CPI	new CPI
1950	72.1	24.9
1951	77.8	26.9
1952	79.5	27.5
1953	80.1	27.7
$\vdots$	$\vdots$	$\vdots$

12-24. Current production is much higher than sixteen months earlier, and higher by still more than that (slightly) than it was eight months earlier.

12-25. A simple price index reflects changes in a single price variable of time, relative to a single base time.

12-26. Index numbers are used as deflators for comparing values and prices over time in a way that prevents a given inflationary factor from affecting comparisons. They are also used to provide an aggregate measure of changes over time in several related variables.

12-27. **a.** 1985

b. Just divide each index number by $\dfrac{1990 \text{ index}}{1985 \text{ index}} = \dfrac{163}{100}$

c. It fell, from 145% of the 1985 output down to 133% of that output.

d. Big increase at the start of the '80s, then a sharp drop in 1983, tumbling for three more years, then slowly climbing back up until 1992, then a drop-off.

12-28. Divide each data point by $\dfrac{1990 \text{ value}}{100} = 7.30$:

1981: 108.9   1982: 104.8 ...

12-29. Divide each data point by $\dfrac{\text{Jan. 1995 value}}{100} = 1.44$:

Jun.'94: 98.6   Jul.'94: 95.14 ...

12-30. Since a yearly cycle has 12 months and there are only 18 data points, a seasonal/cyclical decomposition isn't feasible. Simple linear regression, with the successive months numbered $1, 2, \ldots$, gives $\text{SALES} = 4.23987 - .03870\text{MONTH}$, thus for July 1995 (month #19), the forecast is 3.5046.

12-31. Trend analysis is a quick, if sometimes inaccurate, method that can give good results. The additive and multiplicative TSCI models are sometimes useful, although they lack a firm theoretical framework. Exponential smoothing methods are good models. The ones described in this book do not handle seasonality, but extensions are possible. This author believes that Box-Jenkins ARIMA models are the way to go. One limitation of these models is the need for large data sets.

12-32. Exponential smoothing models smooth the data of sharp variations and produce forecasts that follow a type of "average" movement in the data. The greater the weighting factor w, the closer the exponential smoothing series follows the data and forecasts tend to follow the variations in the data more closely.

12-33. **a.** The series is seasonal.

b. Using a computer:
Linear regression trend line: Zhat(t) =   47.1558 + 1.18087 t

t (mon.)	data: Z(t)	trend: Zhat(t)	Centered Moving Average	C(t)= CMA/ Zhat(t)	Ratio Moving Average	Seasonal Index S	[Deseasoned] Z(t)/S%
1 (Jan)	56.00	48.34				110.79	50.54
2 (Feb)	53.00	49.52				104.09	50.92
3 (Mar)	57.00	50.70				97.69	58.35
4 (Apr)	47.00	51.88				91.33	51.46
5 (May)	48.00	53.06				92.90	51.67
6 (Jun)	46.00	54.24				94.19	48.84
7 (Jul)	50.00	55.42	55.71	1.005	89.75	89.71	55.73
8 (Aug)	58.00	56.60	56.79	1.003	102.13	102.08	56.82
9 (Sep)	55.00	57.78	57.58	0.997	95.51	95.47	57.61
10 (Oct)	57.00	58.96	58.38	0.990	97.64	97.60	58.40
11 (Nov)	63.00	60.15	59.50	0.989	105.88	105.83	59.53
12 (Dec)	72.00	61.33	60.83	0.992	118.36	118.30	60.86
13 (Jan)	69.00	62.51	62.25	0.996	110.84	110.79	62.28
14 (Feb)	66.00	63.69	63.38	0.995	104.14	104.09	63.40
15 (Mar)	63.00	64.87	64.46	0.994	97.74	97.69	64.49
16 (Apr)	60.00	66.05	65.67	0.994	91.37	91.33	65.70
17 (May)	62.00	67.23	66.71	0.992	92.94	92.90	66.74
18 (Jun)	64.00	68.41	67.92	0.993	94.23	94.19	67.95
19 (Jul)	66.00	69.59				89.71	73.57
20 (Aug)	69.00	70.77				102.08	67.59
21 (Sep)	70.00	71.95				95.47	73.32
22 (Oct)	71.00	73.13				97.60	72.75
23 (Nov)	74.00	74.32				105.83	69.92
24 (Dec)	90.00	75.50				118.30	76.08

-------------FORECAST-------------
25 (Jan) (Zhat = 76.68)(S = 110.79)/100 = 84.95

12-34. Trend analysis model: $r^2 = .925$ $b_0 = 0.085$ $b_1 = 0.739$
$\hat{Z}(\text{8th year}) = 6.00$
Limitations: the usual ones for trend analysis.

12-35.

a,d. Using MINITAB:

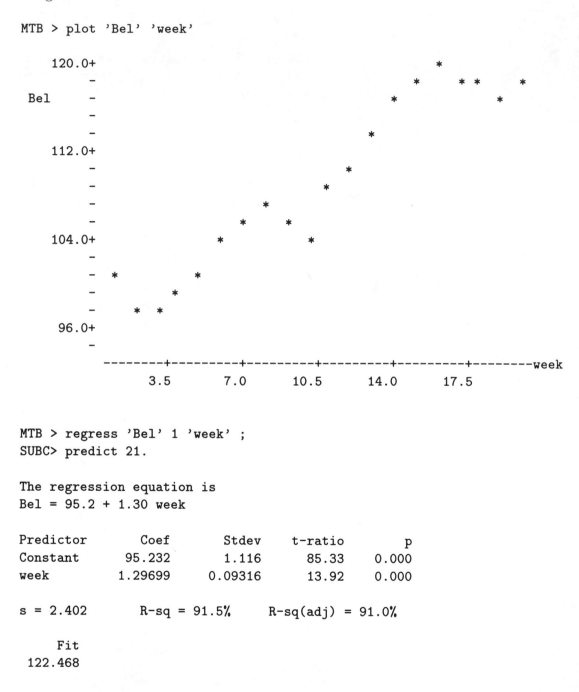

```
MTB > plot 'Bel' 'week'

     120.0+                                                *
          -                              *          *  *          *
Bel       -                          *                       *
          -
          -                      *
     112.0+
          -                  *
          -              *
          -          *
          -      *       *
     104.0+  *                *
          -
          - *            *
          -          *
          -     *  *
      96.0+
          -
          --------+---------+---------+---------+---------+--------week
                 3.5       7.0      10.5      14.0      17.5
```

```
MTB > regress 'Bel' 1 'week' ;
SUBC> predict 21.

The regression equation is
Bel = 95.2 + 1.30 week

Predictor      Coef      Stdev     t-ratio        p
Constant     95.232      1.116       85.33    0.000
week        1.29699    0.09316       13.92    0.000

s = 2.402      R-sq = 91.5%     R-sq(adj) = 91.0%

       Fit
    122.468
```

b. So that comparisons of all later values can be made against the base value = first value for the year.

c. Multiply each value by 100/104.

Case 12.

Since the data are annual, there is no obvious choice for a cycle length. Let's try an exponential smoothing model with a high weighting factor (0.8) so that the model responds quickly to fluctuations in the data.

Using a computer:

```
w = 0.8        Zhat(1) = Z(1) = 2

Zhat( 2): 0.8(2.00) + 0.2(2.00) = 2.00
Zhat( 3): 0.8(4.00) + 0.2(2.00) = 3.60
Zhat( 4): 0.8(3.00) + 0.2(3.60) = 3.12
Zhat( 5): 0.8(1.00) + 0.2(3.12) = 1.42
Zhat( 6): 0.8(2.00) + 0.2(1.42) = 1.88
Zhat( 7): 0.8(4.00) + 0.2(1.88) = 3.58
Zhat( 8): 0.8(0.00) + 0.2(3.58) = 0.72
Zhat( 9): 0.8(1.00) + 0.2(0.72) = 0.94
Zhat(10): 0.8(2.00) + 0.2(0.94) = 1.79
Zhat(11): 0.8(0.00) + 0.2(1.79) = 0.36
Zhat(12): 0.8(2.00) + 0.2(0.36) = 1.67
Zhat(13): 0.8(3.00) + 0.2(1.67) = 2.73
Zhat(14): 0.8(5.00) + 0.2(2.73) = 4.55
Zhat(15): 0.8(6.00) + 0.2(4.55) = 5.71
Zhat(16): 0.8(10.00) + 0.2(5.71) = 9.14
Zhat(17): 0.8(12.00) + 0.2(9.14) = 11.43
Zhat(18): 0.8(12.00) + 0.2(11.43) = 11.89
Zhat(19): 0.8(15.00) + 0.2(11.89) = 14.38
Zhat(20): 0.8(18.00) + 0.2(14.38) = 17.28
Zhat(21): 0.8(15.00) + 0.2(17.28) = 15.46
Zhat(22): 0.8(16.00) + 0.2(15.46) = 15.89
Zhat(23): 0.8(20.00) + 0.2(15.89) = 19.18
Zhat(24): 0.8(15.00) + 0.2(19.18) = 15.84
Zhat(25): 0.8(14.00) + 0.2(15.84) = 14.37
Zhat(26): 0.8(17.00) + 0.2(14.37) = 16.47
Zhat(27): 0.8(18.00) + 0.2(16.47) = 17.69
Zhat(28): 0.8(18.00) + 0.2(17.69) = 17.94
Zhat(29): 0.8(19.00) + 0.2(17.94) = 18.79
Zhat(30): 0.8(14.00) + 0.2(18.79) = 14.96
Zhat(31): 0.8(10.00) + 0.2(14.96) = 10.99
Zhat(32): 0.8(12.00) + 0.2(10.99) = 11.80
Zhat(33): 0.8(11.00) + 0.2(11.80) = 11.16
Zhat(34): 0.8(15.00) + 0.2(11.16) = 14.23
Zhat(35): 0.8(12.00) + 0.2(14.23) = 12.45
Zhat(36): 0.8(10.00) + 0.2(12.45) = 10.49
Zhat(37): 0.8(10.00) + 0.2(10.49) = 10.10
Zhat(38): 0.8(9.00) + 0.2(10.10) = 9.22
Zhat(39): 0.8(12.00) + 0.2(9.22) = 11.44
Zhat(40): 0.8(8.00) + 0.2(11.44) = 8.69
```

```
Zhat(41): 0.8(9.00) + 0.2(8.69) = 8.94
Zhat(42): 0.8(7.00) + 0.2(8.94) = 7.39
Zhat(43): 0.8(5.00) + 0.2(7.39) = 5.48
Zhat(44): 0.8(7.00) + 0.2(5.48) = 6.70
Zhat(45): 0.8(10.00) + 0.2(6.70) = 9.34
Zhat(46): 0.8(11.00) + 0.2(9.34) = 10.67
Zhat(47): 0.8(12.00) + 0.2(10.67) = 11.73
Zhat(48): 0.8(13.00) + 0.2(11.73) = 12.75
Zhat(49): 0.8(16.00) + 0.2(12.75) = 15.35
Zhat(50): 0.8(19.00) + 0.2(15.35) = 18.27
Zhat(51): 0.8(17.00) + 0.2(18.27) = 17.25
Zhat(52): 0.8(4.00) + 0.2(17.25) = 6.65
Zhat(53): 0.8(7.00) + 0.2(6.65) = 6.93
Zhat(54): 0.8(8.00) + 0.2(6.93) = 7.79
Zhat(55): 0.8(10.00) + 0.2(7.79) = 9.56
Zhat(56): 0.8(14.00) + 0.2(9.56) = 13.11
Zhat(57): 0.8(10.00) + 0.2(13.11) = 10.62
Zhat(58): 0.8(12.00) + 0.2(10.62) = 11.72
Zhat(59): 0.8(13.00) + 0.2(11.72) = 12.74
Zhat(60): 0.8(15.00) + 0.2(12.74) = 14.55
Zhat(61): 0.8(13.00) + 0.2(14.55) = 13.31
Zhat(62): 0.8(14.00) + 0.2(13.31) = 13.86
Zhat(63): 0.8(15.00) + 0.2(13.86) = 14.77
Zhat(64): 0.8(14.00) + 0.2(14.77) = 14.15
Zhat(65): 0.8(16.00) + 0.2(14.15) = 15.63

------------FORECAST------------
Zhat(66): 0.8(17.00) + 0.2(15.63) = 16.73
```

CHAPTER 13

13-1. A production process is monitored by tracking various numeric parameters pertaining to the items produced, the tolerances desired, etc. Quality control/improvement is a means of checking and maintaining standards in the process, with the help of sampling methods and statistical indicators.

13-2. Variance, particularly the effort to minimize it for the production parameters of interest.

13-3. 1) Natural, random variation; 2) variation due to assignable causes.

13-4.
13-5. A center line representing the desired value of a production parameter is given, as well as upper and lower limits for acceptable variation away from the center value. The sampled parameters are then charted, typically in order corresponding to the chronology of the process, and certain anomalous patterns can then be discerned to determine whether the process in "in control" or not, and if not, the direction in which to make corrections.

13-6. The variable being charted must be assumed to have an at least approximately normal distribution. Variation of the random, natural kind cannot be singled out by means of quality control charts.

13-7. A method for determining whether a particular lot or group of items is acceptable. It usually involves making an assumption of a probability that any one item is acceptable, then checking a sample of outcomes for whether the proportion of acceptable items in the sample falls within a certain range in a binomial distribution corresponding to the assumed probability.

13-8. Various experiments in the design and production methods used are made to determine which factors most affect the parameters of interest. ANOVA methods are often used to make this determination. By adopting modified methods in the full-scale production process, the overall quality control results may be improved.

13-9. Instead of merely ensuring that each individual parameter of interest in a production process is within an allowable tolerance, one can define a function measuring the overall defect of quality of the output by combining the various individual deviations; then one works to modify the process to as to minimize this overall "loss function" and thus minimize the total variation in quality.

13-12. Both the average number of bugs (i.e., the "process mean") and the variance in number of defects over all projects are steadily decreasing over time.

13-13. Since the sample mean is a random variable which tends toward a normal distribution, we expect it to cluster around the process mean over repeated observations. Thus a time plot of sample means of aggregated observations is a way to see whether this clustering behavior is in fact taking place, so we will be able to detect any major shift in the process mean (the process then being out of control). The chart is constructed by means of estimates of the parameters of interest: process mean and process standard deviation.

13-14. The "waiting time" process in in control:

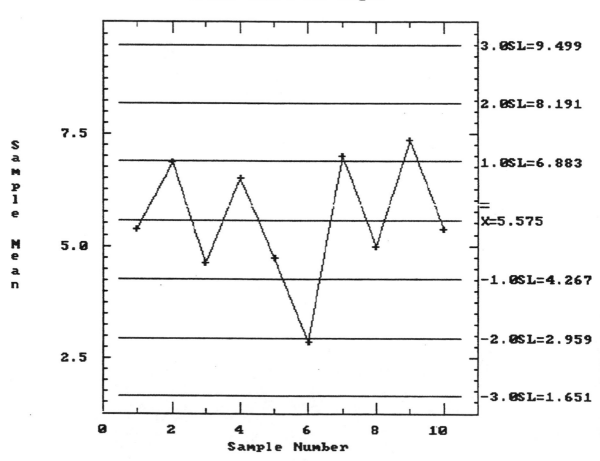

13-15. Random sampling, so that the observations are independent.

13-16. Sixth group mean is above the UCL line.

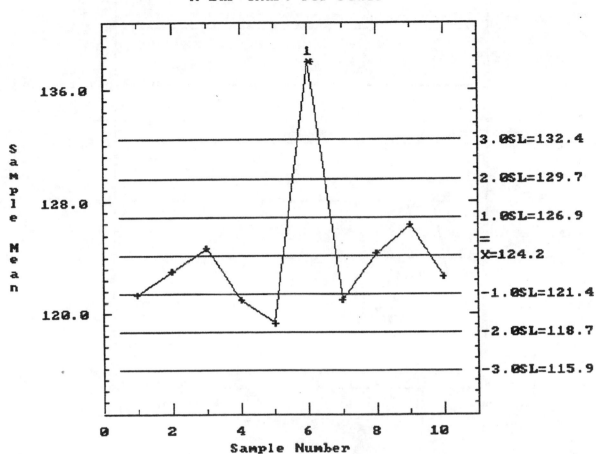

X-bar Chart for Power

13-17. Process in is control:

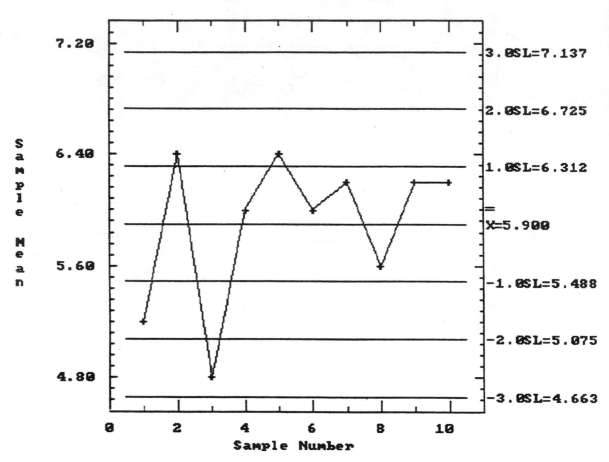

X-bar Chart for Pounds

13-18. We wish to monitor and control the process variance.

13-19. An *R*-chart is easier to calculate by hand, but an *s*-chart gives information more directly related to the actual process standard deviation.

13-20. Sample range and sample standard deviation, as random variables, actually have skewness (are not symmetrically distributed about their means).

13-21.

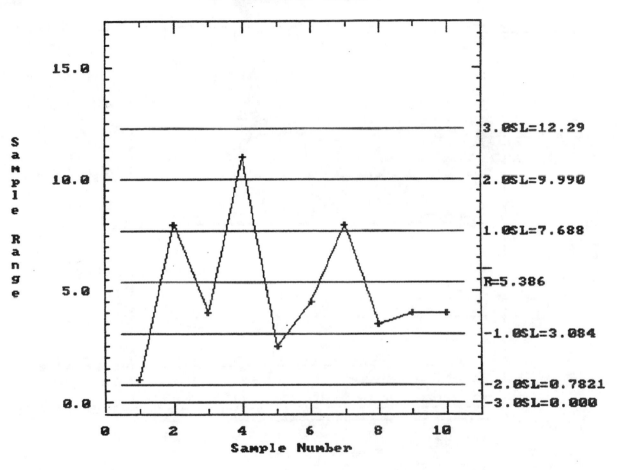

R Chart for Legal

15.0

3.0SL=12.29

2.0SL=9.990

10.0

1.0SL=7.688

R=5.386

Sample Range

5.0

-1.0SL=3.084

-2.0SL=0.7821

0.0

-3.0SL=0.000

0   2   4   6   8   10

Sample Number

13-22.

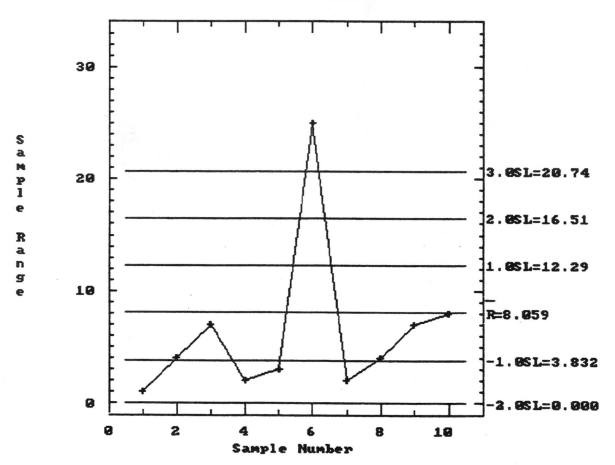

13-23.

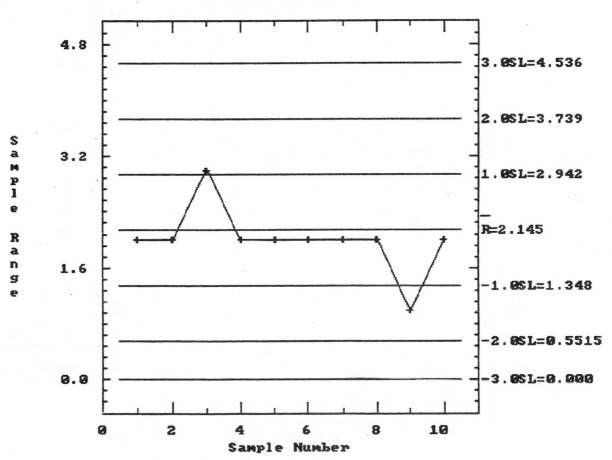

R Chart for Pounds

13-24.

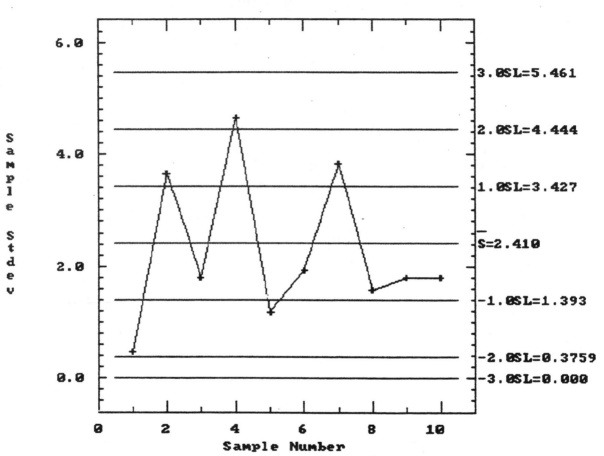

3-25.

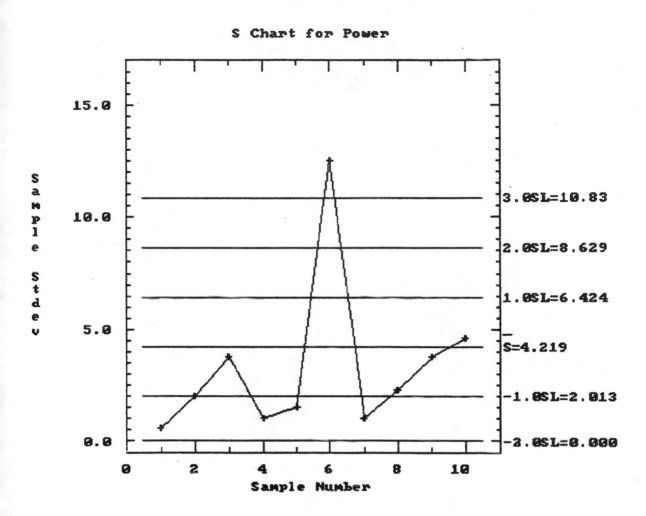

S Chart for Power

3-26. Yes, the process standard deviation is in control.

3-27. All points are well within the p-chart limits; process is in control.

3-28. From a p-chart: $\bar{P} = 0.0333$ UCL = 0.1317
The 12th sample exceeds the UCL.

13-29. All points are well within the p-chart limits; process is in control.

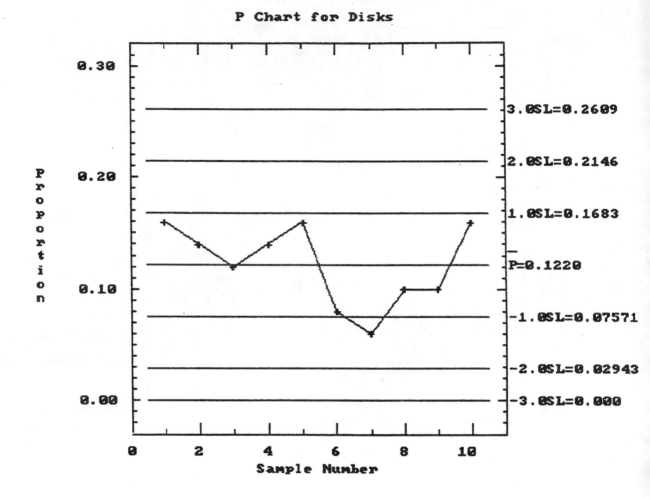

P Chart for Disks

13-30. It may be very hard to detect any defective items at all.

13-31. The tenth sample barely exceeds the UCL = 8.953; otherwise in control.

13-32. The 12th observation exceeds the UCL = 34.33; otherwise in control.

3-33. All points within c-chart limits; process is in control.

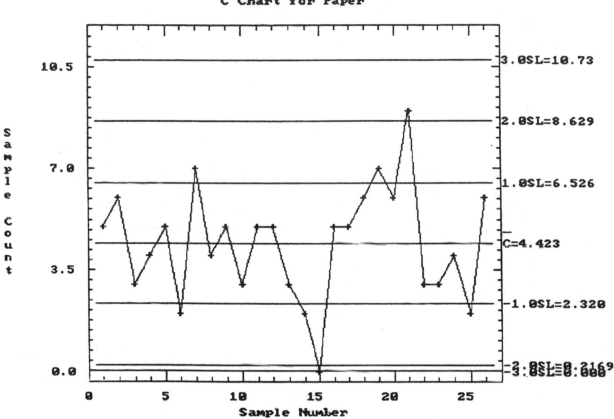

C Chart for Paper

3-34. The number of defectives is assumed to follow a Poisson distribution.

3-36. Using a c-chart, we find that the 10th observation exceeds the UCL = 27.01.

3-37. The twentieth observation far exceeds the UCL = 8.92/100; also, the last nine observations are all on one side of the center line $\bar{P} = 3.45/100$.

13-38. Process variation is in control:

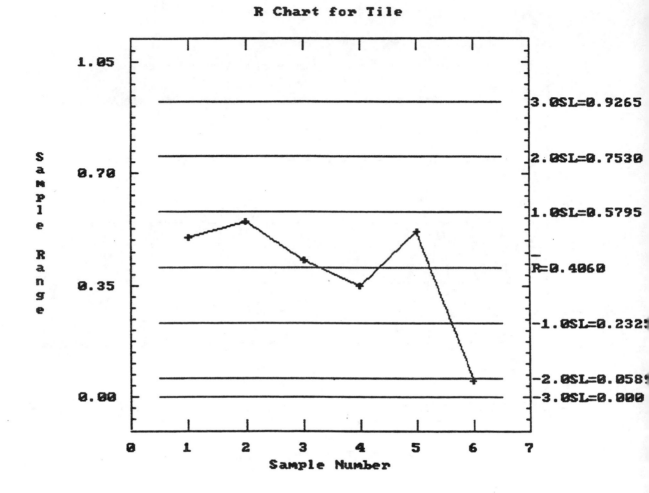

13-39. Last group's mean is below the LCL = 2.136:

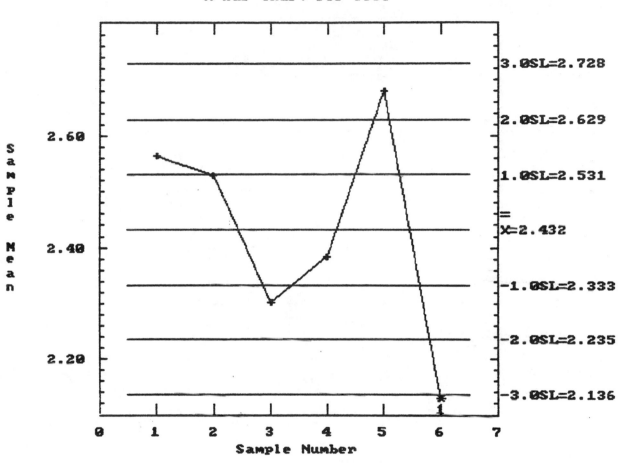

X-bar Chart for Tile

Sample Mean

3.0SL=2.728

2.0SL=2.629

1.0SL=2.531

$\overline{\overline{X}}$=2.432

-1.0SL=2.333

-2.0SL=2.235

-3.0SL=2.136

Sample Number

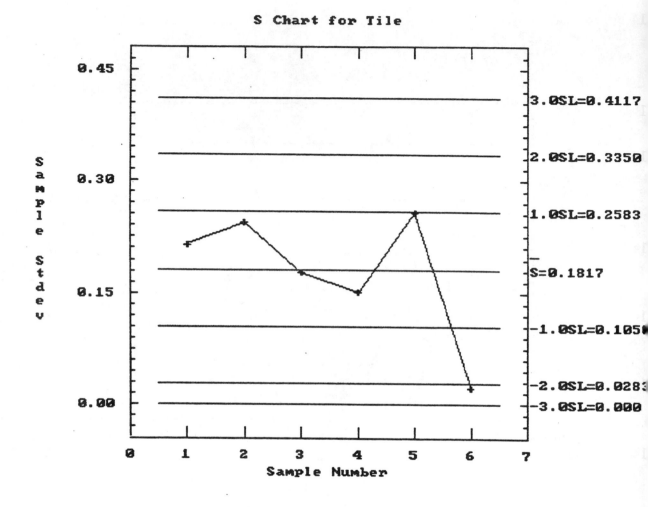

S Chart for Tile

Case 13.

Of the eight tests for an X-chart, only test #6 fails, the test for four out of five consecutive points falling outside the 1σ limit. In this case, all but one of the observations #12–#16 are higher than $\mu + \sigma$, and all but one of the observations #19–#23 are higher than $\mu + \sigma$ while the remaining one is lower than $\mu - \sigma$. The process is essentially in control, with an apparent slight bias toward heavier coating.

CHAPTER 14

14-1. $n = 15$ $\quad T = \sum + = 10$

Critical pts. at $\alpha = 2(.0176) = .035$ are 3 and $n - 3 = 12$.

Cannot reject H_0 (p-value $= 0.18$)

14-2. $\sum + = 10$ $\quad$ p-value $= 0.006$. Reject H_0.

14-3. $n = 25$ $\quad$ Use z (because $25(.5) = 12.5 > 5$).

$T = \sum + = 20$ $\quad$ $z = (2T - n)/\sqrt{n} = (40 - 25)/5 = 3$

Reject H_0. (Program is probably effective.)

14-4. $\sum + = 19$ $\quad$ p-value $= 0.0015$. Reject H_0. There is evidence that the second fund is better.

14-5. $n = 42$ $\quad T = \sum B(+) = 27$ $\quad z = (54 - 42)/\sqrt{42} = 1.85$

At $\alpha = .05$, cannot reject H_0 (no preference).

14-6. $T = 1.52$. The critical point for chi-square with 1 df and $\alpha = 0.05$ is 3.841. Therefore, we cannot reject H_0.

14-7. Before 324 out of 1,000, 129 changed to other network while 75 changed to our network.

$T = (b-c)^2/(b+c) = (129-75)^2/(129+75) = 14.29$ $\quad$ Crit. pt. $\chi^2_{(1)}(.005) = 7.88$

Reject H_0. There is evidence that the network loses more viewers than it gains. p-value $< .005$.

14-8. $n = 6$ $\quad \sum + = 5$ $\quad$ p-value $= 0.1095$. We cannot reject H_0. Due to the small sample size, the test is weak and hence the acceptance of H_0.

14-9. $T = (58 - 15)^2/(58 + 15) = 25.33$ $\quad$ Reject H_0. Campaign is probably effective. (Crit. pt. for $\alpha = 0.05$ is 7.88.)

14-10. $T = 9$ $\quad$ p-value $= 0.01$. Reject H_0. There is evidence of an increasing trend.

14-11. After being divided into the two halves of 8 points each, every data point in the first half is less than its corresponding second-half point. The binomial probability of this is $\binom{8}{8}(0.5)^8(1-0.5)^0 = 1/256 = 0.00391$. Thus there is strong evidence of an upward trend, with that as the p-value.

14-12. $n = 6 \qquad T = 6 \qquad p\text{-value} = 0.016$. Reject H_0. There is evidence of a positive correlation.

14-13. The t test requires the assumption of a normal distribution. When this assumption cannot be justified, the variation of the sign test for correlation should be used.

14-14. The t test requires an assumption of a normal population distribution. When the distribution is not believed normal, but is believed to be symmetric, a test for the population median is equivalent to a test for the population mean and the sign test may be used. When a normal distribution can be assumed, the t test is more powerful and should be used.

14-15.

$-$	$-$	$-$	$-$	$-$	$-$	$-$	$+$	$+$	$-$
$-$	$+$	$+$	$+$	$+$	$-$	$-$	$-$	$+$	$-$
$-$	$+$	$+$	$+$	$-$	$-$	$-$	$-$	$+$	$-$

$T = 19 \qquad n = 30 \qquad z = (2T - n)/\sqrt{n} = 8/\sqrt{30} = 1.46$
We cannot reject H_0 that median is \$78.50.

14-16. $T = 5 \qquad n = 5 \qquad p\text{-value} = 0.032$. Yes, there is evidence of an increasing trend.

14-17. $b = 355 \qquad c = 122 \qquad T = (b - c)^2/(b + c) = 113.8$
Reject H_0. There is evidence that the newspaper lost readers.

14-18. $T = 4 \qquad n = 5 \qquad p\text{-value} = 0.1875$. We cannot reject H_0.

14-19. $n_1 = 41 \qquad n_2 = 17 \qquad R = 10 \qquad E(R) = (2n_1n_2)/(n_1 + n_2) + 1 = 25.034$

$$\sigma_R = \sqrt{\frac{2n_1n_2(2n_1n_2 - n_1 - n_2)}{(n_1 + n_2)^2(n_1 + n_2 - 1)}}$$

$$z = \frac{R - E(R)}{\sigma_R} = \frac{-15.034}{\sqrt{\dfrac{2(41)(17)[2(41)(17) - 41 - 17]}{(58)^2(57)}}} = -4.82$$

Reject H_0. Not random.

14-20. $n = 72$ Runs $= 46$ $z = 2.145$ p-value $= 0.032$. Reject H_0. The sequence is probably not random.

14-21. $$z = \dfrac{4 - \left[\dfrac{2(12)(18)}{30} + 1\right]}{\sqrt{\dfrac{2(12)(18)[2(12)(18) - 12 - 18]}{(30)^2(29)}}} = -4.42$$

Reject H_0. The regression errors are probably not random.

14-22. $n = 17$ Runs $= 2$ $z = -3.756$. The p-value is very small. If assignments are truly random, such an occurrence would happen less than once in 2,500 days. If messengers work 5 days a week, this should occur about once in ten years! Discrimination is likely.

14-23. $n_1 = 30$ $n_2 = 12$ $R = 10$

$$z = \dfrac{10 - \left[\dfrac{2(12)(30)}{42} + 1\right]}{\sqrt{\dfrac{2(12)(30)[2(12)(30) - 12 - 30]}{(42)^2(41)}}} = -3.13$$

Reject H_0. Foreign firms can claim discrimination.

14-24. $n = 17$ Runs $= 2$ $z = -3.756$. Reject H_0. There is evidence that ad 1 is preferred to ad 2.

14-25. $R = 6$ $n_1 = 7$ $n_2 = 8$ Cannot reject H_0. (The sample size is probably too small.) p-value $= 2(.149) = 0.298$.

14-26. $U = 100 + (110/2) - 151.5 = 3.5$. Reject H_0; p-value < 0.0002. Nautical Design seems to be preferred.

14-27. $R_1 = 228$ $U = 18(16) + 18(19)/2 - 228 = 231$ $z = (231 - 144)/28.98 = 3.00$

Reject H_0. The concentration in Antarctica is probably lower.

14-28. Both the Wald-Wolfowitz and the Mann-Whitney tests are nonparametric and do not require the assumption of normality required for the t test. Mann-Whitney requires that the data be on an ordinal scale, and in such cases the test should be used as it is a powerful alternative to the t test, more powerful than Wald-Wolfowitz.

14-29. $R_1 = \sum R = 160 \qquad U = (12)(11) + 12(13)/2 - 160 = 50$

$E(U) = 12(11)/2 = 66 \qquad \sigma_U = \sqrt{[11(12)(24)]/12}$

$z = (50 - 66)/16.248 = -0.984 \qquad$ Do not reject H_0.

14-30. $U = 8(8) + 8(9)/2 - 88 = 12 \qquad$ Reject H_0; p-value $= 2(0.019) = 0.038$. There is some evidence that the Chicago investment may be better.

14-31. $U = 16(17) + 17(18)/2 - 229.5 = 195.5 \qquad z = \dfrac{59.6}{\sqrt{\dfrac{16(17)(16 + 17 + 1)}{12}}} = 2.14$

Reject H_0. The black-market commissions are probably cheaper.

14-32. The Wilcoxon signed-rank test is a useful alternative to the paired-difference t test when it may not be assumed that the differences between the paired observations are normally distributed.

14-33. $T = 6$. We cannot reject H_0 at $\alpha = 0.05$. p-value $= 0.10$.

14-34. $T = 23$. Do not reject H_0; no evidence of differences in management style.

14-35. $T = 56$. Reject H_0 at $\alpha = 0.05$

14-36. The sign test is appropriate since the data are binary (0 or 1 depending on the sound preference).

14-37. Use the parametric t test (actually use z since the sample is large). This is the appropriate test since commissions can be assumed to be normally distributed.

14-38. Use the Wilcoxon signed-rank test for the mean of a single population.

14-39. $T = 18 \qquad n = 14 \qquad$ Reject H_0 at $\alpha = 0.025$. The main limitation of the analysis is that we have time-series data, which are likely correlated. This is not a random sample. (Another limitation is that the operation is just beginning and may not have yet reached a stable level.)

14-40. $n = 12 \qquad T = 27 > 17$, so we cannot reject H_0 at $\alpha = 0.10$.

14-41. $n = 10 \qquad T = 4.5 < 5$. Reject H_0 at $\alpha = 0.01$.

14-42. p-value < 0.001. There is evidence that the airline's delays have increased after the deregulation.

14-43. Using SYSTAT: p-value $= 0.468$, so we do not reject H_0.

14-44. $H = 12.5 \qquad p$-value $= 0.002$. Reject H_0. There is evidence that the frequency of use is not the same in all three industry groups.

14-45. $R_1 = 75 \qquad R_2 = 116 \qquad R_3 = 55 \qquad R_4 = 160$

$$H = \frac{12}{28(29)}\left(75^2/7 + 116^2/7 + 55^2/7 + 160^2/7\right) - 3(29) = 13.716$$

Compare with $\chi^2_{.005}(3) = 12.84$. Reject H_0; p-value $< .005$

14-46. $H = 29.61 \qquad p$-value < 0.001. Reject H_0. Not all three songs are equally liked. Now continue with further analysis:

$D_1 = |\bar{R}_R - \bar{R}_A| = |(366/12) - (214.5/12)| = 12.625$
$D_2 = |\bar{R}_R - \bar{R}_B| = |(366/12) - (85.5/12)| = 23.375$
$D_3 = |\bar{R}_A - \bar{R}_B| = |(214.5/12) - (85.5/12)| = 10.75$

Using $\alpha = 0.05$, we find $C_{\text{KW}} = \sqrt{(7.38)\dfrac{(36)(37)}{12}\left(\dfrac{1}{12} + \dfrac{1}{12}\right)} = 11.68$. This number is greater than D_3 but smaller than both D_1 and D_2. Hence there is proof that "Revolution" is favored over other songs and Nike should definitely pay the Beatles for its use.

14-47. $R_1 = 79 \qquad R_2 = 103 \qquad R_3 = 28$

$$H = \frac{12}{20(21)}\left(79^2/8 + 103^2/6 + 28^2/6\right) - 3(21) = 13.54$$

$\chi^2_{(2)}(.005) = 10.6$. Reject H_0. [Using SYSTAT: p-value $= 0.001$.]

14-48. $H = 13.01 \qquad p$-value $= 0.001$. Reject H_0. Returns on investment in the three areas are probably not all equal.

14-49. $R_1 = 228 \qquad R_2 = 192 \qquad R_3 = 135 \qquad R_4 = 62 \qquad R_5 = 49$

$$H = \frac{12}{36(37)}\left(228^2/7 + 192^2/8 + 135^2/8 + 62^2/7 + 49^2/6\right) - 3(37) = 26.49$$

$\chi^2_{(4)}(.005) = 14.9$. Reject H_0. Further analysis shows that, at $\alpha = 0.05$, the only significant differences are between New York and Orlando (NY > Orlando).

14-50. We assume that the samples are random and independent of each other, the variables under study are continuous, and the measurement scale is ordinal. We do not assume a normal distribution of the populations under study. If we test for differences among population means, we must assume that when differences exist they are differences in the means.

14-51. $X^2 = \dfrac{12}{12(4)(5)}(14^2 + 32^2 + 42^2 + 32^2) - 3(12)(5) = 20.4$

Compare with $\chi^2_{(3)}(.005) = 12.8$. Therefore, reject H_0. Not all fragrances are equally liked (p-value < 0.001).

14-52. $X^2 = 12.60 \qquad p$-value $= 0.002$. Reject H_0. Not all managers are equally effective.

14-53. $X^2 = \dfrac{12}{9(3)(4)}(16^2 + 24^2 + 14^2) - 3(9)(4) = 6.22$

Compare with $\chi^2_{(2)}(.05) = 5.99$. Therefore, reject H_0; p-value $< .05$.

14-54. $X^2 = 16.35 \qquad p$-value $= 0.001$. Reject H_0. Not all four processes are equally good.

14-55. $H_0: \rho \leq 0 \qquad H_1: \rho > 0$

$r_s = 1 - 6\left(\sum d^2\right)/n(n^2 - 1) = 1 - 6(406)/15(224) = 0.275$

From Table 11 of Appendix C, for $n = 15$, the critical point for $\alpha = 0.05$ is 0.441. Do not reject H_0 of no positive correlation.

14-56. $n = 11 \qquad r_s = 0.791 \qquad$ From Table 11 of Appendix C, for $n = 11$, the critical points for $\alpha = 0.05$ in a two-tailed test are ± 0.623. Reject H_0. There is evidence of a positive correlation.

14-57. $n = 10 \qquad r_s = 0.486 \qquad$ For the positive one-tail test at $n = 10$, the table value is greater than this; there is no evidence of rank correlation.

14-58. $n = 11 \qquad r_s = -0.755 \qquad$ There is certainly no evidence of a *positive* rank correlation between the two variables here.

14-59. $n = 10 \qquad r_s = 0.297 < 0.564$, which is the critical point in a two-tailed test at $\alpha = 0.10$. Hence we do not reject the null hypothesis of no rank correlation between color intensity and appeal.

4-60. We convert the article's table percentages to expected counts within the sample:

UK: $0.402(212) = 85.22$ G: $0.0909(212) = 19.27$

N: $0.195(212) = 41.34$ Other: $0.312(212) = 66.14$

Next we use the observed counts together with the above expected counts and compute: $X^2 = \sum_i (O_i - E_i)^2/E_i = 21.80$. This value is far greater than the critical point for $\chi^2_{(3)}(0.005)$, which is 12.838. We thus reject H_0. The p-value is very small. The percentages of all European firms who invested in the U.S. in 1992 are very probably different from what the article reported.

4-61. $X^2_{(4)} = \dfrac{(4-20)^2 + (12-20)^2 + (34-20)^2 + (40-20)^2 + (10-20)^2}{20} = 50.8$

Reject H_0; p-value $< .005$.

4-62. The expected counts are as follows:

NB: $0.729(1,000) = 729$ PL: $0.23(1,000) = 230$ G: $0.041(1,000) = 41$

The observed counts are, respectively: 610, 290, and 100. We now compute the value of the test statistic: $X^2 = \sum (O - E)^2/E = 119.97$. Strongly reject the null hypothesis.

4-63. **a.** No. E(count) in cell A is < 5, and the same is true for cell E.

b. Combine cells A and B, and cell E with Other.

c. $X^2_{(3)} = 10 + 10.28 + 4.65 + 1.62 = 26.56$. Reject H_0. p-value < 0.005.

4-64. For a normal distribution with mean 11 and standard deviation 2, we expect 0.3413 of the observations to be between 11 and 13; 0.3413 of the observations to be between 9 and 11; 0.1587 of them below 9; and the same proportion above 13. [Here we use one standard deviation.] The observed counts are as follows: Below 9: 5;   9 to 11: 12;   above 11 and up to 13: 9;   above 13: 4. Expected counts are (respectively): $30(.1587) = 4.76$; $30(.3413) = 10.24$;   10.24;   4.76. The test statistic value is: $X^2_{(3)} = (5 - 4.76)^2/4.76 + (12 - 10.24)^2/10.24 + (9 - 10.24)^2/10.24 + (4 - 4.76)^2/4.76 = 0.586$. Do not reject H_0. [Note that two expected counts are slightly below 5. However, other partitions also lead to non-rejection of the null hypothesis.]

14-65. The test statistic now has 2 fewer degrees of freedom: df $= 4 - 3 = 1$. We have: $\bar{x} = 11.21$ and $s = 2.71$. Forming a partition using $z = 0.44$ and $z = -0.44$ leads to: $X^2_{(1)} = 1.7 + 0.86 + 0.24 + 0.082 = 2.88$. At $\alpha = 0.05$, we cannot reject H_0.

14-66. $X^2 = 12.193$ df $= 2$ Reject H_0.

14-67. $X^2 = 6.81$ df $= 3$ Do not reject H_0.

14-68. $X^2 = 6.94$ df $= 4$ Do not reject H_0 at $\alpha = 0.05$.

14-69. $X^2 = 6.65$ df $= 1$ Reject H_0 at $\alpha = 0.01$.

14-70. In this problem, some cells have expected counts below 5. Therefore, we will combine the income level categories so that the first one is 0 to $24,999 and the last one is $40,000 and above. All intermediate categories remain as they are. We get: $X^2 = 50.991$ df $= 8$ Strongly reject H_0.

14-71. **a.** $X^2 = 33.958$ df $= 12$ Reject H_0.

     b. $X^2 = 32.90$ df $= 1$ Reject H_0. There is evidence of a difference in preference for red versus blue in the two cities. Since this single subsequent test was proposed before looking at the data, it is valid.

14-72. $X^2 = 109.56$ df $= 4$ Strongly reject H_0. The proportion is probably not equal across the five locations.

14-73. $X^2 = 4.23$ df $= 3$ Do not reject H_0.

14-74. $X^2 = 16.15$ df $= 2$ Reject H_0.

14-75. $X^2 = 10.86$ df $= 2$ p-value $< .005$ Reject H_0. The proportions are probably not equal in all 3 shipments.

14-76. $X^2 = 24.36$ df $= 6$ Reject H_0.

14-77. Median $= 15$ $X^2 = 4.159$ df $= 2$ Do not reject H_0.

14-78. $X^2 = 1{,}626.004$ df $= 4$ Reject H_0. The p-value is extremely small.

4-79. Let $1, 0$ denote predicting and missing the buyouts, respectively. Then the data in order are:

$$1, 1, 1, 1, 1, 1, 0, 1, 1, 1, 1, 1, 1, 0, 0, 0, 0, 0, 1, 1, 1$$

A MINITAB runs test on this sequence, for runs of data points above and below 0.5, rejects H_0, p-value $= 0.0113$. The analyst's performance is probably not random.

4-80. $X^2 = 0.15 \qquad df = 2 \qquad$ Do not reject H_0.

4-81. **a.** The Friedman test.

b. $R_1 = 27 \qquad R_2 = 24 \qquad R_3 = 25 \qquad R_4 = 24 \qquad n = 10$
$$X^2 = \frac{12}{10(4)(5)}(27^2 + 24^2 + 25^2 + 24^2) - 3(10)(5) = 0.36$$
$\chi^2_{(3)}(0.10) = 6.25.$ Thus, do not reject H_0. There is no evidence of differences among any of the 4 announcers.

4-83. $n = 12 \qquad R_1 = 18 \qquad R_2 = 27 \qquad R_3 = 39 \qquad R_4 = 36$
$$X^2 = \frac{12}{12(4)(5)}(18^2 + 27^2 + 39^2 + 36^2) - 3(12)(5) = 13.5$$
Compare with $\chi^2_{(3)}(.005) = 12.8$; p-value $< .005$. Reject H_0. Not all four brands are equally appealing.

4-84. The Pearson product-moment correlation coefficient is the most useful one. It requires the assumption of normal populations of the two variables involved. Spearman's correlation coefficient, based on ranks, is a nonparametric alternative. For testing for an association between variables, the Cox and Stuart test may also be used, or a chi-square test for independence.

4-85. Using SYSTAT: p-value $= 0.031$. Reject H_0. There is evidence of an increasing trend.

4-86. $r_s = -0.125 \qquad n = 9 \qquad$ Do not reject H_0. There is no evidence of a correlation. Note: there are many ties here. One should get a larger sample.

4-87. Use the Wilcoxon signed-rank test. Using SYSTAT, the reported 2-tailed p-value is 0.209. Thus the one-tailed p-value for this test is either 0.105 or a large number—depending on which rank sum is greater. Do not reject H_0. There is no evidence that the Hyatt card is preferred to the airline card.

14-88. $n_1 = 14$ $n_2 = 12$ $R_1 = 232.5$
$U = (14)(12) + 14(15)/2 - 232.5 = 40.5$ $E(U) = (14)(12)/2 = 84$
$\sigma_U = \sqrt{(14)(12)(27)/12} = 19.44$ $z = (40.5 - 84)/19.44 = -2.24$
Reject H_0. System A is probably rated higher, on average, than system B.

14-89. We use the Kruskal-Wallis test. $H = 7.43$, df $= 2$, p-value $= 0.024$. Not all three systems are equally well liked (as we already know from Problem **14-88**).

14-90. The Mann-Whitney test and the Kruskal-Wallis test are the most powerful alternatives to the two-sample t test and ANOVA, respectively, when the assumption of normal populations may not be justified.

14-91. Distribution-free methods are methods that do not rely on particular distributional assumptions, usually the normal-distribution assumption. Non-parametric methods are methods that do not deal with particular population parameters, such as the mean or the median.

14-92. $\bar{x} = 31.55$ $s = 5.09$ Form a partition using one standard deviation and the expected proportions 0.1587, 0.3413, 0.3413, and 0.1587. Computing the expected and observed cell counts gives us: $\chi^2_{(1)} = 1.65$. Do not reject H_0. There is no evidence here that the distribution of salaries is not normal.

14-93. You should combine this cell with another, so that the expected count will be at least 5. However, if only one cell has an expected count below 5, some rules of thumb say the chi-square analysis may still be carried out.

Case 14.

This is an interesting case. First, we need to convert the reported percentages in all three tables to counts so that we can carry out a chi-square analysis. We do this by multiplying each percentage in the table, expressed decimally as a proportion, by the total count at the bottom of the appropriate column. Then check the counts by adding across each row and testing against the reported row totals.

Next, we find that the expected counts in some of the cells are less than 5. The categories "sense of belonging" and "fun-enjoyment-excitement" were thus combined, although "fun-enjoyment-excitement" can be combined with another category to solve the problem of its low expected counts. In Exhibit 3, it is also necessary to combine The Islands with The Empty Quarter because of low expected counts. Next we carry out the analysis.

The results are as follows:

For the Census Regions (Exhibit 2): $\chi^2_{(48)} = 79.162$ p-value $= 0.003$.

For the Nine Nations (Exhibit 3): $\chi^2_{(36)} = 59.452$ p-value $= 0.008$.

For the Quadrants (Exhibit 4): $\chi^2_{(18)} = 46.69$ p-value $=$ "0.000."

If we consider the p-value a measure of the discrimination among regions, then the Quadrants division seems to work best, then comes the Census division, and the Nine Nations seems least effective. There are, however, some problems with this analysis. It seems that The Islands may be expected to be different from other regions in culture, nature of the people, etc. The combination of this category with another (due to low expected count) in effect removes this category from the analysis and important information may thus be lost. A larger sample should be selected from this Nation. These results call for further analysis of this problem in order to reach a more definite conclusion.

CHAPTER 15

15-1. $P(\theta \mid x) = \dfrac{P(x \mid \theta) P(\theta)}{\sum_i P(x \mid \theta_i) P(\theta_i)}$ $\hat{p} = x/n = 6/20$

s	$P(s)$	$P(x \mid s)$	$P(s)P(x \mid s)$	$P(s \mid x)$
.1	.2	.0089	.00178	.02531
.2	.3	.1091	.03273	.46544
.3	.1	.1916	.01916	.27247
.4	.1	.1244	.01244	.17691
.5	.1	.0370	.00370	.05262
.6	.1	.0049	.00049	.00697
.7	.1	.0002	.00002	.00028
	1.0		.07032	1.00000

Credible set of posterior probability 0.9148 is [0.2, 0.4].

15-2. $\hat{p} = x/n = 7/17$

s	$P(s)$	$P(x \mid s)$	$P(s)P(x \mid s)$	$P(s \mid x)$
.1	.02531	.0007	.000018	.000205
.2	.46544	.0268	.012474	.142496
.3	.27247	.1202	.032751	.374131
.4	.17691	.1927	.034091	.389438
.5	.05262	.1483	.007804	.089149
.6	.00697	.0571	.000398	.004546
.7	.00028	.0095	.000003	.000035
	1.00000		.087539	1.000000

Credible set of posterior probability 0.9061 is [0.2, 0.4].

15-3. Using Table 15-3:

s	$P(s)$	$P(x \mid s)$	$P(s)P(x \mid s)$	$P(s \mid x)$
.1	.049	.0547	.0027	.0126
.2	.619	.2013	.1246	.5829
.3	.293	.2668	.0782	.3658
.4	.038	.2150	.0082	.0384
.5	.0006	.1172	.00007	.0003
			.21377	1.0000

15-4. $\hat{p} = x/n = 1/18$

M	P(M)	P(X | M)	P(M)P(X | M)	P(M | X)
.05	.3	.3763	.11289	.53849
.15	.5	.1705	.08525	.40665
.20	.1	.0811	.00811	.03869
.25	.1	.0339	.00339	.01617
	1.0		.20964	1.00000

Note that the mode of the distribution changed from .15 to .05 in view of the data.

15-5. $\hat{R} = x/n = 3/10$

R	P(R)	P(X | R)	P(R)P(X | R)	P(R | X)
.25	.1	.2503	.02503	.1129
.30	.2	.2668	.05336	.2407
.35	.2	.2522	.05044	.2275
.40	.3	.2150	.06450	.2909
.45	.1	.1665	.01665	.0751
.50	.1	.1172	.01172	.0529
	1.0		.22170	1.0000

15 6. $\hat{p} = x/n = 4/12$

R	P(R)	P(X | R)	P(R)P(X | R)	P(R | X)
.25	.1129	.1936	.02186	.10291
.30	.2407	.2312	.05565	.26198
.35	.2275	.2366	.05383	.25341
.40	.2909	.2129	.06193	.29155
.45	.0751	.1699	.01276	.06007
.50	.0529	.1208	.00639	.03008
	1.0000		.21242	1.00000

A credible set of posterior probability 0.97 is [0.25, 0.45].

A credible set of posterior probability 0.91 is [0.25, 0.40].

15-7.

R	P(R)	P(X | R)	P(R ∩ X)	P(R | X)
.1	.111	.0574	.0064	.0633
.2	.111	.2013	.0224	.2216
.3	.111	.2668	.0296	.2928
.4	.111	.2150	.0239	.2364
.5	.111	.1172	.0130	.1286
.6	.111	.0425	.0047	.0465
.7	.111	.0090	.0010	.0099

.8	.111	.0008	.00009	.0009
.9	.111	.0000	.0000	.0000
			.10109	1.0000

15-8. $x/n = 17/20$

S	$P(S)$	$P(X \mid S)$	$P(S)\,P(X \mid S)$	$P(S \mid X)$
.70	.1	.0716	.00716	.0423
.75	.2	.1339	.02678	.1584
.80	.3	.2054	.06162	.3644
.85	.2	.2428	.04856	.2872
.90	.1	.1901	.01901	.1124
.95	.1	.0596	.00596	.0352
	1.0		.16909	1.0000

15-9.

S	$P(S)$	$P(X \mid S)$	$P(S)\,P(X \mid S)$	$P(S \mid X)$
.70	.0423	.0278	.00118	.0071
.75	.1584	.0669	.01060	.0638
.80	.3644	.1369	.04989	.3001
.85	.2872	.2293	.06585	.3962
.90	.1124	.2852	.03206	.1929
.95	.0352	.1887	.00664	.0399
			.16622	1.0000

15-10. $\hat{p} = d/n = 2/15$

x	$P(x)$	$P(d \mid x)$	$P(x)\,P(d \mid x)$	$P(x \mid d)$
.05	.1	.1348	.01348	.055503
.10	.2	.2669	.05338	.219788
.15	.4	.2856	.11424	.470375
.20	.2	.2309	.04618	.190143
.25	.1	.1559	.01559	.064191
	1.0		.24287	1.000000

A credible set of posterior probability 0.9445 is [0.10, 0.25].

A credible set of close to the same probability is [0.05, 0.20].

15-11. $M' = 8,500 \qquad \sigma' = 1,000 \qquad n = 35 \qquad M = 9,210 \qquad \sigma = 365$

$$M'' = \frac{8,500/(1,000)^2 + 35(9,210)/(365)^2}{1/(1,000)^2 + 35/(365)^2} = 9,207.3$$

$$\sigma''^2 = \frac{1}{1/1,000^2 + 35/365^2} = 3,792 \qquad \sigma'' = 61.58$$

The posterior distribution of the population mean is normal with mean 9,207.3 and standard deviation 61.58.

15-12. $M' = 15{,}000 \qquad \sigma' = 4{,}000 \qquad n = 12 \qquad M = 9{,}867 \qquad \sigma = 1{,}055$

$$M'' = \frac{15{,}000/(4{,}000)^2 + 12(9{,}867)/(1{,}055)^2}{1/(4{,}000)^2 + 12/(1{,}055)^2} = 9{,}896.58$$

$$\sigma''^2 = \frac{1}{1/4{,}000^2 + 12/1{,}055^2} = 92{,}217.498 \qquad \sigma'' = 303.67$$

The posterior distribution of the population mean is normal with mean 9,896.58 and standard deviation 303.67. A 95% HPD credible set for average expected monthly sales is: $9{,}896.58 \pm 1.96(303.67) = [9{,}301.39,\ 10{,}491.77]$.

15-13. $M' = 94 \qquad \sigma' = 2 \qquad n = 10 \qquad M = 96 \qquad$ Assume $\sigma = 1$

$$M'' = \frac{94/4 + 10(96)/1}{1/4 + 10/1} = 95.95$$

$$\sigma''^2 = \frac{1}{1/4 + 10/1} = .0976 \qquad \sigma'' = 0.312$$

The posterior distribution of the population mean is normal with mean 95.95 and standard deviation .312.

15-14. $n = 15 \qquad M = 95 \qquad \sigma = 1$

$$M'' = \frac{95.95/.0976 + 15(95)/1}{1/.0976 + 15/1} = 95.386$$

$$\sigma''^2 = \frac{1}{1/.0976 + 15/1} = .03961 \qquad \sigma'' = 0.199$$

The posterior distribution of the population mean is normal with mean 95.386 and standard deviation 0.199. A 95% HPD credible set for the mean rating of the *foie gras* is: $95.386 \pm 1.96(0.199) = [94.996,\ 95.776]$.

15-15. $M' = 22 \qquad \sigma' = 2 \qquad n = 14 \qquad M = 24 \qquad \sigma = 3$

$$M'' = \frac{(1/4)(22) + (14/9)(24)}{(1/4) + (14/9)} = 23.72$$

$$\sigma''^2 = \frac{1}{(1/4) + (14/9)} = .5538 \qquad \sigma'' = .7442$$

The posterior distribution of the population mean is normal with mean $M'' = 23.72$ and standard deviation $\sigma'' = 0.7442$.

15-16. $n = 20 \qquad M = 25 \qquad \sigma = 2$

$$M'' = \frac{(1/.5538)(23.72) + (20/4)(25)}{(1/.5538) + (20/4)} = 24.66$$

$$\sigma''^2 = \frac{1}{(1/.5538) + (20/4)} = .1469 \qquad \sigma'' = .3833$$

The posterior distribution of the population mean is normal with mean $M'' = 24.66$ and standard deviation $\sigma'' = 0.3833$. A 99% HPD credible set for the population mean is: $24.66 \pm 2.576(.3833) = [23.67, 25.65]$.

15-17. Governor: D (largest s.d.) \qquad ARCO expert: C (smallest s.d.) \qquad Most embarrassed: C (prediction far off, with smallest s.d. implying greatest confidence).

15-19. 95% from 1.5 to 3.5

$1.5 = \mu - 2\sigma \qquad 3.5 = \mu + 2\sigma$

$5 = 2\mu \qquad \mu = 2.5$

$1.5 = 2.5 - 2\sigma \qquad 2\sigma = 1 \qquad \sigma = 0.5$

15-20. Decision analysis is a quantitative method of evaluating decision problems and may be used as an aid in reaching an optimal decision in a given situation.

15-21. Human decision problems may not always be quantified, and when they are quantifiable, there is no assurance that values are correctly assessed.

15-22. Actions—taken by the decisionmaker; chance occurrences—the "actions" of chance; probabilities—assessments of the likelihood of chance occurrences; additional information—used in further assessment of probabilities; final outcome—the aim of the decision problem. This is when the final payoff (or loss) is obtained.

15-23. Probabilities are needed as quantitative measures of likelihood of chance occurrences. They are obtained using the most appropriate method for any given situation; often these are subjective probabilities elicited from experts. The probabilities are used in evaluating expected values of outcomes.

15-24. A decision tree is a graphical display of the interconnection of actions and chance occurrences that captures the sequential nature of a decision problem.

15-25. Cost = 180($20,000) = $3.6 million.

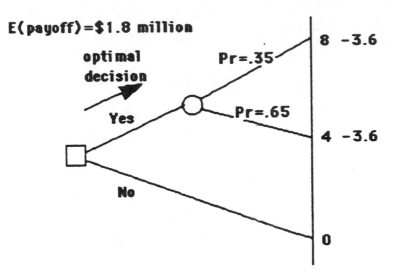

15-26.

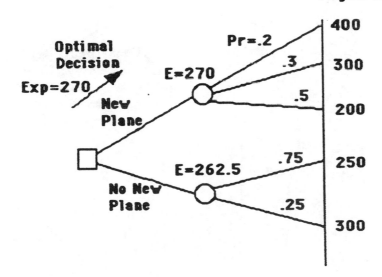

15-27. Buy Federated Stores: E = $65.5 million

Start own chain: E = $58 million

Make new computer: E = $86 million

The optimal decision is therefore to make a new computer.

15-28.

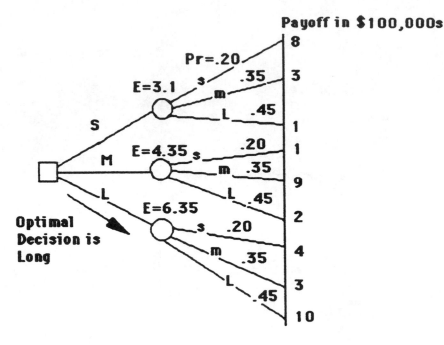

15-29.

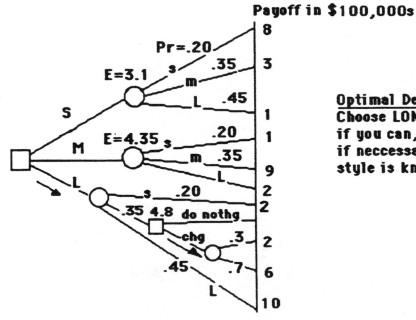

$$E(L) = 4.8(.35) + (.2)(4) + (.45)10 = 6.98$$

15-30. The optimal decision is to invest, then pull out if necessary. The expected monetary value of the decision is $3,040. When you pull out, the expected value is −$4,100.

15-31. The expected value of the limited partnership is $2,500. Hence the optimal decision is as in the previous problem: invest in wheat futures. The expected value is $3,040.

15-32. In a decision problem, it is often necessary to incorporate probabilities describing the reliability of a test or survey. In order to transform such probabilities to the probabilities of states of nature given the test or survey results, Bayes' theorem is needed.

15-33. A predictive probability is the unconditional probability of a given test or survey result. It is obtained using the law of total probability.

15-34. The optimal decision now is to hire the consultants; the expected monetary value is $7.46 million. Then follow subsequent arrows in Figure 15-18 in each possible consultant's finding.

15-35. Don't test; go for it: E = 1.8. If you must test, still make the decision to advertise on television, regardless of the test results.

15-36.

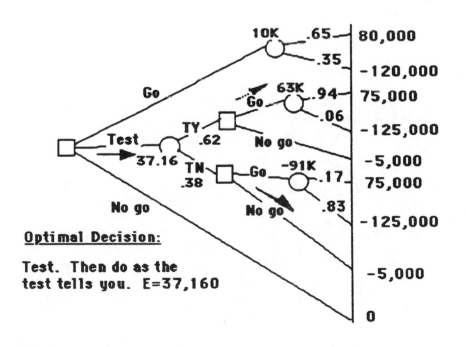

15-37.

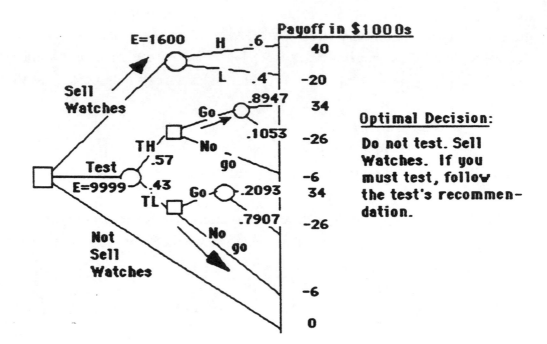

15-38. Test, then do as test recommends. E = $752,000.

15-39. Optimal decision: test and follow the test's recommendation. E = $587,000

15-40. Go with discount broker. E = $225.

15-41. A utility function is a value-of-money function of an individual.

15-42. Since people's attitudes toward risk and toward money should be accounted for, an analysis using utility rather than money may be more meaningful.

15-43. A risk-averse individual has a concave utility function. A risk-seeking individual has a convex utility function.

15-44. This investor is risk-averse.

15-46. Additional information in a decision problem helps us make better decisions. The value of such information may be assessed *a priori*.

15-47. The expected value of perfect information is computed as the expected monetary value of the decision situation when perfect information is available minus the expected value of the decision situation without any additional information. We use the expectation because the actual information is not known.

15-48. See Problem **15-49** below.

15-49. EVPI = E(payoff with perfect information) − E(payoff without info)
= 8(.2) + 9(.35) + 10(.45) − 6.35 = 2.9 [in $100,000's].
Buy information if it is perfect.

15-50. EVPI = 0 because the optimal decision is to go ahead in any case.

15-51.

x	$P(x)$	$P(y \mid x)$	$P(x)\,P(y \mid x)$	$P(x \mid y)$
.1	.1	.0137	.00137	.01142
.2	.3	.1201	.03603	.30043
.3	.2	.2099	.04198	.35004
.4	.2	.1623	.03246	.27066
.5	.1	.0667	.00667	.05561
.6	.1	.0142	.00142	.01184
	1.0		.11993	1.00000

15-52. The set [0.2, 0.4] has posterior probability 0.9211.

15-53.

x	$P(x)$	$P(y \mid x)$	$P(x)\,P(y \mid x)$	$P(x \mid y)$
.1	.01142	.0319	.00036	.0026
.2	.30043	.1746	.05245	.3844
.3	.35004	.1789	.06262	.4589
.4	.27066	.0746	.02019	.1480
.5	.05561	.0148	.00082	.0060
.6	.01184	.0013	.00002	.0001
	1.00000		.13646	1.0000

15-54. The Bayesian approach allows for the use of prior information; the classical approach uses only the data. In the Bayesian approach, parameters are viewed as random variables with which we may associate probability distributions.

15-55. The family of normal probability distributions is closed under the operation of Bayesian updating of information: if the prior is normal and the likelihood is normal, so is the posterior.

15-56. $M' = 45$ $\sigma' = 5$ $n = 100$ $M = 102$ $\sigma = 10$

$$M'' = \frac{(45/25) + 100(102)/100}{(1/25) + (100/100)} = 99.81$$

$$\sigma''^2 = \frac{1}{(1/25) + (100/100)} = 0.9615 \qquad \sigma'' = 0.9806$$

15-57. 95% HPD region $= 99.81 \pm 1.96(.9806) = [97.888, 101.732]$

15-58. $n = 60$ $M = 101.5$

$$M'' = \frac{(99.81/.9615) + 60(101.5)/100}{(1/.9615) + (60/100)} = 100.43$$

$$\sigma''^2 = \frac{1}{(1/.9615) + (60/100)} = 0.6097 \qquad \sigma'' = 0.781$$

95% HPD region $= 100.43 \pm 1.96(.781) = [98.89, 101.96]$

15-59. A payoff table is a matrix of possible outcomes of a decision problem. A decision tree is a graphical way of showing a decision problem. A payoff table can certainly be used without a decision tree.

15-60. A subjective probability is one obtained by anything other than an objective frequency-based approach. Such probabilities may vary depending on the person assessing them. Lack of objectivity is the main limitation of these probabilities.

15-61. The main principle behind the de Finetti game is the gauging of a subjective probability against an objective hypothetical lottery with known probabilities. The game is somewhat simplistic as it does not allow for checking the coherence of the probability assessments.

15-62. The main complaint against Bayesian methods relates to their use of prior information, which may be of unknown reliability.

15-63. E(gamble) $= (.2)5,000 + (.8)500 = 1,400 < 3,000$, therefore, I am a risk taker.

15-64. The investment has expected monetary value \$2,650. The alternative investment has expected monetary value \$4,000. Hence, the alternative investment is optimal. Limitation: this analysis does not incorporate attitude toward risk.

15-65. Depending on the degree of risk-aversion, the investment may become optimal.

15-66. Optimal decision: Merge. The expected monetary outcome is $2.45 million.

15-67.

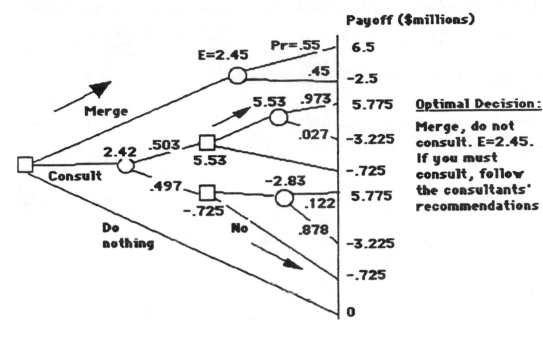

Optimal Decision:

Merge, do not consult. E=2.45. If you must consult, follow the consultants' recommendations

15-68. EVPI = (.55)(6.5) + (.45)(0) − 2.45 = $1.125 million.

15-69.

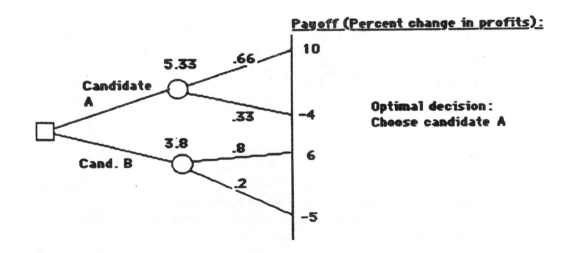

Optimal decision:
Choose candidate A

15-70. Not hiring a new manager has value 0, which is dominated by the decision to hire either A or B. So hire candidate A.

15-71. $P(TS \mid S) = .9 \qquad P(TF \mid F) = .9$
$P(TS \mid F) = .1 \qquad P(TF \mid S) = .1$

Use these probabilities in conjunction with Bayes' theorem and augment the tree in Problem **15-69**. The optimal decision now is to test candidate A.

15-72. Let c, a, h be the probabilities of the mutually exclusive outcomes: conviction, acquittal, and hung jury. Both kinds of contracts have a value of $100, but a Conviction contract costs $65 while an Acquittal contract costs $25. If we make a decision tree with the four choices: Do Nothing, Buy Conviction, Buy Acquittal, and Buy Both, each of these subject to the three possible outcomes above, we calculate that the payoff for Do Nothing is 0; the payoff for Buy Conviction is $-65 + (100c + 0a + 0h) = 100c - 65$; the payoff for Buy Acquittal is $-25 + (0c + 100a + 0h) = 100a - 25 = 100(1 - c - h) - 25 = 75 - 100c - 100h$; and the payoff for Buy Both is the sum: $10 - 100h$. The investor can play the de Finetti game or use some other means to determine prior probability values for c, a, h and, having those values, can immediately determine which choice has the maximum payoff.

Case 15.

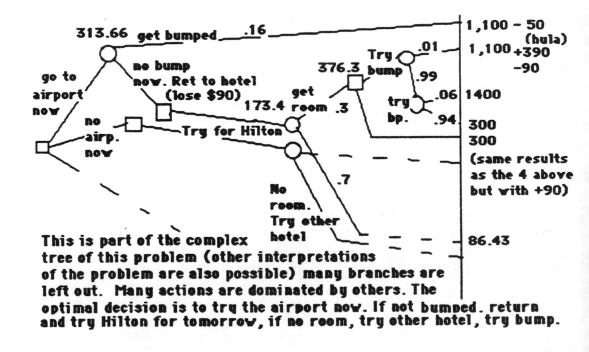

This is part of the complex tree of this problem (other interpretations of the problem are also possible) many branches are left out. Many actions are dominated by others. The optimal decision is to try the airport now. If not bumped, return and try Hilton for tomorrow, if no room, try other hotel, try bump.

CHAPTER 16

16-1. Discriminant analysis is used in statistically classifying elements into one of several groups.

16-2. Overall percentage of correct classification is 57%. However, $125 + 89 = 214$, and the relative size of one group is $125/214 = 0.584$. Thus, classifying any given point as belonging to the larger group gives us a classification power as good as the discriminant analysis. The results of the analysis should not be used. Seek a more meaningful model.

16-3. $D = -0.995 - 0.0352\,\text{Assets} + 0.0429\,\text{Debt} + 0.483\,\text{FamSize}$
$\quad = -0.995 - 0.0352(23) + 0.0429(12) + 0.483(3) = 0.1592$
Since the score is greater than zero, classify as Default.

16-4. $D = -0.995 - 0.0352\,\text{Assets} + 0.0429\,\text{Debt} + 0.483\,\text{FamSize}$
$\quad = -0.995 - 0.0352(54) + 0.0429(10) + 0.483(4) = -0.5348$
Since the score is less than zero, classify in the repay group.

16-5. A holdout data-set is used for testing how well the discriminant model performs with data not used in the estimation procedure. Simply withhold some of the observations when estimating the model, then use them for testing the model's performance.

16-6. (1) The hit ratio must be better than 92%. (2) Use the proportional chance criterion: $C = p^2 + (1 - p)^2 = 0.8528$.

16-7. This prior information may be used in a Bayesian formulation of a discriminant function, using $P(G)$, $P(D \mid G)$, leading to $P(G \mid D)$.

16-8. Group 2.

16-9. $F_1 = -1.713$, $F_2 = 3.29$. Group 3.

16-10. A stepwise routine has similar advantages to those of a stepwise regression routine: the best discriminating variable is chosen first, then variables are added each for its own additional contribution.

16-11. The discriminant function is not statistically significant and should not be used.

16-12. $P(G \mid D)$ is the posterior probability that a given point belongs to group G, given its score D on the discriminant function. This probability is obtained via Bayes' theorem using prior probability and the likelihood $P(D \mid G)$.

16-13. 5 functions; some may not be significant.

16-14. "Hold"

16-15. The main purpose of factor analysis is to break down a large set of variables into a smaller set of latent factors where each factor accounts for a subset of the variables that measure something in common.

16-16. In principal-component analysis the aim is not to reduce the dimensionality of the problem, as in factor analysis, nor do we care whether the components may be identified with meaningful extracts of the information in their associated variables. Here, our aim is to find components that are orthogonal, i.e., uncorrelated with each other.

16-17. Q-factor analysis is a technique similar to cluster analysis and is aimed at grouping elements into meaningful groups. R-factor analysis, the more commonly used technique, is aimed at grouping variables.

16-18. Rigid rotations maintain the orthogonality of the factors; oblique rotations allow for non-orthogonal factors. The rotations help us find the best distribution of factor loadings in terms of what the factors mean.

16-19. VARIMAX maximizes the sum of the variances of the loadings in the factor matrix. Two other rotation methods are QUARTIMAX and EQUIMAX.

16-20. Factor 1 is Overall Supplier Evaluation, Factor 2 is Who Must Yield, and Factor 3 is Argument Evaluation.

16-21. Factor 1 is Price Items, Factor 2 is Retailing/Selling, Factor 3 is Advertising, and Factor 4 is negative (or opposite) of Product ratings.

16-22. Factors are: Importance, Displeasure, Sign, Risk Probability.

16-23. Pricing policies variable: associate with Factor 2;

communality $= (.331)^2 + (.626)^2 = 0.501$

Record and reporting procedures variable: associate with Factor 2;

communality $= (.136)^2 + (.242)^2 = 0.077$

Similarly obtain the communalities of the other variables.

16-24. Factor 1: business/operational practices; Factor 2: development/promotion.

16-26. The multivariate normal distribution is a useful model for many multivariate situations. It is justified by central-limit arguments, and is used to satisfy the assumptions required for most of the techniques discussed in this chapter.

16-27. 3 functions.

16-28. Yes, there may be only one significant discriminant function.

16-29. The hit ratio is the proportion of cases in a discriminant analysis that are correctly classified. 67% is not good enough when 200 out of 300 items belong to one group. Arbitrary assignment to the larger group performs as well.

16-30. Principal-component analysis identifies orthogonal components of variables out of a large set of variables. It can be used as the first stage in a factor analysis: after the component analysis we rotate the components to better identify factors with variables in a meaningful way (this may even be done by nonrigid rotation so the orthogonality of factors does not have to be preserved).

16-31. This is not a worthwhile result since the dimensionality of the problem has not been reduced.

16-32. When the latent factors in a problem are not independent of each other, an oblique rotation may identify these factors better than a rigid rotation by allowing the factors to be correlated (allowing them to be unorthogonal).

16-33. Communality is the proportion of the variance of each variable that is explained by the common factors. The communality of a variable is the sum of its squared factor loadings.

16-34. Communality $= (.17)^2 + (.62)^2 + (.46)^2 + (.12)^2 = 0.6393$.

16-35. Multiple regression analysis. If multicollinearity is present, running a regression on the principal components of the variable set may be a good alternative.

16-36. The factor loadings are the coefficients of the variables in the estimated equations of the common factors. The factor loadings measure sample correlations between each variable and each factor.

16-37. Wilks' $\Lambda = .412$ $F_{(3,21)} = 9.987$ p-value $= .000$
Univariate tests:
Production cost: p-value $= .009$
Number of sponsors: p-value $= .066$ (n.s.)
Promotions: p-value $= .004$

Standardized canonical discriminant function coefficients:
for production cost $= 0.945$
for promotions $= 0.996$
84% correct prediction.

16-38. This analysis is fine (from the standpoint of reducing dimensionality).

Case 16.

This was an example of discriminant analysis, in which we are not privy to the weights that were used. One possible way to improve the performance would be to refine these weights by examining more historical data.

CHAPTER 17

17-1. **a.** $\bar{x}_{\text{st}} = 46(.44) + 9(.15) + 29(.41) = 33.48\%$

b. $s^2 = (1/n) \sum W_i s_i^2 = (1/200)[(.44)8^2 + (.15)4^2 + (.41)16^2] = .6776$
$s = 0.823$

c. 95% C.I. for μ is: $33.48 \pm 1.96(.823) = [31.87, 35.09]$

17-2. **a.** Under proportional allocation, $n_i/n = N_i/N$. Hence the proportions are: production $1,200/2,100 = 0.571$, marketing $600/2,100 = 0.286$, management $100/2,100 = 0.048$, other $200/2,100 = 0.095$. If 100 employees are to be sampled, get (about) 57 from production, 28 from marketing, 5 from management, and 10 from the Other category.

b. An optimum allocation will be based on Equation (17-16) using estimates of the costs of sampling and the internal variability in each category.

17-3. **a.** $\bar{x}_{\text{st}} = 152.43(.18) + 15.33(.82) = \$40.01$

b. $s = \sqrt{(1/n) \sum W_i s_i^2} = \sqrt{(1/300)[(.18)25.77^2 + (.82)5.11^2]} = .6854$

c. 90% C.I. for μ is: $40.01 \pm 1.645(.6854) = [38.88, 41.14]$

d. Measurements are not normally distributed: people either buy jogging suits or they do not (the population has many zero values).

17-4. First Chicago $33/175 = 0.189$, Manufacturers Hanover $27/175 = 0.154$, Bankers Trust $21/175 = 0.12$, Chemical Bank $19/175 = 0.109$, Wells Fargo $19/175 = 0.109$, Citicorp $16/175 = 0.091$, Mellon Bank $16/175 = 0.091$, Chase Manhattan $15/175 = 0.086$, Morgan Guarantee $9/175 = 0.051$.

Problems with study: percentage of profit may not be a good indicator of the average loan amount; neither may the bank's involvement in foreign loans be an indicator of the average loan amount.

17-5. $\bar{x}_{\text{cl}} = \$35,604.5 \qquad \bar{n} = 565.2$
$(M - m)/Mm\bar{n} = 0.00000062 \qquad SE = 5,635.7$
C.I. $= [26,333.8, 44,875.2]$

17-6. $M = 282 \quad m = 15$. The cluster means are: $4.5/4$, $2.8/2$, $8.9/6$, $1.2/2$, $7.0/5$, $2.2/3$, $2.3/2$, $0.8/1$, $12.5/8$, $6.2/4$, $5.5/3$, $6.2/3$, $3.8/2$, $9.0/5$, $1.4/2$

$\bar{x}_{cl} = 1.4288 \quad s_{cl} = 0.26$

95% C.I. is $[0.912, 1.945]$ \$million.

17-7. Cluster sampling should be used when it is convenient to define and select clusters from an entire population. In two-stage cluster sampling, elements are randomly selected from the random sample of clusters.

17-8. $M = 27 \quad m = 6 \quad \bar{n} = 153 \quad \sum n_i = 918$

$\hat{p}_{cl} = (1/918)[80 + 75 + 100 + 65 + 45 + 200] = 0.615$

$$s = \sqrt{\frac{21}{(27)(6)(153)^2(5)}\left(\begin{array}{c}120^2(.00267)+150^2(.0132)+200^2(.0132)\\+100^2(.001225)+88^2(.0107)+260^2(.02378)\end{array}\right)} = 0.053$$

99% C.I. is $0.615 \pm 2.576(0.053) = [0.478, 0.752]$

17-9. a) No; b) No; c) No. For cluster sampling, the ships need to be randomly selected (the first 5 ships of the season are not a random sample). d) Consider the companies as strata, ships as clusters. Choose a random sample of clusters from each stratum. Then randomly select people on each ship. Thus, combine 2-stage cluster sampling with stratified sampling for high precision.

17-10. $11,000/50 = 220$. Select a random number from 1 to 220; this is the number of the first element in the systematic sample. Add to this number 220 to get the number of the next sampled tire, and so on until you have 50 tires.

17-11. The nearest integer to $855/30$ is either 28 or 29. Arrange elements in a "circle," randomly choose a number from 1 to 28, and then add 28 to element number until you have a sample of 30 sales.

17-12. a) This is not systematic sampling since the first element is not randomly selected. b) Sampling bias may occur.

17-13. If k is a multiple of 7, systematic sampling may result in a sample of Mondays (or any other single, particular day of the week). This will cause a significant bias due to the cyclicity of sales over the entire week.

17-14. $\bar{x} = 27.3$ $s = 5.58\sqrt{90/1{,}000} = 1.67$ 90% C.I. for μ is:

27.3 ± 1.645(1.67) = [24.55, 30.05].

17-15. The systematic sampling of Problem **17-14** is equivalent to stratified random sampling where one element of each stratum is selected. The added feature here is that the number of the chosen element within the stratum is the same in all strata.

17-16. $\bar{x}_{st} = (.25)65 + (.35)87 + (.15)52 + (.35)38.5 = 67.975$

$n = 1{,}000$, proportional allocation.

$V(\bar{X}_{st}) = \dfrac{1}{n}\sum W_i s_i^2 = \dfrac{1}{1{,}000}[.25(123) + .35(211.8) + .15(88.85) + .35(100.4)] = .1533$

$SE(\bar{X}_{st}) = 0.3916$ 95% C.I. for μ is:

67.975 ± 1.96(.3916) = [67.207, 68.743]

17-17. Yes, with each vehicle a cluster.

17-19. This is fine unless a non-negligible proportion of the businesses in the community are unlisted in the Yellow Pages.

17-20. 17, 40, 63, 86, 109, 12 (= 132 − 120 because there are 120 in the population).

17-21. $M = 1{,}000$ $n = 100$ $m = 12$ $\hat{p}_{cl} = \dfrac{\sum n_i \hat{p}_i}{\sum n_i} = .0733$

95% C.I. for p is: .0733 ± .018 = [0.055, 0.091]

17-22. Stratified random sampling is appropriate—each factory is a stratum.

17-23. A four-stage cluster sampling method may be covenient here.

17-24. $\bar{x}_{st} = \sum W_i \bar{x}_i = .25(90) + .55(82) + .20(88) = 85.2$

$s(\bar{x}_{st}) = \sqrt{\dfrac{1}{1{,}000}(.25(25) + .55(121) + .20(36))} = 0.2828$

95% C.I. for μ is: 85.2 ± 1.96(0.2828) = [84.646, 85.754]

17-25. Optimum allocation $\qquad n_i/n = \dfrac{W_i\sigma_i/\sqrt{C_i}}{\sum_j W_j\sigma_j/\sqrt{C_j}}$

Children: $\qquad \dfrac{(.25)(5)/\sqrt{2}}{(.25)(5)/\sqrt{2} + (.55)(11)/1 + (.20)(6)/1} = .10866$

Children: 0.10866, so sample about 109 children out of the total sample of 1,000.

Young Adults: 0.74380, so sample about 744.

Older People: 0.1475, so sample about 147.

17-26. Define groups such that $\mathrm{Cum}\sqrt{f(x)}$ is approximately equal. $\sqrt{f(x)}$ is (in order): .316, .316, .224, .224, .387, .387, .316, .316, .224, .224, .224, .224. The underlined groups have *approximately* equal cumulative $\sqrt{f(x)}$. Strata may be constructed as: 15 years and under, 16 to 25, 26 to 35, 36 to 45, 46 and over. (Other breakdowns are possible.)

17-27. Regression and ratio estimators.

17-28. Poststratification.

17-29. No. Benefits from stratification are not substantial when the number of strata is much greater than 6. Combine some of the strata.

Case 17.

The purpose of this case is to have students look at the map of the Roxbury area and think about planning a survey using the ideas of sampling methods: Stratification by subdistricts (some may be combined), cluster sampling, and more. Relative cost (time) of reaching different parts of the area may also be estimated from the map.